W9-ANA-235

GRAMLEY LIBRARY
Salem Academy and College
Winston-Salem, N. C. 27108

English Medieval Theatre
1400–1500

Theatre Production Studies

General Editor
John Russell Brown
Associate of the National Theatre of Great Britain
and
Professor of Theatre Arts, State University of New York
at Stony Brook

PN
2587
.T93
1986

English Medieval Theatre
1400–1500

William Tydeman

Routledge & Kegan Paul

London, Boston and Henley

GRAMLEY LIBRARY
Salem Academy and College
Winston-Salem, N. C. 27108

First published in 1986
by Routledge & Kegan Paul plc

14 Leicester Square, London WC2H 7PH, England

9 Park Street, Boston, Mass. 02018, USA and

Broadway House, Newtown Road,
Henley on Thames, Oxon RG9 1EN, England

Phototypeset in Linotron Plantin 10 on 12pt
by Input Typesetting Ltd, London
and printed in Great Britain
by The Thetford Press
Thetford, Norfolk

© *William Tydeman 1986*

No part of this book may be reproduced in
any form without permission from the publisher,
except for the quotation of brief passages
in criticism

Library of Congress Cataloging in Publication Data

Tydeman, William.
English medieval theatre, 1400–1500.

Bibliography: p.
Includes index.
1. Theater—Great Britain—History—Medieval, 500–1500.
2. English drama—To 1500—History and criticism.
I. Title.
PN2587.T93   1986   792'.0941   85–18317

British Library CIP Data also available

ISBN 0–7100–9850–2

To Jackie with love

No thing on erth more would I have
Save that I have to have it still.
Wyatt

Contents

Illustrations

Plates

Figures and Drawings (all by Josephine Tydeman)

Preface

Writing this book has enabled me to set aside the wide-angle lens employed on the more panoramic *Theatre in the Middle Ages*, and to bring into sharp focus a small selection of representative plays staged in England during the fifteenth century. Although I provide a general introduction to the medieval repertoire in Part One, my main concern has been to examine the texts of *Mankynde*, the Croxton *Play of the Sacrament, The Castel of Perseveraunce*, the Passion sequence from York, and *Fulgens and Lucres*, to establish their probable manner of staging, and to show how these texts might have come to life in performance. A discussion of certain aspects of medieval theatrical practice follows in Part Three.

It may be objected that I concentrate too extensively on religious drama but only scanty remnants of secular pieces survive from this period, and Christian drama therefore assumes inevitable prominence. Similarly, if too much material cited in the final section seems to post-date the centuries usually designated as 'medieval', it is because precise information about staging methods is comparatively sparse until the sixteenth century, thus forcing one to gather evidence from outside the bounds of conventional chronology. As F. M. Salter once wrote, 'it is the type of drama, rather than the period, that is in question'.

I have tried to avoid merely reproducing in these pages data which can be found in *The Theatre in the Middle Ages*. Where duplication has proved impossible to prevent, the facts are set in a different context, and I have attempted to draw fresh conclusions from them wherever feasible. Much of what appears here must prove more speculative than in my previous book, since I have often been forced to abandon a neutral position in order to make positive assumptions from ambivalent evidence. Because some readers will wish to search out particular areas for attention rather than assimilate the whole work, I have aimed to make each chapter as self-contained as possible.

As before, I remain heavily indebted to the leading authorities on the subject, perhaps most of all to Dr Richard Southern, whose pioneering researches into actual production-methods have put all subsequent writers under a vast debt of gratitude to him. Where I have disagreed with Dr Southern's findings in the ensuing pages it has only been after long periods of hard thinking. I must thank John Russell Brown for his act of faith in inviting me to undertake this volume, and for the exemplary kindness and patience he displayed in helping me to achieve greater clarity of expression and conciseness of effect. Several fellow-investigators have answered questions, provided photographs, or simply encouraged me: they include Sandy Johnston, Keith Ramsay, Meg Twycross, and Glynne Wickham. The whole manuscript has benefited from the commonsense comments of my wife, with whom I have visited many places mentioned in the text: for many reasons, personal and professional, this work is dedicated to her.

My daughter Josephine has undertaken the original artwork which the satisfactory presentation of my ideas has required: I offer her my deepest thanks for her painstaking devotion. Joyce Williams has cheerfully typed order out of chaos; our Faculty Photographer, Douglas Madge, has rendered valued and willing assistance. Finally, the staff of Routledge & Kegan Paul have been immensely helpful, and I thank Philippa Brewster in particular for bringing my ship safely into harbour. Needless to say, the errors which remain after such generous ministrations are my own responsibility.

William Tydeman
November 1984

A Note on Texts and Spellings

All quotations are given in a form as close as possible to the original. The relevant sources are indicated in the notes. I have, however, adopted the usual policy of exchanging ff, i, j, u, v, and vv for their modern equivalents, and of replacing þ and ȝ with the appropriate letters. Capitals have been modified in keeping with present-day usage, and numerals etc. are spelled out. I have on the other hand retained most of the original punctuation, without always being convinced that it bears the significance in play-texts that some critics have claimed. My own editorial emendations and glosses are placed within the customary square brackets.

I have also adhered to the original spellings of titles and names, but am convinced that this should cause no confusion, even for those familiar with their modernized versions. It seems incongruous to quote from texts in the original and then adapt titles and proper names to twentieth-century styles. So readers must bear with such apparitions as *The Castel of Perseveraunce* and *Mankynde*, Dethe, Flesch, and Lucres. They will quickly recognize them; they may even come to like them.

Abbreviations

For reasons of space and convenience books and periodicals referred to frequently in the notes appear in the following abbreviated forms. Complete publishing details are given in the Select Bibliography.

Chester	Lumiansky and Mills (eds), *The Chester Mystery Cycle*, I
Coventry	Craig (ed.), *Two Coventry Corpus Christi Plays*
Digby	Baker *et al.* (eds), *The Late Medieval Religious Plays*
DMC	Young, *The Drama of the Medieval Church*
EES	Wickham, *Early English Stages*
EETS (OS)	Early English Text Society (Ordinary Series)
EETS (ES)	*ibid.*, Extra Series
EETS (SS)	*ibid.*, Supplementary Series
EMI	Wickham (ed.), *English Moral Interludes*
ERD	Craig, *English Religious Drama of the Middle Ages*
JEGP	*Journal of English and Germanic Philology*
LC	Block (ed.), *Ludus Coventriae*, or *The Plaie called Corpus Christi*
LSE	*Leeds Studies in English*
Macro	Eccles (ed.), *The Macro Plays*
MD	Bevington (ed.), *Medieval Drama*
MDC	Salter, *Mediaeval Drama in Chester*
MED	Taylor and Nelson (eds), *Medieval English Drama*
MES	Nelson, *The Medieval English Stage*
METh	*Medieval English Theatre*
MLN	*Modern Language Notes*
MLQ	*Modern Language Quarterly*
MLR	*Modern Language Review*
MP	*Modern Philology*
MS	Chambers, *The Mediaeval Stage*
MTR	Southern, *The Medieval Theatre in the Round*
N&Q	*Notes and Queries*

NCP	Davis (ed.), *Non-Cycle Plays and Fragments*
OED	*Oxford English Dictionary*
PFRC	Dutka (ed.), *Proceedings of the First* [REED] *Colloquium*
REEDC	Clopper (ed.), *Records of Early English Drama: Chester*
REEDN	*Records of Early English Drama Newsletter*
REEDY	Johnston and Rogerson (eds), *Records of Early English Drama: York*
RORD	*Research Opportunities in Renaissance Drama*
SP	*Studies in Philology*
SPS	Southern, *The Staging of Plays before Shakespeare*
TMA	Tydeman, *The Theatre in the Middle Ages*
TN	*Theatre Notebook*
Towneley	England (ed.), *The Towneley Plays*
TS	*Theatre Survey*

Introduction

If we go into a bookshop and purchase a recently-written play or even one composed during the last hundred years, we may reasonably expect to discover from it a good deal concerning its theatrical presentation. Along with the dialogue, our text will usually contain a plentiful supply of stage directions, instructing the players where to sit and when to stand, how to deliver a particular line, or suggesting the mood that they are to convey by means of gestures and movements. The characters' physical appearances will often be delineated, along with at least some notion of what they are wearing. The setting will probably be described in even greater detail (especially if the play was written early in the twentieth century), establishing the exact position of each table, chair, sofa, cocktail cabinet and kitchen sink. Frequently, as an additional aid to visualizing the scenic effect, a stage-plan will be included: there may even be some photographs of the set or of actual performances. Those taking an interest in such things will almost certainly find that the book includes full data on the original presentation in the form of a cast-list, the date of the first night, the names of author, director, designer, and that of the theatre where the play first saw the glare of the spotlights. From all this, we can easily piece together a fairly adequate picture of the play in performance, even if we have never witnessed such a thing for ourselves.

This is far from being the case with the dramatic literature of the Middle Ages. If we take as an example the best-known English play of the years between 1400 and 1520, the celebrated morality piece known as *Everyman*, we shall quickly realize that its original text offers us hardly any overt clues as to the nature of its first encounter with the public gaze. There is no record of when, where, or in what circumstances the work was first presented, no evidence regarding its earliest audiences, its author-ship, or its cast. We have no notion as to whether the piece was staged indoors, perhaps in a place of worship or a banqueting-hall, or out of doors on a village green, in a market-square, or within an inn-yard. We do not know the size or shape of the venue selected: we cannot necessarily assume that the play was even set forth on a raised platform, since many medieval plays shared the same street or floor as spectators were expected to occupy. Did the actor presenting God appear on a higher level than his fellows, or was his occupation of 'the hevenly spere' (line 95)[1] left to the audience's imagination?

How did characters enter and leave the scene? Did Everyman, prior to Dethe's summons, emerge on stage through a rear curtain, or did he simply climb up on to the platform from among the audience? Did the performance-area contain any scenery? It certainly seems as if Knowlege's reference to a 'hous of salvacyon' may allude to a scenic structure of some kind, but it is not capable of proof. It may also be significant that Goodes announces in lines 394–6 that he lies 'here in corners, trussed and pyled so hye', so weighed down with possessions that he 'can not styre': does this suggest that he must be 'discovered' already on stage rather than making an entrance, and if so, must we postulate the presence of an alcove within the playing-area, hidden by a curtain until Everyman draws it and exposes Goodes within it?[2] Such a facility would also assist with the problem implicit in Good Dedes's later announcement that she too 'can not stere' but lies 'colde in the grounde' (lines 486–8). Perhaps this figure was also 'discovered' by drawing back a curtain. Everyman's grave creates difficulties too: did it consist of a portable wooden framework brought forward when required, or was it a permanent feature of the set, a 'trap' in the floor of the stage, for instance?

Analogous problems occur when considering the appearance of the play's characters. The dramatist left few indications as to how his hero and the other figures should be costumed. John Skot's edition of the play does contain two woodcuts depicting some of the cast (see Plate 1), but these cuts were standard illustrations used to embellish other works of the period,[3] and nothing indicates that they bear any relationship to the appearance on stage of the earliest performers. However, Everyman's dress clearly has the required degree of flamboyance, representing suitable attire to justify Dethe's 'Whyder arte thou goynge/Thus gayly?' – 'gayly' being taken here to imply 'dressed up to the nines' – so pains were plainly taken to garb the leading character as a well-to-do burgher, in contrast to the penitential robe he dons later in the action, and which he wears as he ultimately travels to meet his death.

Enough has been said to explain why this book must deal in speculation and surmise to a far greater extent then many other works in this series: the vital evidence is too often missing. However, the present study embodies the belief that even without such vital evidence we can still go some way towards recreating the theatrical experience of which a dramatic text forms an all-too-inadequate record. In medieval drama entrances and exits, movements and gestures, setting and staging, usually have to be

1 Woodcuts from Skot's edition of *Everyman* (c. 1530) (Photo: British Library)

ascertained from the dialogue, and failing that, through the cautious exercise of that essential qualification for reading any play, namely 'theatrical imagination'. From such a combination of careful textual scrutiny and the judicious development of a sensitive awareness of what the medieval stage both permitted and demanded, we can overcome some of the drawbacks inherent in such playscripts as *Everyman*. In this way the apparently uninformative texts of anonymous medieval playwrights can be made to yield up the secrets of their abundant theatrical potential.

Moreover, an awareness of the vigour and variety, the excitement and integrity of the medieval stage, can also enhance our response to the theatre of our own times. In the past that excellence and appeal were largely overlooked by a theatrical establishment unprepared to shift its eyes from contemplating the glories of its own proscenium arch. Today this particular myopia is nearly cured, but though the theatre of the present is ready to admit that drama manifests itself in many diverse forms, directors and players could still learn much from the imaginative vision and artistic range of their medieval predecessors, and from that sense of democratic integration taken for granted by pre-Renaissance actors and auditors. It is in the belief that medieval theatre techniques are by no means outdated that this enquiry has been undertaken.

Part One

The Repertoire

I

Ask a typical modern reader what he or she would rate as the chief glory of our national literature, and the chances are that the reply will be: 'the Elizabethan and Jacobean drama'. A survey of the complete range of English stage-plays, published in 1981,[1] devotes almost 100 of its 209 pages to the 'golden age' of Shakespeare and his distinguished contemporaries, and there is little doubt that in the public mind this degree of attention is justified. Yet it is arguable whether the theatre industry during the period of 'Eliza and our James' could have offered its clientele the sheer variety of dramatic forms and theatrical modes deployed by its medieval counterpart between 1400 and 1500. Certainly, if we possessed even a fraction of the lost English drama of this epoch, we might be moved to agree that the great era of Elizabethan and Jacobean theatre performances represented not the first but the second burst of major achievement in the British dramatic tradition.

Allusions to plays and performances in medieval documents remind us that a mass of plays extant during the period survives no longer. It is even more chastening to reflect that there must once have been other plays whose existence is not even recorded. Time and chance have dealt particularly harshly with secular works, since these were unlikely to have been set down in written form, at a time when writing materials were scarce. Even sacred drama, often no doubt copied down more for its doctrinal content than its theatrical excellence, fared badly, especially when it later fell into the hands of the zealous reformers of the Protestant persuasion. As a result the whole corpus of extant medieval drama in the English tongue can be contained within the covers of a very modest series of volumes. Even if one includes works in the Celtic tongues, what remains is a small particle of what must have once existed, and it may also form a far from representative selection of what is now lost to sight.

However, we may derive consolation from the realization that such medieval drama as abides is usually of excellent quality. Admittedly, we must make the effort initially to adjust our modern sensibilities and tastes to those of the original creators, presenters, and patrons of the surviving plays, if we are not to experience a certain sense of alienation on first looking into them. Medieval drama is almost totally non-naturalistic in presentation and characterization: 'authenticity' is not its aesthetic goal. Expositions are bold and unashamed, story-telling uncompromising and undisguised, while stylization and symbolism form central features of its characteristic technique. In the main we should not expect to find elaborately structured and involved plots in which each tiny incident contributes its share to the smooth running of the whole, like a minute cog-wheel in some intricate piece of machinery. Medieval plots can sometimes prove surprisingly 'well-made', particularly on close inspection, but they can also prove episodic in the extreme, their various elements assisting the total effect only as the separate members of a tug-of-war team combine to achieve victory for their side. Characters too are hardly ever conceived as psychological studies of subtly motivated individuals, but rather as types of humanity whose traits are determined by the given facts of their situation or dramatic function, rather than being inherent in their personalities. Herod brags and blusters by virtue of his role as a pagan tyrant, and Mankynde falls into wickedness not through personal disposition but because his human condition ordains it.

A highly formal impulse often informs plays of this period, found chiefly in a ceremoniousness of diction whose presence may appear to conflict with the vibrant colloquialisms or vernacular exchanges found in other sections of the same piece. Again this stems from the medieval playwright's freedom from the insistent desire to make verisimilitude the dominant criterion of his work. A medieval writer will certainly make us believe, for example, in the truth-to-life of the shepherds who appear in the Nativity scenes of the cycle plays; he will take pains to impress us that their opinions and their language might easily be heard in any Yorkshire market town or village inn during the fifteenth century. But he will not hesitate either to make them exchange prophecies concerning the coming of Christ drawn from the Old Testament, or to present their gifts at the manger with a wealth of rhetorical skill and iconographical allusion, with no concern for the unlikelihood of their doing so in reality. In the same way we may be irked at first by the ostensibly didactic function of much of the medieval repertory, but here too we must recall that it was the function of drama in the Middle Ages not to conduct a pragmatic exploration of the potentialities of the human condition which might vary from individual to individual, but rather to demonstrate a pre-determined theosophy which remained valid for all sorts and conditions of men at all times and in all places. For this reason medieval drama is predominantly celebratory and confirmatory rather than questioning or revolutionary: the *status quo* is more often upheld and justified rather than challenged or subverted – although this might not be the case if we possessed a larger number of secular works from which to draw our conclusions.

II

Such is the diversity of medieval religious plays in English and to such a degree do the principal types overlap that it is difficult to assign them to precise categories. Existing works appear to fall most happily, however, into five basic classes: plays of a generally biblical character which form no part of a longer series of related pieces; plays which celebrate the life and work of some saint or equally venerated upholder of the Christian faith; dramas whose central feature is the performance of one or more miracles to God's greater glory; sequences of cyclic episodes depicting the Christian view of mankind's salvation through Christ and covering a span stretching 'from Creation to Doomsday'; morality plays which teach their audiences to aim for higher standards of personal conduct in the mundane and spiritual spheres by illustrating the human potential for salvation or damnation. These were the principal forms of religious drama written in the vernacular which came to flourish alongside the Latin music-dramas of the Roman Catholic Church, the so-called liturgical plays which enjoyed their heyday between about 1000 and 1200 AD.

The precise causes which led to the emergence of religious plays in the European vernaculars, or to the apparent passing of the creative initiative from the compilers of indoor liturgical pieces with a strongly devotional character to the authors of saints' plays, moralities, and lengthy sequences of plays based on Biblical history are unknown. But it now seems obvious that the Roman Catholic Church did not simply abandon religious drama to the lay community by casting plays forth from its hallowed interiors with cries of distaste and disgust at their increasing secularization, and ceasing to bestow any further care upon them. Liturgical performances continued to be given, even though their truly creative phase was over by about 1200, but the Church also watched over and indeed supervised the new vernacular plays, despite their 'secularized' nature, the fact that their finances were frequently in the hands of the medieval trade guilds, and that the plays on many occasions were performed entirely by laymen. Far from wishing to demote the demotic dissemination of Christian doctrine or to condemn its manifestation on the street and in the market-place rather than within a sacred building, the Church was in many ways striving to bring the story of Christ's life and the message of his teaching into closer contact with the ordinary Christian's everyday habitat and the temporal life of the medieval community in general. So-called 'secular' and comic elements in the vernacular dramas were not concessions to the frivolousness and worldly preoccupations of a lay audience, but skilfully employed touches to reinforce the play's doctrinal message or to emphasize that Christ in his human as well as his divine role had a place in men's daily lives, and was concerned with their temporal as well as their spiritual needs. For this reason, while there is no basic doctrinal discontinuity between drama staged as part of a religious service within a church and drama presented amid the distractions of a medieval street or market-place, a radical shift of mood and tone is perceptible as one turns from the Latin music-dramas which form an integral part of official church worship to the vernacular plays with their stronger 'human interest' and their less devotional atmosphere.[2]

Many commentators now agree that some new theological impulse has to be sought in order to clarify the development of what appears to be a new phase in the history of medieval play-making.[3] Some find what they consider to be the vital key in the well-attested missionary activities of the monastic orders of the Franciscans and the Dominicans in the first part of the thirteenth century, a period when the evangelizing zeal of members of these fraternities helped to publicize and make familiar a fresh attitude to the figure of Christ. Formerly viewed in his supernatural role as a member of the Holy Trinity and as the Judge of Mankind, a new emphasis was placed during the twelfth century on his incarnation as humankind – the Word made Flesh – and on his redemptive role in suffering a human death on the cross in order to save humanity from the effects of its sin. The image of Christ in majesty was replaced by those of the baby in Mary's arms and of the tortured naked body hanging from the cross at Calvary. An awareness of Christ's self-immolation as a member of suffering humankind also led to a fresh appreciation of the gift of the sacraments of bread and wine partaken at Mass, symbolizing Christ's offer of himself as a sacrifice at the Crucifixion; and in 1215–16 at the Fourth Lateran Council the doctrine of transubstantiation was promulgated, enshrining the belief that Christ actually became present during the consecration of the bread and wine at the Mass service, and that the faithful literally consumed his body and blood. At the same time it was recognized that to merit salvation individual Christians required a fresh approach to their religious duties, and penance was now solemnly enjoined on all those who sought redemption through Christ's agency. Recognition of the urgent importance of this spiritual necessity opened the way for the creation of a new didactic drama addressed to the common people, which had as its aim the promulgation of the Church's teachings on the availability of salvation to the repentant sinner, on the example and sacrifice offered by Christ, and on God's life on earth as a divine phenomenon in every way as remarkable as his power and majesty manifested outside historical time.

It must be admitted that this attractive account does not entirely square with the facts as we know them. Two centrally important Anglo-Norman plays, *Le Mystère d'Adam*, and *La Seinte Resureccion*, which date from the middle of the twelfth century, show firm resemblances to the newer type of non-liturgical play. Written in the vernacular and, though often liturgically-inspired, seemingly independent of the decorum imposed by the devotional framework particularly in their diction and characterization, these pieces appear to represent a well-established dramatic mode, which in the case of *Adam* in particular rises to considerable heights of theatrical success. *Adam* also contains a cleverly integrated comic element supplementing the play's general tendency towards greater realism which co-exists with its obvious religious purpose. Such a blend of humour and piety is characteristic of the best of medieval drama in England, but its appearance in *Adam*, usually dated between 1146 and 1174, suggests that, even before the followers of St Francis and St Dominic began their proselytizing, plays treating scriptural incidents with greater freedom and inventiveness were in production.

Perhaps the most that can be safely concluded is that the trend towards public performances of free-ranging scriptural drama was probably given additional impetus as a result of the missionary fervour of the later twelfth and early thirteenth centuries, and in this the fresh emphasis on Christ's ministry and passion and the renewed insistence on repentance and penance as necessary preliminaries for salvation had a role. Whether the institution of the Feast of Corpus Christi, which provided for a celebration of Christ's twin gift of himself in the Eucharist and on the cross to take place on the first Thursday after Trinity Sunday, supplied the motive force behind the development of the Corpus Christi cycle plays in Britain is not easily determined. But it is not impossible that the processions which were such an important feature of public ceremonies carried out on that day (see Plate 2) gradually turned into a mobile display of tableaux, and that these acquired successively a mimed element, a set of brief speeches, and finally enough exchanges in dialogue-form for them to be regarded as plays. At the same time, not all cycle-sequences were performed on Corpus Christi Day, Whitsuntide being another favourite period for their staging. Furthermore, there is evidence that sequences of episodes were already a feature of liturgical drama. It may well be that records of productions in which scenes were linked together show that the cyclic impulse was in being well before the Corpus Christi procession established itself as part of the medieval Christian year.[4] There are even

GRAMLEY LIBRARY
Salem Academy and College
Winston-Salem, N. C. 27108

2 A Corpus Christi procession, showing the Host carried beneath a canopy (Harley MS 7026) (Photo: British Library)

those who claim that plays such as *Le Mystère d'Adam* demonstrate the germ of the cyclic tendency, in that three separate episodes based on inter-related scriptural materials are here linked to form one dramatic whole, and that since the text breaks off incomplete, there are grounds for arguing that further matter gleaned from the life of Christ originally followed, and that *Adam* is in fact a fragment from an early vernacular cycle-drama.

Considerable weight must also be attached to the view that the circumstances of their performance determined the nature of the vernacular plays. Merely by taking drama out of doors and presenting it to the general public, the organizers of religious presentations changed the basis of the dramatic premise. Church plays could count on an audience of worshippers whose principal motive for entering the church could be assumed to be spiritual rather than diversionary in origin. But once outside the church, plays had to be devised to appeal to spectators whose primary impulse was to be entertained. Thus the didactic substance of Christian literature was re-worked in order to present its message in forms of entertainment associated with outdoor places of public assembly and recreation. The authors of the newer forms of religious drama were constrained to give their work the popular appeal of secular sports and pastimes, games and 'shows', so as to command public attention and to compete with the more traditional and light-hearted diversions the populace had enjoyed for centuries.

III

Whatever the exact circumstances which fostered their genesis,[5] the artistic achievements of the vernacular theatre in medieval England were considerable and deserve careful attention. As early as 1170–80 William Fitzstephen praising London in his *Life of St Thomas* [À Becket] says of it:

> London, in place of [Rome's] theatrical spectacles and stage-shows,
> possesses much holier dramas, representations of the miracles
> wrought by holy confessors, or of the passions by which the constancy
> of martyrs was demonstrated.[6]

It would be unwise to assume that Fitzstephen was familiar merely with plays celebrating miracles or the lives of saints and martyrs, but there is no doubt that this type of drama is found in existence early in the history of medieval vernacular theatre, and was one of its most popular and enduring forms. The Church's custom of celebrating saints' days and the common habit of dedicating a church-building to an individual patronal saint offered ample opportunities for dramatized celebrations of suitably holy men and women at appropriate times of the year, and the colourful figures of certain saints and the stirring or bizarre legends attached to them supplied the playwright with invaluable subject-matter with which to enliven his drama. In around 1100 it is known that Geoffrey of Le Mans staged a play on the life of St Katherine with the pupils of his choir-school at Dunstable, possibly a Latin music-drama since he borrowed copes from the abbey of nearby St Albans for the purpose. Some twenty or so years later Hilarius, a 'wandering scholar' possibly English in origin, created his delightful *Ludus super Iconia Sancti Nicolai* (*The Play of St Nicholas's Image*). Later allusions to saints' plays abound from a wide variety of centres: London had a play of St Katherine in 1393 and there is mention of another from Coventry in 1490–1. Lincoln and King's Lynn staged plays of St Thomas in the fourteenth century; St Susannah features at Lincoln in 1447–8, as does a play of St Clara in 1455–6. The genre proved resilient: the insertion of anti-government propaganda into a play of St Thomas the Apostle at York in August 1536 angered Henry VIII, and even as late as 1557 the parishioners of St Olave's in London staged a piece about their patron saint to raise funds.[7]

Most of the texts of saints' plays now accessible survive from very late in the fifteenth and early in the sixteenth centuries, though the incomplete *Duk Morawd* which dates from c. 1300 might prove to be of this type, did we possess the entire text. The fragment remaining consists of lines spoken by the actor playing the title role, but the complete story can be reconstructed as that of a boastful ruler who in his wife's absence commits adultery with his own daughter; she afterwards kills her mother and then gives birth to a baby, who is also done away with. Shortly afterwards the father repents of his sin, confesses, and is enjoined to undertake some form of penance, but before he can do so his daughter murders him, the fragment ceasing at this point. Possibly a local saint or the Virgin Mary may have intervened at some later junction in order to save the father's immortal soul, or the play may have run on to trace the daughter's downfall until she repented or was saved by some act of divine intervention.[8] Alternatively, we may have here the opening of an early exemplary morality play, in which the soul of Duk Morawd or his daughter might be fought over by the Virtues and Vices, although the text as it stands contains none of the personifications of abstract qualities which feature in surviving examples of the genre such as *The Castel of Perseveraunce* or *Mankynde*.

Three English works may, however, be claimed as saints' plays. They are the two 'Digby Plays', *The Conversion of St Paul* and *Mary Magdalene*, and the Cornish epic-drama *Beunans Meriasek* (*The Life of Meriasek*), which all date from the years 1480–1510.[9] These must serve to represent a highly popular type, even if we have no means of knowing whether or not they typify it. Strictly speaking, neither St Paul nor Mary Magdalene conforms to the saintly criteria exemplified in St Nicholas or St George, but the plays in which they feature adhere to the pattern of sin–repentance–conversion, which distinguishes the genre in general.

The miraculous conversion of Saul into Paul on the road to Damascus was a familiar medieval dramatic subject, often composed for presentation on the Feast of St Paul's Conversion, 25 January. The English play traces Saul's development from fanatical persecutor of Christians – characterized as 'an aunterous knyth' supported by feudal attendants – to religious convert and apostle. The central incident shows Saul setting off for Damascus on horseback, the provision of a 'palfray' providing the cue for some farcical comedy between his servant and a groom which may satirize Saul's own initial arrogance. If so, this low-life echo of the main plot is an interesting foretaste of Marlowe's *Dr Faustus*. The third portion of the action is the least satisfactory; learning of Saul's apostasy, a pair of devils threaten to be revenged on him, and the saint is imprisoned after preaching a lengthy sermon on the Seven Deadly Sins. But the play peters out tamely with the narrator informing us of Paul's escape in a basket: we neither see the escape nor does the apostle have the last word.

Mary Magdalene, a much fuller work of some 2140 lines, appears more episodic and loosely organized than *The Conversion*. *Magdalene* contains some sixty-five roles, not surprising in a work which must have taken most of one day to present. The play is unified by little more than the presence of its eponymous heroine. The action begins with an abbreviated cycle sequence of some 1100 lines tracing Christ's relationship with Mary culminating in the events of Easter morning. The writer then abandons his scriptural allegiances and plunges into an exotic round of pagan kings, long sea-voyages, miraculous pregnancies, romantic reversals of fortune, and a triumphant outcome for the Christian faith. Magdalene, finally alone in the wilderness after her harrowing vicissitudes, is fed with manna, given the Last Rites and assumed into heaven. The whole is a blend of incidents and moods not entirely unrelated to one another, but despite the lively action and the refreshing comedy of such disreputable figures as the Priest and his Boy, the overall impression is of a lack of artistic control, akin to that derived from the stimulating but overloaded political dramas of Auden and Isherwood in the 1930s. Very similar in method and impact is the Cornish *Beunans Meriasek*, or the *Life of Meriasek*, copied down in 1504. Like *Mary Magdalene* its action is immensely protracted, amounting to some 4670 lines, and it also involves a vast cast, almost a hundred parts being featured. Though the work is full of interest, it is scarcely a polished product.

The unique surviving example of an English miracle play, the so-called

Croxton *Play of the Sacrament*, forms the subject of the second chapter of Part Two. This recounts in a lively and skilful fashion the widely-disseminated legend of a Jew who acquires the Host or Communion wafer, and by a series of desperate assaults attempts to destroy it and so prove its purely corporeal nature. All his efforts ending in failure, he ultimately receives a vision of Christ, and as a result is converted to the faith and receives baptism. The play is notable for the inclusion of a comic interlude featuring a quack doctor and his boy which has clear affinities with similar episodes in the traditional English Mumming Play, though it may not necessarily form the irrelevant interpolation that some have claimed.[10]

A fine line may divide the miracle or saints' plays from what are generally referred to as the moralities or the moral plays. The lost York Creed play, for example, possibly consisted of twelve episodes or scenes in which a different apostle played the leading part, since it was commonly believed that each apostle (with Mathias substituted for Judas) was involved in the composition of the Apostles' Creed. It may be that the play of St Thomas at York in 1536 which caused riots and angered Henry VIII was a portion of the complete series. The earliest apparent allusion to the morality form in England occurs in one of the writings of John Wycliffe, his *De Officio Pastorali* (*Of the Pastoral Function*) of 1378. In it the divine alludes to the York Pater Noster plays, in which the doctrine that each of the seven principal petitions of the Lord's Prayer had power to save men from one of the Seven Deadly Sins was evidently set forth in dramatic guise. A Pater Noster play possibly on similar lines is mentioned as being presented at Lincoln in 1397, and another example is recorded at Beverley in 1469. Extant moralities with their emphasis on reformation of conduct based on an awareness of human propensity to sin, together with their telling use of abstract personification of virtue and vice, suggest that they may well have had their origins in the Pater Noster and Creed plays. On the other hand, it is equally possible that their source was not dramatic but rather to be found in the medieval sermon, with its graphic imagery and its penchant for illustrating doctrinal points through illuminating anecdotes or *exempla*.

The first true morality known in English is again fragmentary: known as *The Pride of Life*, it dates from around 1400, and depicts the haughty King of Life (Rex Vivus) defying Death despite warnings from his queen and bishop, and supported by Strength and Health (Fortitudo and Sanitas). He sends Death a challenge that he will do battle with him, confident that he cannot be overcome. Since the text terminates at this point the rest of the action must be pieced together from the prologue, which reveals that Death accepts the challenge, and slays the king. Fiends carry off the soul to Hell, but the action no doubt concluded with the intercession of the Virgin Mary, much as in the French *Miracles de Nostre Dame* or in the ending outlined in the Banns of *The Castel of Perseveraunce*.[11]

The Castel is without doubt the longest, most ambitious, most grandly conceived English morality that survives.[12] Probably slightly later in date than *The Pride of Life*, it dramatizes the traditional battle between the Virtues and the Vices for man's soul – a theme often known as the *Psychomachia* from the title of its vivid treatment in Latin verse by the Spaniard Prudentius in about 400 AD. The staging of the play will occupy Chapter 3 of Part Two of the present study; the plot centres on the spiritual fortunes of Humankind or Humanum Genus from the time of his birth to beyond the grave, as he is assailed by the wiles of the World, the Flesh, and the Devil, assisted by the Seven Deadly Sins. Rescued by his Good Angel, he is lodged in the castle under the protection of the Seven Moral Virtues; but he succumbs to the temptations of Covetousness (Avaricia) and dies in a state of sin, though he cries out for mercy with his last breath. This fact, coupled with the pleas of Mercy and Peace, persuades God to redeem his soul from Hell, and the soul is finally seated at God's right hand.

Mankind is also the hero of a later play of that name, dating from c. 1465–70; like *The Castel of Perseveraunce*, *Mankynde* contains a great deal of stage movement and linguistic energy, but its colloquial vigour and earthy humour should not divert us from the play's serious didactic purpose. It constitutes a highly successful attempt to mingle doctrinal impact with theatrical enjoyment, and its mode of presentation forms the theme of Chapter 1 in Part Two. Its basic theme is not unlike that of *The Castel* but on a smaller scale: it concentrates not on the entire span of human life but on an allegorical incident epitomizing the constant warfare between man's spiritual friends and foes.

Wisdom Who is Christ, or *Mind, Will, and Understanding* (c. 1460–70), which shares the Macro Manuscript with *Mankynde* and *The Castel of Perseveraunce*, has been overshadowed by its more prestigious and accessible companions. Its theme is similar to theirs, in that it presents the three human faculties of mind, will, and understanding as subjected to the corrupting influence of Lucifer, and so imperilling the fate of the Soul or Anima who has declared her allegiance to Wisdom; the latter, in this instance, stands not for worldly knowledge or sagacity but for the 'Wisdom Who is Christ'. Mind becomes proud, Understanding avaricious, and Will turns to lechery, each indulging in song and dance with a band of followers. Absorbed in their wicked plans and quarrelling among themselves, they are brought to their right minds by the rebukes of Wisdom, particularly when Anima, disfigured by their excesses, appears looking 'fowlere than a fende [fiend]'. Repentance and confession cleanse her from sin, and the play closes with the Soul praising Christ for his capacity to redeem mankind. Lacking the epic dimension of *The Castel of Perseveraunce* and less enjoyable as theatre than *Mankynde*, *Wisdom* is a far better play than its relative neglect suggests, and it can repay stylish treatment if special prominence is given to dances which in some measure anticipate the sixteenth-century masque.

Everyman, the best-known of the English moralities, has been touched on in the preface to this book. While it is said to be the least typical of its genre because of its tone of almost unrelieved seriousness and its concentration on the final phase of its hero's career, it is rash to make any assumptions concerning its atypicality in the light of the small handful of analogous plays which survive. In its relative brevity it may be said to characterize the spate of moral interludes of similar length which proliferate from the early sixteenth century – partly as a result of the extremely adaptable nature of the form which could be pressed into a variety of uses, not least as a vehicle for religious polemic, both pro- and anti-Catholic in bias.

If we exclude *Le Mystère d'Adam*, the cycle form in Britain is almost certainly first represented in terms of extant materials by the impressive three-part sequence of plays from Cornwall, now usually referred to as the Cornish *Ordinalia*; this is divided into the *Origo Mundi* (The Creation), the *Passio Domini* (The Lord's Passion), and the *Resurrexio Domini* (The Resurrection of the Lord), each of which occupied a day's playing-time.[13] The date of composition remains problematic: *Annals of English Drama* offers a date between 1300 and 1325, while David C. Fowler suggests the third quarter of the fourteenth century as more likely. Certainly the latter would confirm one's general impression that something approaching full cycle sequences of scriptural dramas were known by 1400.[14] The earliest known record of a Corpus Christi play comes from Beverley in 1377, but as early as c. 1335 Robert Holcot in his commentary *Super librum Sapientiae* alludes to a type of play 'of devotion and spiritual joy, such as Christians perform on the day of Corpus Christi'.[15] However, with such early references it is impossible to tell whether the terms 'pageant' and 'play' allude to a silent tableau, a single play with dialogue and action, or a full sequence. A York record of 1378 mentions a pageant which may imply the existence of dramatic performances, and Chester may well have had plays at about this time too. A Coventry record of 1392 alludes to a *domum pro le pagent pannarum* [quarters to house the Bakers' pageant-waggon], but unfortunately there is no evidence to indicate what kind of spectacle was mounted on the 'pagent'. Certainly we know that Old Testament plays were being given under the auspices of St Paul's in London by 1378, and that plays of a cyclic nature were staged by clerics at Skinner's Well in August 1384 in a production occupying five days –

though that was probably the length of the 'run'. Clerics too presented something similar in July 1391 when 'as much of the Old as the New Testament' was performed, and the chronicler tells us that the proceedings lasted four days. In 1409, according to John Stow the Tudor historian, eight days were devoted to presenting 'matter from the creation of the world', information expanded by the keeper of the royal wardrobe accounts in these terms: 'How God created Heaven and Earth out of nothing, and how he created Adam and so on to the Day of Judgment'. Two years later a seven-day play 'from the begynnyng of the worlde' was also presented by clerics: the cyclic pattern seems to be well attested by the first decade of the fifteenth century.

Records from the fifteenth and sixteenth centuries suggest that a wide range of towns and cities throughout the British Isles possessed cycle series of one kind or another, although only communities sufficiently populous and devoted to their own corporate reputation could have staged the magnificent large-scale dramas associated with such centres as York, Chester, Beverley, Coventry, Lincoln, Norwich, Wakefield and others which, where they survive, are one of the chief glories of English dramatic literature. Lincoln may have been the home of the so-called Hegge or N-Town Cycle, although some of the evidence points to this as having been a peripatetic sequence; King's Lynn and Norwich have also been canvassed as possible centres from which this cycle sprang. Lincoln certainly had its own biblical cycle plays, now lost, which may have been staged in the nave of the cathedral, but on St Anne's Day (26 July) rather than on Corpus Christi Day itself. Aberdeen in Scotland staged a Passion Play at Corpus Christi, but also presented some kind of Nativity sequence on Candlemas Day (2 February); in New Romney in Kent a combined Passion and Resurrection play was presented at Whitsuntide from about 1428 onwards. And so the list might be multiplied at length for the entire country.

The five great English cycle sequences are the end-products of possibly two centuries of successive revisions and rewritings by a body of anonymous playwrights: the sequences are the Cornish *Ordinalia*, and the York, Wakefield or Towneley, Chester, and N-Town (or Hegge) Cycles, the latter of which is sometimes referred to erroneously as the *Ludus Coventriae*. Two individual plays survive from the Coventry Cycle, which once consisted of at least eleven pageants: the celebrated Nativity pageant presented by the Shearmen and Tailors of the city, and Christ's Presentation in the Temple, performed by the Weavers, are all that remains. There also exist some few isolated Biblical plays, apparently remnants of fuller series, which have perished: two fragments of an Adam and Eve play from the Grocers of Norwich; a play of Noah from Newcastle-upon-Tyne; two affecting treatments of the story of Abraham's putative sacrifice of Isaac from Northampton and from Brome in Suffolk, make up the total of what is now left of a once-proud dramatic tradition.[16]

The three-day *Ordinalia* from south-west Cornwall totals about 8,600 lines of Middle Cornish verse. Like the English cycles, it consists of plays dealing with such Old Testament incidents as the Fall of Man, the Flood, and the Exodus from Egypt as were felt to have relevance to the later theme of Man's redemption from death through Christ's Passion, Death, and Resurrection, which form the subject of Plays II and III. However, unlike the English sequences, the Cornish Cycle contains no plays on the Nativity; Play II opens with the Temptation in the Wilderness and the Entry into Jerusalem. A number of its most characteristic plays are unique to the Cornish trilogy: these include King David's planting of three rods symbolizing the Trinity, his courtship of Bathsheba, the Building of the Temple at Jerusalem, and the Death of Pilate. The Ascension is seen as the high point of the Cornish plays where it receives a far more extended treatment than is accorded to it in any of the English cycles.

The Cornish Cycle is an accomplished and often vigorous rendering of biblical history, in no way inferior to the better-known English versions which – at least in their present state – post-date it. The astute characterizations and zestful dialogue still give great pleasure to modern audiences, though much is lost by translation into even idiomatic contemporary slang. The scriptural figures are perhaps a trifle flat, but the earthy, non-Biblical, unidealized characters still make an impact: the Torturers who martyr the female saint Maximilla and later put Christ to death, the carpenters at work on the Temple, the soldiers guarding the tomb, and above all, the Jailor, his insubordinate Boy, and the Wife of the Smith who, in forging the nails for the Cross, has a scene of amazing *double-entendre* with one of the Torturers.

The York Cycle may not be the oldest extant cycle in the English language, but it certainly appears in one of the oldest texts, a fair copy preserved in the British Library and made in the fifteenth century to serve as the official civic register of the plays as they then existed, though even this is clearly not the earliest version of the plays ever presented. Into this manuscript other material was copied at a later period, alterations and additions being recorded here in order to keep the register up-to-date. The version thus secured for posterity consists of forty-eight separate plays and a fragment, but there is no evidence that all forty-eight episodes were presented in sequence at any one time; this is a point to which we shall return in Part Two of this book, where the staging of the York Passion plays will be analyzed. The contents of the York sequence are notable for the leisured treatment of the Creation and Fall of Man, six separate plays being devoted to this aspect of the Christian story, and the Passion sequence is also broken down into a large number of plays, possibly to cater for the large number of guilds in the city who wished to take part in the performances. The York Passion sequence is also distinguished by the fact that it contains the work of one of the few anonymous playwrights whose literary and dramatic style can be identified, and who has been awarded the label of 'the York Realist'.

While the cyclic principle lying behind all the sequences must never be lost sight of, it is inevitable that certain highlights should help to give individual cycles their particular flavour for readers and spectators, and the York Plays contain a number of memorable episodes. Notable are a long *Exodus* play, a delightful comedic rendering of Joseph's suspicions concerning Mary, a somewhat formalized Entry into Jerusalem, and a highly dramatic *Dream of Pilate's Wife*; but it is perhaps in the plays depicting Christ's suffering and death (and the Crucifixion in particular) that the sequence reaches the height of its artistry, although the solemn majesty of its opening and close with their verbal patterns of proposition and response demonstrates medieval stage rhetoric at its best.

The Towneley Plays (usually, though not necessarily correctly, associated with the town of Wakefield; the name 'Towneley' refers to the Burnley family in whose hands the manuscript rested until 1814) are linked with those of York, not merely in their use of a similar dialect, but more directly. It seems that early in the fifteenth century the Wakefield authorities borrowed the text from neighbouring York, six of the Wakefield plays being almost identical to those in the York register. The Wakefield text as we now have it was copied down in about 1450, and since several of the plays written out there are considerably more bald and basic than their York counterparts, it appears that episodes which received revision at York were left untouched at the other Yorkshire centre. At the same time, several of the Wakefield versions are considerably more advanced in technique and execution than their York originals, notably the six plays attributed to the revising pen of the so-called 'Wakefield Master'; he is the most theatrically sophisticated dramatist among all the cycle-play authors, being a skilled versifier, a masterly creator of character and dialogue exchanges, and a comic writer with a lively sense of irony. The most telling plays in the Wakefield sequence are those by the 'Master': indeed, the Murder of Abel, the Noah play, the two Shepherds' Plays (including the celebrated version featuring Mak the Sheepstealer), the play of Herod the Great, and the Buffeting of Christ at his trial before Caiaphas and Annas, are among the best plays in the medieval repertoire.

In about 1468 a scrivener copied out the text of the N-Town or Hegge Cycle into another unique manuscript which eventually found its way from the custody of the Hegge family to the British Library. The N-Town cycle had as its chief redactor a man of considerable knowledge and theological sophistication, and with an eye for spectacular dramatic effects. It seems clear that it was never presented in processional form, at least as a totality, although parts might be staged in that way. The work appears to have been made up into a complete cyclic structure of the orthodox kind by conflating a number of separate sets of plays together, and producing a sort of edited anthology which does not hang together as satisfactorily as it should. It has even been suggested that the manuscript was never intended as a basis for stage performance at all, and that its compilation was simply a literary exercise, or intended for reading or devotional purposes. However, the degree of theatrical expertise exhibited renders it virtually certain that live presentation was never far from the minds of the N-Town authors. The chief glories of the sequence include a poignant Creation and Fall, an excellent rendering of the Sacrifice of Isaac, a version of Joseph's Suspicion to rival York's, the apocryphal but theatrically effective Trial of Joseph and Mary, and the best of all those plays dealing with Christ's Ministry, that of the Woman Taken in Adultery, which takes full advantage of the theatrical potential of the Gospel episode.

Equally successful, although in an entirely different mode, is the Chester Cycle, five manuscripts of which survive, although these are regrettably late in date, being copied between c. 1590 and 1610. The Chester *Play of Antichrist* also exists in an earlier version, and there is a separate manuscript of *The Trial and Flagellation*, roughly contemporary with the complete versions. The Chester plays were almost certainly presented in processional manner by the guilds of the city using the traditional pageant-waggons, a procedure which has come to typify medieval staging methods for many people. The plays themselves are not strongly steeped in a sense of robust human vigour and warmth, and they have therefore been undervalued by some commentators. But they have a simplicity of feeling and economy of expression which has its own appeal, and in at least a handful of plays the Chester playwrights achieved effects which were outside the scope of even such experts as the York Realist and the Wakefield Master. Their treatment of Noah and the Flood is the most accomplished of any; their Shepherds are quite as memorable as their York and Wakefield counterparts. Chester scores heavily, too, in a comparison of the plays of the Ministry, notably in the Healing of the Blind Chelidonian and the Raising of Lazarus; and if the Passion sequences do not rise to the heights of rival depictions, the Harrowing of Hell and the post-Resurrection plays are successful at points where the other, more lofty cycles often convey a sense of anti-climax. It is characteristic that the Chester *Judgement* concludes not with the majestic tones of the exultant Christ or the satisfied God, but with the rueful statements of the Four Evangelists that their warnings went unheeded by sinful man until Doomsday overtook him.

IV

Our knowledge of secular dramatic activity in England during the late Middle Ages is regrettably confined to a handful of texts and a few partisan accounts.[17] For this we must blame a combination of forces: the ravages of time and the instincts of disapproving ecclesiastical censors are two of the major reasons why many exciting scripts have disappeared from view, although perhaps the best of this type of dramatic entertainment was never committed to paper. Traces of ritual folk-dramas, such as Plough Monday routines, Wooing and Mumming Plays, Combat pieces, still exist, along with remnants of popular 'games' of a dramatic nature. The influence of these ceremonies can often be detected in literary drama, but sadly, few of these can properly convey the flavour of demotic theatrical activities. Plays with the best chances of surviving were undoubtedly aristocratic pageants, mummings, and similar devices primarily prepared for the delectation of the royal court. Courtly conditions obviously favoured the preservation of such pieces far more than those circumstances which prevailed in obscure hamlets or country fields. As it is, there are only about twenty or so dramatic texts and fragments which represent Britain's secular stage between the Norman Conquest and the end of the fifteenth century.

The principal candidate for the honour of being the earliest English secular dramatic fragment to survive must be the *Interludium de Clerico et Puella* (The Interlude of the Clerk and the Girl), dated between 1300 and 1325.[18] This consists of the two opening scenes of an anonymous farce, starring the eponymous protagonists and an old crone, Mome Helwis or Mother Eloise. The clerk or student of the title is a typical young lover aching to enjoy a girl living 'at the tounes ende', who, whilst welcoming him to her parents' house in their absence, is still unwilling to satisfy his passionate desires. He seeks the aid of an aged dame to further his cause, and the fragment breaks off at her hypocritical protest that she is not in the habit of acting as a pimp. However, the outcome of similar narratives which form the subject of the Latin dramatic poem *Pamphilus* and the Middle English verse *fabliau Dame Sirith* makes it obvious that girlish resolution will ultimately succumb to male persistence and antique guile.

De Clerico et Puella is almost the only English example of a genre of bawdy domestic farces which survive in rather greater profusion on the

Continent; a puzzling remnant of a possible Cornish example has been preserved on the back of a charter from around 1400.[19] Like the liturgical 'Shrewsbury Fragments' it is in the form of a copy of an actor's part. A young traveller is offered a seemingly docile wife by an older man, and is pleased to accept her; on his departure the elderly man instructs the girl how to get the better of her new husband, by never yielding to him, despite the fact she finds him attractive. She is warned that she must get the upper hand and never allow him to dominate her! It has been claimed as part of a saint's play, but its content appears to be sexual, and it could well belong to a piece in which adulterous activities formed the core of the action.

Roughly seventy-five years after the Cornish piece, on Good Friday 16 April 1473, Sir John Paston II wrote to his brother from Canterbury complaining of the ingratitude of some of his servants. These included one W. Woode who had promised never to leave his service, and whom Paston had retained 'to pleye Seynt Jorge *and* Robynhod *and* Shryff off Notyngham', an ironic way of saying that the man in question had spent more time acting in interludes than looking after his master's horses![20] From about the same date there occurs a fragmentary text, now in Trinity College Library, Cambridge, of a play which seems to feature both Robin Hood and the Sheriff, though the text lacks all speech-ascriptions. This may possibly be part of the script for the performances in which Woode took part, although it is clearly incomplete as it stands. From the evidence of the parallel ballad of 'Sir Guy of Gisborne' it has been argued that it is he who appears in the play as Robin Hood's opponent in a series of sporting contests: they compete at archery, at stone-casting, at wrestling, and lastly at duelling to the death. Robin finally cuts off Sir Guy's head, but his band of outlaws are captured by the Sheriff, whereupon the fragment ends. The ballad conclusion is that Robin Hood disguised as Sir Guy hoodwinks the Sheriff by pretending that the severed head is his own not Gisborne's, and as a result is able to claim Little John's life as his reward. They are then able to turn the tables on the Sheriff and release the rest of the outlaws. But David Wiles has put forward a more plausible reconstruction in which the Sheriff is locked in his own prison. There must always be doubts as to whether or not this composition is a true play, and not some kind of recited ballad, but the opportunities for spirited action, admittedly of an athletic more than a histrionic kind, suggest that it is correct to regard it as a dramatic script.

Henry Medwall's *Nature* and *Fulgens and Lucres* date from the 1490s, and these 'moral interludes' appear to have been intended for performance at the home of Cardinal John Morton, Archbishop of Canterbury from 1486 until his death in 1500; Thomas More served as a youth in his household, and Medwall was chaplain there. The entertainment of players seems to have been a speciality of Morton's house; More's biographer, William Roper, left a vivid picture of his celebrated father-in-law stepping in among the players presenting the Christmas diversions and improvising a part for himself in the action, 'which made the lookers-on more sport than all the players beside'. The views of the players on the subject are fortunately not recorded.

Medwall deserves well of posterity for pioneering the new vogue for secular morality dramas which was to flourish during the early decades of the sixteenth century, and led on in some measure to the exploration of ethical and moral principles in Elizabethan plays.[21] His two-part work *Nature* features the abstract personifications familiar from religious moralities such as *The Castel of Perseveraunce* and *Mankynde*, but adapts the theme of the *Psychomachia* to reflect humanistic concerns in that Man is shown abandoning Reason in youth and succumbing to Pride, but ultimately learning self-control and returning to more abstemious habits as he grows older. *Fulgens and Lucres*, probably presented during a banquet in 1497, is a more radical departure from the conventional morality framework. Based on a translation of a Latin humanist treatise on the nature of true nobility, but incorporating something of the lively horseplay of folk festivities into its comic sub-plot, *Fulgens and Lucres* rejects the potentially rigid structure of the morality convention for a more flexible approach to humanized characters in a secularized society. The final chapter of Part Two discusses how the earliest performance of this delightful comedy might have been arranged.

Dramatic entertainments forming part of the texture of medieval court society fall into two principal categories: mummings presented for the amusement of the assembled court, and pageants staged by urban communities at the visitation of a royal or noble personage as a mark of respect and loyalty. Both types usually consisted of tableaux and static dumb-shows mimed by costumed figures often representing abstract qualities (as in the morality plays) or popular mythological characters, accompanied by somewhat undramatic speeches often narrated by a presenter. Both frequently culminated with some kind of presentation, sometimes linked to a request for royal redress of some real or spurious complaint, but the mummings which survive have a more light-hearted tone than the more solemn pageants, as befits a form of diversion mainly intended for private enjoyment.

One of the earliest scripts for such a presentation dates from the fifteenth century, and is found in Trinity College, Cambridge MS 599. Christened 'The Mumming of the Seven Philosophers' by R. H. Robbins, it consists of twelve, rather laboured stanzas in the rhyme-royal form so common in the fifteenth century, recited by a 'Nuncius' or messenger from the Roman philosopher 'Senek' and the seven philosophers themselves, and addressed to the 'kyng of Crystmas'; he is greeted in stanza 2 and offered wise counsels for a successful life in the remainder of the poem.[22] Since ceremonies featuring a 'kyng of Cristemesse' are recorded, including one notable account from Norwich in 1443, it may be that we have here a mumming or pageant incorporating a popular folk ritual.

Almost all the courtly mumming texts to survive emanate from the pen of John Lydgate, generally reckoned as Chaucer's principal and most successful literary disciple. Between c. 1424 and c. 1431 Lydgate devised at least seven entertainments under the labels of mummings or disguisings either for the pleasure of the boy-king Henry VI, or to fulfil commissions from various of the London Livery Companies for tributes in dramatic form to be staged before the Lord Mayor.[23] The earliest was presented before Henry VI and his mother during the celebrations for Christmas 1424 at Eltham Palace, site of several previous 'lost' mummings staged before Richard II and Henry IV; it depicted the descent to earth of Bacchus, Juno and Ceres. Classical figures also featured in Lydgate's roughly contemporary 'Mumming at Bishopswood' performed at Stepney before the sheriffs of London at a May Day dinner, while Jupiter's poursuivant acted as presenter for a mumming commissioned by the London Mercers in January 1429 to entertain the Lord Mayor. However, although in the following month the expositor in the Goldsmiths' Mumming is the classical figure of Fortune, the other participants are King David and representatives of the twelve tribes of Israel. Fortune again appears along with other personifications in the lengthy and some- what pompous 'London Mumming' of c. 1427 presented apparently by an all-female cast before 'the great estates of England'; this attempt at grandiloquence holds little appeal beside the more attractive and vivacious Christmas 'Mumming at Hertford' in which the young Henry VI was invited to watch 'a disguysing of the rude upplandisshe [rustic] people compleynynge on hir wyves, with the boystous aunswere of hir wyves' and adjudge which of the sexes had most reason to denigrate the other. Henry was also the recipient of the last of Lydgate's mummings to survive, that presented at Windsor shortly before the king crossed the Channel to be crowned King of France on 16 December 1431.

Lydgate also composed the libretti for the pageants which welcomed Henry back to London on 21 February 1432, such ceremonies being of course a familiar feature of civic life in Britain from at least the early thirteenth century onwards, though their textual content only becomes apparent in the fifteenth century.[24] Records of seven pageants staged for Henry's entry to the city are extant, and they present a farrago of giants, allegorical personifications, the liberal sciences and their practitioners, virgins representing both the Christian and the secular virtues, Old Testa- ment prophets, a Jesse tree, and the Holy Trinity! When Henry's queen,

Margaret of Anjou, entered London thirteen years later the pageants (again by Lydgate) were predominantly religious, featuring such biblical tableaux as Noah's Ark, The Wise and Foolish Virgins, the Resurrection and the Day of Judgment, which may well reflect the influence of the pageantry of the Corpus Christi processions.

A few examples and fragments of similar pageants remain, but the majority have perished, and in this instance it would be hypocritical to regret the loss of material so clearly lacking in literary or dramatic merit. Most of what survives is turgid, mechanical, and pretentious, and the few exceptions such as Lydgate's Hertford mumming only accentuate the frigid dullness of the rest. It is the great gap in our knowledge of less portentous and less inhibited secular drama in the Middle Ages which constitutes the true tragedy.

Part Two

Plays in Performance

The five chapters which follow aim to reconstruct the original performances of some major medieval English plays, using a mixture of scholarly
evidence and informed guesswork, but there is one important caveat to
be kept in view. A medieval drama which comes down to us as a written
text may have assumed a totally different face when set forth on stage
before an audience. Many surviving texts were almost certainly never
played in their extant form; many others were doubtless altered radically
in the course of production. All conjectures as to their original presentation must take this into account and be regarded not as firm proposals
but rather as fallible efforts to deduce the treatment existing scripts *could*
have received when prepared for staging in the Middle Ages.

I · The Booth Stage: *Mankynde*

The anonymous fifteenth-century morality play of *Mankynde* has enjoyed a revival of scholarly status and critical interest in the last few decades, without attracting comparable attention in the theatre.[1] Changes in contemporary taste are partly responsible for the enhanced stature of this fast-moving and often bawdy piece, yet it is largely due to a fuller perception of the playwright's skills that *Mankynde* now ranks high among pre-Elizabethan dramas. Misunderstanding of its effect in the past has largely come about through failure to comprehend the carefully-engineered relationship between humour and 'doctryne', and from an imperfect appreciation of the psychological knowledge which underlies the generous use of the scatological in the action. What were formerly dismissed as authorial incompetence and indecorum are today viewed as parts of a subtly-contrived scheme for reinforcing the didactic ends of the drama without sacrificing entertainment-value.

The script dating from c. 1465–70 derives from East Anglia; its word-forms are of East Midland origin, and Cambridgeshire, Norfolk, and Suffolk place-names occur in the text.[2] Speculation regarding its auspices of performance partly centres on the intriguing question of whether this piece was presented indoors, possibly in the hall of a large house or a chamber of a tavern, or out of doors, perhaps in an inn-yard.[3] Textual evidence alone must help us decide on the most probable performance-site, and the most likely methods employed in *Mankynde*'s staging.

There is another point of interest. It has sometimes been claimed that *Mankynde* is part of the repertoire of a professional band of strolling players, and that a demand in lines 457–70 that spectators must stump up a cash donation if they wish to see the devil Titivillus denotes a professional company at work. However, there is no necessity to make this assumption, since amateurs were not averse to making a collection if the need arose. At Sutterton in Lincolnshire in 1525–6, 3s 6½d was 'Resavyd of Gaderyng [taken by collecting]' at a performance by local amateurs, and the fund-raising *quête* or house-to-house collection featured in many amateur folk-dramas including the Mumming Play and Robin Hood ceremonies.[4] Even if *Mankynde* is the earliest English text to integrate the need for such a collection into its dramatic structure, it does not follow that we are dealing with a company which relied on such support for its main source of livelihood. Even if we are confronting the work of professionals here, the local references suggest that players confined their strolling to a fairly limited area and did not stray beyond it. In view of the difficulties of fifteenth-century travel, the reasons are not hard to comprehend.

Of greater interest is the evidence for the play's performance-site. The usual inference that *Mankynde* was presented on the premises of an inn or tavern has customarily been supported by Mercy's allusion to

ye soverens that sytt and ye brothern that stonde ryght wppe [up]
     (line 29);[5]

by Mankynde's greeting to Mercy:

Ye be welcom to this house (209);

by New Gyse's request at line 467 for 'the goodeman of this house' to start the collection rolling with a generous contribution; by Mankynde's explanation when he seeks to relieve himself that

I wyll into thi yerde [yard], soverens, and cum ageyn son [soon] (561);

by his summons to the tapster in line 729, followed by New Gyse's call to the ostler to lend him a football at line 732.

Some of the arguments are not irrefutable. Mercy's reference to the audience could apply to any auditorium where some spectators were seated while others stood; the 'house' alluded to might be any secular building, while its 'goodeman' might simply be the owner, even the lord of the manor in whose hall the players were performing; Mankynde's retreat into the yard seems only to suggest that to 'do that nedys must be don' he goes outside a building. Yet there are several objections to the view that *Mankynde* was staged in some notable's hall. The taking of a collection does not accord with what we know of presentations of this nature, where the spectators were probably dinner-guests of the householder who might object to a request to sanction a 'whip-round' in his own home, while the sustained bawdry of the piece does not entirely accord with a private occasion. Moreover, considerable weight must be given to the calls to the tapster and the ostler respectively: even if an ostler might plausibly be found within the environs of a manor-house or castle, a tapster would surely only be located within a hostelry. Mankynde's departure to answer a call of nature in the 'yard' seems more aptly sited on licensed premises too, even if no particular significance attaches to Nought's reference to a door and a 'way' at line 159 – especially as it quotes a common proverbial tag of the period. Thus it seems that an inn-site must be preferred to that of a great hall, if only because the conjunction of so many appropriate details supports it.

Two locations are then possible: within the inn itself, and outside in an enclosed courtyard of the type which survives at the New Inn, Gloucester, and the George Hotel, Huntingdon (see Plates 3 and 4) a model familiar to many playgoers today from its close resemblance to the interior of an Elizabethan playhouse. The principal support for indoor performance comes from Mankynde's reference to going into the yard, which at first sight only seems intelligible if the player is assumed to be inside a building when he says it, and from Nought's allusion to a door. On the other hand, these impressions may be countered with another line drawn from a later point in the action when Mankynde, disconcerted by Titivillus and the Vices, announces:

Adew, fayer masters! I wyll hast me *to the ale-house*
Ande speke wyth New Gyse, Nowadays and Nought (609–10; my
    italics).

This seems absurd if he is already *inside* an ale-house, even if in the upshot he does not actually make the trip there. It seems imperative to select a location for the performance of *Mankynde* which satisfies the following criteria:

(a) proximity to a site where ostlers and tapsters are normally found;
(b) proximity to a courtyard where natural functions are often
    exercised;
(c) proximity to an inn to which Mankynde can conveniently
    withdraw.

The most satisfactory solution is to maintain that the presentation took place in an inn-yard, where the simple booth-stage familiar since Roman times with its portable platform divided in two by a curtained framework provided a raised playing-area (see Plate 5). Setting up such a stage within the yard fulfils all three criteria set out above: it provides for ostlers and tapsters to be within plausible hailing-distance; it offers Mankynde easy access to the 'toilet facilities' when he descends 'into the yerde' without rendering that remark tautologous; at the same time it does not render ridiculous his reference to hurrying to the ale-house – and we may note that the formulation '*the* ale-house' rather than '*an* ale-house' is employed – by placing him within the tavern already. Moreover, this location is in accordance with the general impression one retains from reading this play that its action is essentially conceived of as taking place under the open sky. It is rare for the authors of any of those pieces which we know were intended for indoor performance such as *Fulgens and Lucres* to introduce natural outdoor activities into them. But while the dancing and horseplay in *Mankynde* could be equally well accommodated indoors as outside, the play lays great emphasis on its hero's efforts to till his ground and sow his

3 The inn-yard of the George Hotel, Huntingdon
(Photo: British Tourist Authority)

4 The yard of the Tabard Inn, Southwark, c. 1780, from a contemporary
engraving (Photo: Douglas Madge)

5 A booth stage erected in a market-square (Detail from David Vinckboons, 'Kirmes') (Photo: Herzog Anton Ulrich-Museum, Braunschweig)

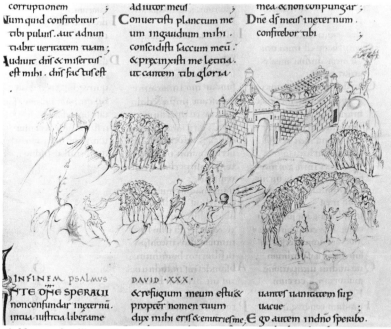

6 Manuscript illustration of a crowd entertained by a bearward, musician, and dancer (Harley MS 603) (Photo: British Library)

1 A conjectural view of *Mankynde* presented on a booth stage within an inn-yard

corn, so that it is at least arguable that open-air staging most appropriately accommodated this *al fresco* dimension.

★ ★ ★

Let us now assume that we are among the spectators assembled in the year 1470 somewhere in East Anglia, to witness a production of *Mankynde*. We are crowded into the yard of a country inn where there is necessarily a limited amount of space vacant for those 'brothern that stonde ryght wppe' like ourselves, and indeed from the back of the yard our view of the stage is not all that it might be. However, unlike the 'soverens that sytt' more comfortably in the first-storey galleries all round the yard, we have not had to pay the landlord for the privilege of watching the play from under cover, although it is rumoured that at some point in the proceedings we shall be invited to contribute something to the funds.

At the far end of the rectangular inn-yard, abutting on to the chief public rooms, a temporary platform about 4 feet 6 ins. to 5 feet in height has been erected on a solid foundation of ale-casks, although in circumstances where such commodities are less readily come by, sturdy wooden trestles could be used. The platform comprises about fifteen planks laid side by side end-on to the audience, and is divided into two: the frontal playing-area, which juts out into the throng of standing spectators and measures roughly 6 to 8 feet deep and some 10 to 12 feet wide, is backed by a curtain suspended before the 'backstage' area from which the players can emerge and into which they can retire. This sector, formed of a wooden framework of poles arranged in a rectangle, is curtained on all four sides to prevent its inhabitants from being seen; access to it is gained by ascending steps at the rear of the structure and then slipping through the back curtain. There are also three ladders or short flights of steps leading down from the front and the leading corners

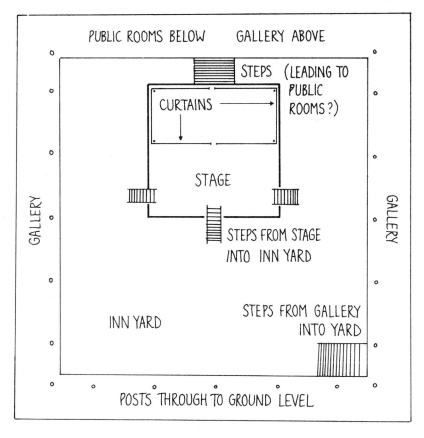

2 A bird's-eye view of the staging of *Mankynde* in an inn-yard

of the platform into the yard, whose use often involves the players in pushing through the throng to gain the comparative peace of the inn itself, or the arcades under the galleries. Departures and arrivals can therefore be effected either through the back curtain, or up and down the steps leading directly on and off the platform; players can appear from and retreat between front curtains, disappear into the inn itself, or even retire under the galleries to await their cues. A relatively sophisticated system of exits and entrances can thus be arranged with a minimum of disruption to the inn's normal function of serving food and drink.

Mankynde begins with the arrival of Mercy characterized as a 'semely father' and therefore dressed as an itinerant friar or a priest. His opening speech in the form of a forty-four line sermon on the urgent necessity for repentance and virtuous conduct confirms this impression. Mercy's initial entry is worth pondering; does he enter through the crowd and climb on the platform to begin his exhortation, stressing his role as a wandering preacher, or does he reinforce that he is a player by stepping out from between the curtains and advancing to the front of the stage to deliver his oration? The latter is more immediately arresting and would gain him swifter attention, but there is a certain attraction if the priest in his long gown emerges from the ranks of the 'groundlings' and climbs the steps, if only because it preserves the sense, at least briefly, that Mercy has stepped up to preach a genuine sermon rather than appearing from the 'green-room' to participate in a play.

The significance of the language of Mercy's opening sermon has been imperfectly understood until recently. There is little doubt that its ornate vocabulary and inflated tone are highly characteristic of the 'aureate' manner popular at a time when many authors felt that the English language was too naked and crude a vehicle to compete with Latin when it came to paying poetic compliments, or coping with the divine mysteries of the Christian faith. In a search for sounding eloquence and stylistic elegance, a fashion for selecting terms rich in elaborate Latinate adornments became widespread, so much so that the virtues of plain homely English speech became disregarded in certain quarters. Mercy's speech abounds in such pompous nouns as 'remocyon' [inclination], 'restytucyon', 'defendawnte [defender]', 'felycyctes', 'premedytacyon'; ponderous phrases such as 'he hade non indygnacyon [disdain]' and 'partycypable of his retribucyon' are typical. The syntax is stiff and formal, the figurative language dull, the sentiments seemingly banal, and the relief felt when Myscheff cheekily interrupts the improving remarks by parodying Mercy's earnest

The corn shall be savyde, the chaffe shall be brente.

I besech yow hertyly, have this premedytacyon (43–4)

with his ribald

I beseche yow hertyly, leve yowr calcacyon [thrashing about the bush].
Leve yowr chaffe, leve yowr corn, leve yowr dalyacyon (45–6)
– is considerable.

Yet suggestions that Mercy is to be regarded as merely a figure of fun to be scoffed at and derided by the audience are wide of the mark. His pretentious tone and conventional sentiments mask two fundamental tenets to which the playwright almost certainly subscribes: one is that the Christian message is not invalidated simply by being conveyed through imperfect agents, and the other is that the truths embodied in the Christian religion *are* ostensibly conventional because they are invariable, the problem being not to grasp them but to act on them. Mercy is not an appealing nor charismatic figure: we warm much more readily to Myscheff, the quick-witted master of repartee and witty abuse, but the spurious appeal of one whose name signifies 'evil' rather than its modern connotation represents the first meretricious allurement prepared for us by a shrewd stage psychologist.

Where does Myscheff appear from to interrupt Mercy's peroration? Again, there is no intrinsic reason why he should not emerge from the booth curtain and march up behind Mercy as he preaches at the front of the stage, but this could take away from the impact of his interruption. It would be much neater, as well as more effective in theatrical terms, if Myscheff began his heckling, if not from the main body of the audience (he might have difficulty inserting and extracting himself!) then at least from somewhere in the yard, almost as if he were a *bona fide* spectator and not a player. (A similar effect is achieved in *Fulgens and Lucres* by the servants A and B, who behave like members of the genuine audience.) Much sensation would result initially if the crowd felt that one of its own members was trying to disrupt proceedings, however welcome the interruption. Myscheff therefore interrupts from the 'floor', swaggers through the throng to confront the speaker, and once on the platform, putting on a mock-serious manner, makes his request for an answer to his flippant query:

But, ser, I prey this questyon to claryfye (48).

The gullible Mercy (who makes the mistake of listening to Myscheff) reacts strongly to his ridiculous patter:

Why com ye hethyr, brother? Ye were not dysyryde (53);

only to be met with further nonsense from the irrepressible Vice-figure who claims that he has been hired as 'a wynter corn-thresher'. This may offer a clue to the play's season of performance: not only is one of its leading theatrical images that of a man preparing the ground ready for sowing his seeds in it, but its theme is amply appropriate to the Lenten season of purgation and repentance. Moreover, the worthless agreement Mankynde is betrayed into entering into with the Vices is dated 'yestern day in Feverere', New Gyse mentions the cold weather in line 323, and even his casual request for the loan of a football reminds us that this sport was a popular Shrove Tuesday amusement enjoyed before the austerities of Lent.

Myscheff proceeds to mock Mercy by picking him up on the words of his sermon, offering to pop a halfpenny in his mouth as payment, and giving out a pseudo-Latin text, quite impervious to Mercy's suggestion that he should take himself off. How long this verbal duelling between these strongly-contrasted types continued is uncertain, since a complete leaf of the text is missing after seventy-one lines, and when the text is resumed Myscheff has gone and three new characters have joined the preacher in the forms of New Gyse, Nought, and Nowadays. It does not appear that they have been present for any length of time, since they still seem to be in the process of establishing themselves. Evidently in his final utterance before their eruption on to the stage Mercy had the occasion to speak some line such as

Men of nought ever follow the new guise nowadays,

supplying the Vices with the verbal cue they require to appear, giving as their excuse that they heard their names called and assumed that Mercy wanted them! Their first line of dialogue is a request to minstrels to 'pley the comyn trace', presumably a popular tune for dancing, so we must assume that musicians are present, entering with the trio of revellers or discovered already ensconced in one of the galleries. At all events a certain amount of horseplay and dancing now ensues.

Since they are unequivocally performers and there is little chance of their being mistaken for members of the public, the three newcomers can be reckoned to enter from the 'backstage' area: of the three, New Gyse and Nowadays are the dominant personalities, Nought (as his name implies) being their butt or stooge. New Gyse, after instructing the minstrels what to play, says to Nowadays:

Ley on wyth thi ballys [whip] tyll hys bely breste [burst]! (73).

Nowadays then gives the callous command to Nought to

Leppe about lyvely! thou art a wyght [nimble] man (76),

and Nought makes his aggrieved response:

Shall I breke my neke to schew yow sporte? (78)

Watch what you're saying, says Nowadays with a flick of the whip, and with a curse Nought makes the best of the matter and reluctantly begins to shuffle about to the music, much as the unfortunate Lucky dances for Pozzo in *Waiting for Godot*. The whole picture becomes still clearer if we adopt Glynne Wickham's inspired suggestion[6] that we have here a deliberate burlesque of a dancing bear with his trainer, a popular roadside and fairground attraction in Britain up to relatively recent times, and another possible indication that the spirit of pre-Lenten Carnival informs this play (see Plate 6). But here the man-with-a-bear routine is given symbolic significance since it equates with brutishness and aggressively cruel foolery the Vices whose aim is to humiliate Nought in the same way that they humiliate Mankynde later in the play. Wickham believes that Nought may even have worn a bear's mask and a skin to match, but this might obscure the fact that he is a man behaving like a bear, and he may well have worn ordinary dress with a bear's head covering his face. Yet it is curious to observe that when Nought suggests that Mercy take his place as the 'bear' he orders:

of [off] wyth yowr clothes, yf ye wyll play (88).

Although Nought may simply be referring to the 'clothes' Mercy wears as a member of his religious order (a meaning not supported by the *Oxford English Dictionary*), this also raises the intriguing possibility that Nought's animality was emphasized by his wearing virtually no clothing, like the bear he is forced to imitate.

Mercy finds the Vices' revelling intolerable and orders them to desist, although Nowadays tells him to mind his own business – 'Thys ys no parte of thi pley' – but Nought, exhausted by his frantic capering, is quite happy to see the 'goode father' intervene if he is prepared to take over the dancing. Nowadays is more than prepared to beat Mercy, and Nought warns him that it is somewhat violent exercise, and that the platform offers little room to escape attention from the whip: 'I tell yt ys a narow space' (97) – which suggests a stage somewhat cramped for expansive movement if four players are on it at any one time. Nought diverts the others' attention by pretending that Mercy called their names; New Gyse complains that he was asleep and Nowadays that he had his cup in his hand and was just about to dine, both reinforcing the notion that they have emerged from the inn behind the stage on hearing Mercy's 'summons'. Mercy criticizes their impudence and curt manner of speech, which they defend as being the latest style, and when he objects to it, the bully Nowadays threatens him with a 'bofett' from his whip. Nought, encouraged that his former tormentors have at last found a fresh victim, actually trips the holy man up. There is no stage-direction, but presumably Mercy gets to his feet in as dignified a manner as possible, and defends himself from having called them by enquiring their names, being horrified when he learns they are those of infamous corrupters of morals, although the Vices protest that all they do is merely make men 'fresch and gay'. Informed in their turn that he is Mercy, they sneer at his 'Englysch Laten' diction, which they claim will make him explode ere long, and they accuse him to being 'a stronge cunnyng clerke', while Nowadays asks him to translate a vile couplet into Latin for him. (It is worth noting here that the frequent excremental imagery employed by the Vices, far from being mere casually obscene colouring, is an integral feature of the moral differentation by verbal means which forms such a marked aspect of *Mankynde*.) Nowadays then asks Mercy's advice on a marital problem, and when Nought ventures to offer his opinion, Nowadays suggests he kiss Mercy's buttocks. Some business between Nought and Mercy follows, though what form it took is obscure: Nought seems to claim to have found a papal pardon on Mercy's person, and it is likely that this character, in trying to carry out Nowadays's lewd suggestion by burrowing among Mercy's garments, lights on a scroll which he holds up and pretends is a pardon. Mercy is furious at such blasphemy – 'Thys ydyll language ye shall repent' – but the sport of baiting virtue begins to grow tame for all three Vices who take themselves off, variously abusing the priest. It is at this point (line 159) that Nought remarks that 'Here ys the dore, her ys the wey'. There is no necessity to assume that this supports an interior setting: apart from the fact that Nought is using a popular tag, he also wishes Mercy 'good night' which is almost certainly not to be taken literally, so that the door may also be figurative. If not, two interpretations of Nought's words are compatible with an inn-yard location: one is that he treats the front curtain of the booth stage as a door, the other that he exits through the audience and makes his remark standing at one of the doors in the yard which leads to the street.

Left alone, Mercy protests that the Vices are worse than beasts since their pleasure is in deriding Christ and speaking idle words; his own language is now purged of its outward affectations, and becomes direct and lucid. His pithy remarks are interrupted by the entry of Mankynde himself, an honest, respectable Everyman-figure in a long old-fashioned gown; again, he might appropriately climb on to the stage from among his own kind, whom he piously blesses. His formalized diction is akin to that of Mercy's initial speeches and like his long robe is possibly intended to demonstrate that he is in a state of grace but lacks experience of the world. Conscious of temptation and fearful of damnation he approaches Mercy who has possibly been quietly telling his beads at one side of the platform where the hero does not notice him for some time. Mankynde's 'Ye be welcom to this house' can quite legitimately refer to the inn; he clearly falls on his knees at the feet of Mercy who bids him rise. A brief exchange ensues in which Mankynde is warned to beware of the ravages of the world, the flesh, and the devil, and to practise rigorous self-control to defeat them, but before the holy man's teaching can be developed, the voice of New Gyse is heard mocking Mercy's words once more. From Mankynde's puzzled enquiry it seems clear that New Gyse does not actually appear at this point:

Wher spekys this felow? Wyll he not com nere? (253).

In the absence of stage-directions Southern wrestles with the problem for some time.[7] Possibly New Gyse spoke from the back-stage area, but it is more likely that he was positioned somewhere the audience could see and enjoy him and Mankynde could not, and no better location can be found than up in or under one of the galleries, where he could 'barrack' Mercy, and yet plausibly dodge back to evade the curious gaze of the hero.

Mercy warns Mankynde that New Gyse and his friends will 'com nere' all too soon, especially once he has departed as he must. 'The sooner the better', calls Nowadays, 'it will soon be evening, you've been away from home too long, and people don't care for sermons which are no fun to hear.' Nought pipes up too with the suggestion that it is time for Mercy to dine, and adds a few biographical details about his own lifestyle. Again it is clear that Nowadays and Nought are not present on stage, since Mercy observes to Mankynde in line 278:

Yowr enmys wyll be here anon, thei make ther avaunte [boast];

this suggests that like New Gyse they too are somewhere in the auditorium, possibly under the galleries where they are free to heckle without Mankynde being too sure where they are stationed.

Mercy now makes a last effort to impress on Mankynde the necessity for suffering adversity and resisting temptation offered not only by the Vices but also by Titivillus, the invisible devil who traditionally collects idle words and so is a fit companion for those who speak nothing else. Mercy then gives Mankynde the kiss of peace, urges him to labour and never be idle, and so departs with a blessing on his pupil and on the audience. The hero is now left to encounter his foes alone.

To guard himself from evil harm, he apparently sits down and writes on a paper '*Memento, homo, quod cinis es et in cinerem reverteris*' ('Remember, o man, that thou art ashes and to ashes shalt return') – though it has been suggested that he merely draws a cross. The handiest source of paper is the back of the so-called pardon which Nought could have flung down in disgust on his departure at line 161; this Mankynde pins to his breast, where a rosary hangs from his neck for use later in the play.[8] But hardly has Mankynde told the audience that he has pinned his 'badge' on than New Gyse takes up the allusion to ashes with a joke about fires in cold weather; he scoffs at Mankynde's faith in scriptural tags, quoting ominously from the psalm 'See how good and pleasant it is for brothers to dwell together in unity', predicting the arrival of the diabolical fraternity before long. Again the text makes it plain that New Gyse and his companions are not yet on stage: Mankynde simply remarks 'I her a felow speke' and decides to begin digging his ground, his spade perhaps having lain to hand on the platform, or being ready behind the back curtain for him to collect – or, as Southern suggests, Mankynde may have brought it with him on his first entrance and laid it aside until needed.[9] He sets to work, miming the act of digging.

No sooner has he begun than New Gyse, Nowadays, and Nought resurface from within the auditorium, pushing their way noisily and jovially through the crowds, whom Nowadays addresses with hearty roughness:

Make rom, sers, for we have be longe [been a long time]!

Once at the front of the stage they ingratiate themselves by announcing that they will lead the assembly in a 'Crystemes songe' in which all are invited to 'join in the chorus'.

Now I prey all the yemandry that ys here

To synge wyth ws [us] wyth a mery chere (333–4)

says Nought, and proceeds to render an unlovely ditty on an excremental subject. Once more the author's tactic appears to be to lure the audience into a false position, trading on their preference for 'mery chere' and high spirits to involve them in the process of sneering at goodness, and becoming parties to scurrility, riot and evil; the point is taken further by the Vices' vile perversion of the Christian refrain 'Holy, holy, holy' into 'Hole-lick, hole-lick, hole-lick'.

The song completed, New Gyse greets Mankynde with mock-respect: 'Gode spede yow wyth yowr spade!'. But he proceeds to more obscenity, wishing that the labourer's mouth and the arse of the man who made his spade were united. Mankynde tells the sniggering trio to clear off, his 'I must nedys labure, yt ys my lyvynge' accenting the contrast between those who toil and those who idle. Nowadays protests that they have only just arrived, and sneers at Mankynde's meagre patch of dug soil while Nought, calling him 'fadere' and pretending he is a priest, offers him the help of a wife. The harassment continues until the labourer having tried protestation – 'Why stonde ye ydyll?' he asks pointedly – resorts to physical violence and beats them off with his spade. New Gyse is struck in the testicles, Nowadays on the head, and Nought escapes with a blow on the arm, and they scatter across the stage bewailing their injuries, leaving Mankynde in possession of his field. He kneels to thank God for his deliverance, and shows the audience his spade which, he implies, he has been reluctant to use, since the Lord does not rejoice in spears or swords. No, he prefers spades, moans Nought ruefully, and the trio take themselves out of range to nurse their wounds, but they do not disappear from view. Mankynde confidently informs the audience that they have seen the last of the Vices, and goes off taking his trusty spade, to fetch corn to sow in his ground.

He has no sooner disappeared through the booth curtain than Myscheff takes the stage: he must obviously appear from some other quarter, and he probably enters from the inn through the audience at one side of the platform, speaking as he goes. Much of his speech consists of tearful lamentation that since he was last here his menials have suffered at

Mankynde's hands. Hark, he says, you can hear them weeping, and the woebegone trio are indeed making a commotion somewhere. They cannot retreat backstage since not only would their crying be less effective there, but this is the area to which Mankynde has retired: they probably occupy the foot of the steps opposite to those which Myscheff has mounted, where they can stay in the audience's view but lead Mankynde to believe they have departed.

Myscheff mothers them now in a comic way, declining to inspect New Gyse's injury but offering to cure Nowadays's broken head by taking it off and replacing it (a possible echo of the comic doctor of the traditional mumming play; see p. 69 below), scaring Nought and New Gyse lest he should try a similar treatment on them, and all three rapidly begin to recover. Nowadays calls for a conference on the subject of Mankynde, and it is tacitly assumed that the devil Titivillus will chair it since Myscheff immediately calls for a minstrel to summon him. Nought volunteers to play the 'Walsyngham wystyll', though presumably the musicians who accompanied the Vices' first entry are still present, having provided the backing for the 'Crystemes songe'. Nought plays none the less, and the voice of Titivillus is heard roaring off-stage. This is clearly a device to stimulate public desire to see him, for this devil was traditionally invisible, a property he employs later in the play, and the Vices, trading on the crowd's natural but spiritually reprehensible curiosity to see a live devil, now take up a collection, most of which will ultimately find its way into Myscheff's pocket. He departs, leaving his underlings to organize the levy which they do through the time-honoured techniques of blackmail and cajolery:

He [i.e. Titivillus] ys a worschyppull man, sers, savyng yowr reverens.
He lovyth no grotys, nor pens of to [two] pens.
Gyf ws rede reyallys [Give us red royals] yf ye wyll se hys
    abhomynabull presens (463–5).

The three Vices now pass among the audience, collecting the money in their hats, New Gyse urging the host of the inn to set an example to the others; from his 'Gode blysse yow, master' he seems not to be disappointed. Southern argues against this interpretation of 'goodeman of this house', but that Mine Host should have been briefed in advance to stimulate his customers' generosity seems more than probable.[10] The process of collecting continues 'a fayer wyll [while]' according to Nought, but when sufficient cash has been extracted, the Vices return to the stage where Nowadays calls to Titivillus 'Cumme forth now yowr gatus!' and then warns the crowd to clear a way for his entry:

He ys a goodly man, sers; make space and be ware! (474)

Hereupon yet another character enters through the audience: the arrival of the ugly fiend, masked and armed not with his traditional sack in which he collected idle talk and mumbled prayers, but with a net to ensnare Mankynde, would undoubtedly create great consternation as he rushed past a concourse of countryfolk only too willing to give him passage. (The actor assigned to this part could well have been the one who played Mercy, as there is ample opportunity for him to change costumes between appearances.) Once arrived on stage, Titivillus proceeds to warn horse-owners to watch out for thieves and to demand money from each of the Vices, each of whom protests that he is penniless, the joke being that we know each has just solicited money from the spectators which he has safely stowed away before the devil arrived – the repetition of the word 'purse' in lines 479, 482, and 488 highlighting the point to amuse the crowd.

Titivillus, having obligingly warned the audience that the Vices are thieves, now changes his tactics, and orders the trio to embark on a spree of pillaging in the surrounding countryside, promising them as recompense that he will avenge the injuries Mankynde has inflicted on them, of which Myscheff has informed him. Each Vice resolves to visit certain notables of the district, many of them no doubt known to the audience, though they promise to spare magistrates and 'Hamonde of Soffeham' for fear of being hanged. New Gyse warns that if any of them are captured they will not return to tell the tale. They go off in different directions, Titivillus cursing them and leaving little doubt in our minds that his only use for his henchmen is to steal for him.

The devil next confides in the audience that he intends to frustrate Mankynde's efforts at labouring honestly by placing a board under the surface of his dug ground, preventing his spade from entering the earth, and by mixing weeds with his corn, like the traditional enemy in Christ's parable. There is no need for Titivillus to do more than lay a convenient loose plank across the stage at the spot where Mankynde had been digging: Southern suggests that the devil carried a board in under his cloak.[11] Watching from the front of the stage he notices Mankynde returning through the curtains, and once more treats the crowd of spectators as his confederates in evil-doings:

Yondyr he commyth; I prey of cownsell [for secrecy] (539).

In acquiescing in the conspiracy they again expose themselves to spiritual risk. Mankynde, oblivious of Titivillus, now carries in his bag of corn; Mankynde's putting the bag down while he completes his digging gives Titivillus the perfect opportunity to doctor it with seeds from his pouch; the farmer crosses himself and gets to work, but the board beneath his spade resists, and he grows tired, Titivillus no doubt hampering him further by the use of his net which might be the source of a good deal of comic business. Eventually Mankynde vows to sow his seed regardless of the untilled portion of his field, but on opening the bag he finds weeds mixed inextricably with it:

Alasse, my corn ys lost [ruined]! (547)

It is worth noting that the corn is deemed to be spoilt not stolen as some commentators including Southern suggest. However, when Mankynde flings down his spade in disgust, the stage-direction tells us that

Here TITIVILLUS *goth out wyth the spade*

– using no doubt the rear exit between the curtains. Mankynde kneels to say Evensong in the fields, and as he begins to tell his beads for the Paternoster, Titivillus re-enters behind him. Announcing himself with a knowing leer to the audience, he creeps up behind the praying man and whispers in his ear that he should cease from prayer and relieve himself instead. Mystified, Mankynde apologizes to the audience that he 'wyll into thi yerde, soverens, and cum ageyn son', and jumps down from the platform to seek the nearest privy under the gallery, leaving his rosary behind, a sure sign that he has abandoned his best defence as well as putting his bodily needs before his spiritual ones. Titivillus makes the point crudely but tellingly:

He ys conveyde, be Cryst, from hys dyvyn servyce . . .

I have sent hym forth to schyte lesynges [lies] (566, 568).

Deception is easy, and if Mankynde does not soon hurry back, Evensong will be over: so saying, Titivillus flings the rosary aside, and again confides in the people that they will see good sport if they stop where they are. He points out Mankynde returning through the throng, and asserts that he plans to divert him from his purpose. Again, by enjoying the sport, the auditors are again subconsciously aiding the villainy.

Mankynde's ardour to pray has waned by his return. He complains that it takes too long to say Evensong and that he goes to church too often anyway; in answering his body's needs he has lost the urge to labour and to pray. Even if it displeases Mercy, he must rebel, and Mankynde promptly lies down and goes to sleep, having succumbed to the temptation of yielding to sloth. Titivillus, enjoining the spectators to silence if they want to see a 'praty game', gloats over him as he snores, and bending down whispers in his ear a sequence of lies: Mercy has stolen a horse and a cow and been hanged, so that his advice is no longer to be trusted; Mankynde ought therefore to ask pardon of the Vices he has injured, seek their good will, and elicit their help to find himself a whore.

The devil departs (perhaps to change back for the role of Mercy), and Mankynde wakes, convinced that his dream was the truth, and that he should hasten to 'the ale-house' to beg forgiveness of New Gyse, Nowadays, and Nought. Their arrival forestalls him. First comes New Gyse desperately hurtling through the crowd crying 'Make space' and obviously fearful of pursuit: he would have been hanged on the gallows but for the rope breaking; he still has the halter round his neck to prove it, though he loses no time in wrenching it off. Mankynde enquires kindly after him, referring to him as 'sir', but New Gyse is sufficiently ashamed of his exploit to pretend that his halter is a silk neck-band and the cicatrice 'a runnynge ryngeworme'. They are joined by Nowadays and by Nought who also push their way up on to the platform. Nowadays has robbed a church, but his escapade is capped by Myscheff who arrives next with broken chains on his wrists, having murdered the gaoler who was holding him prisoner, made love to the man's wife, drunk his fill, and robbed them of a dish and a plate which he still bears with him.

The true viciousness of the quartet is now apparent to all, and the auditors are no doubt intended to be horrified to find Mankynde apologizing to them at this juncture, and anxious to ingratiate himself with his former foes. New Gyse cannot understand this change of heart, but Nowadays shrewdly realizes its cause, and whispers aside to the others:

I sey, New Gys, Nought, Tytivillus made all this:

As sekyr [surely] as Gode ys in hewyn [heaven], so yt ys (659–60).

Mankynde has even gone down on his knees to ask forgiveness.

A highly effective sequence now follows: Mankynde, anxious to be accepted as 'one of the boys', submits to being bound apprentice to the Vices at a court set up by Myscheff, a situation obviously familiar to many of those in the inn-yard, Nought acts as clerk of the court, Myscheff presides, a seat being brought forward for him from the 'back-stage' area. New Gyse seems to form the counsel: it is he who suggests that Mankynde's long 'syde gown' could be cut down to make him a more fashionable short jacket, and the owner eagerly accepts, removing the offending garment and giving it to New Gyse who takes it out through the rear curtains to 'shorten' it. His absence is covered by Nought bringing Myscheff his record of the court proceedings. There is much laughter at his handwriting and incompetent Latin, on which he makes the disarming comment, worthy of Costard in *Love's Labour's Lost*:

I shulde [should] have don better, hade I wyst (685).

Nowadays grows tired of awaiting New Gyse's return, and yells to him to come back, which he does immediately, carrying the jacket which he has substituted for the 'syde gowne' which would obviously be required for future performances. His entry is covered by the line:

Out of my wey, sers, for drede of fyghtynge! (696).

This at first suggests movement through the auditorium, but since New Gyse's departure involves the depositing of one important costume and the collection of another, it is likely that he has to retire backstage to make the substitution, and that his remark is therefore addressed to his cronies and Mankynde, bunched together centre stage reading Nought's transcript of the trial. Similarly, when Nought is still dissatisfied with the brevity of Mankynde's new garment and takes it off-stage to abbreviate it further with the words

Make space, sers, lett me go owte (701),

he too exits to the rear 'green-room' to collect the final version.[12]

The time before Nought's reappearance is devoted to Mankynde's ceremonial oath of allegiance to Myscheff, in which he swears to fornicate, steal, murder, break the Sabbath, neglect religious offices, and turn high-wayman. No doubt similar oaths taken by apprentices are here parodied. Nought then returns with the 'joly jackett' which New Gyse says now resembles a fencing garment, and Mankynde puts it on, New Gyse dancing excitedly round him, exclaiming 'Hay, doog, hay! whoppe whoo!'

At this point affairs are terminated abruptly by Myscheff crying out

Tydyngys, tydyngys! I have aspyede on [someone]!

Hens wyth yowr stuff, fast we were gon! (722–3)

Obviously he has seen somebody whom he and his fellow-thieves must prevent from seeing their 'stuff' which consists of whatever New Gyse said gave him 'no cause to morn' (line 626), what Nowadays stole from the nearby church, and Myscheff's 'dysch and dublere' from the gaol. All this has presumably been piled on the stage since the Vices returned. The 'one' espied by Myscheff must be Mercy who speaks three lines later. He must enter from the auditorium, both to give Myscheff the opportunity to see him and yet allow the Vices enough time to bundle up their gear ready for a hasty flight. They do not retreat quite soon enough to avoid Mercy altogether, for he is able to rebuke Mankynde who, believing him a ghost after Titivillus's falsehoods, makes a fright-ened excuse and explains that he and his new friends are off to celebrate the anniversary of his father's death. Calling for a tapster to draw them all drinks, he rushes off down the steps and into the inn. Myscheff is somehow knocked over in the mêlée of departure, but Glynne Wickham's suggestion that he falls from his judge's seat implies that he has sat there until this point, unworried by Mercy's approach and the chance that the stolen goods will be noticed.[13] It is surely more likely that there is a frantic scrimmage on stage at Myscheff's warning of Mercy's imminent arrival with everyone gathering the goods together, and that Myscheff's fall comes as he quits the platform with the others, tumbling down the steps into the crowd and savagely crying out as he scrambles to his feet:

Hens, away fro me, or I shall beschyte yow all (731).

New Gyse dashes after him, calling to the ostler to find him a football.

A lengthy address of nearly forty lines follows now from Mercy, almost a welcome respite after the riotous violence of the Vices, and one which makes far more impression on us now we have seen evil in action – particularly as the priest directs his tearful words to the audience, lamenting that Mankynde should so easily be diverted from the path of righteousness. He pleads with the Virgin to have mercy on man's frailty and weakness in letting himself be perverted by his new companions, and he vows to seek Mankynde, calling on him to return to one who 'shall never be convicte [convinced] of hys oncurtes condycyon', descending the steps into the auditorium to seek for him there.

Mankynde does not materialize, but Myscheff and two of the Vices erupt on to the scene, their mockery as keen as ever, and they shout a variety of colourful lies as to the hero's whereabouts in order to confuse Mercy. But their location, and also that of Nought, creates a staging problem: Nought is in the process of defecating – a final instance of the excremental imagery that pervades *Mankynde*, and it is appropriate that Nought, the most elemental if not the most vicious of the Vices, should supply it. The lines run:

NOWADAYS: How sey ye, ser? My bolte ys schett [shot].

NOUGHT: I am doynge of my nedyngys; be ware how ye schott [shoot]!

        Fy, fy, fy! I have fowll arayde my fote.

        Be wyse for schotynge wyth yowr takyllys [weapons], for Gode wott

        My fote ys fowly overschett (782–6).

My interpretation is that the pair of Vices appear in different places about the yard, calling out to Mercy different versions of Mankynde's fate: their disparate locations would assist them in confusing the priest. Nowadays stands close to one of the inn's privies, the same one employed by Mankynde earlier in the action, and now containing the unfortunate Nought. Nowadays says his piece and then suddenly bangs on the privy door or partition to ask Nought's opinion with 'How sey ye, ser? My bolte ys schett'. From the gloom within comes Nought's rueful response, complaining that Nowadays's abrupt request has shocked him into carelessness. Emerging doing up his breeches he remonstrates further: take care not to pester me for an answer when I'm otherwise engaged! Such humour may be literally fundamental, but the melancholy Nought is a memorable comic creation.

The play now approaches its crisis. By now Mercy's search has taken him to the rear of the yard or even into the public rooms of the inn, and Myscheff fears that before long he will discover Mankynde, and rescue him. He therefore calls a conference to discuss what is to be done with Mankynde, and the other Vices being closer to the platform, he specifically invites Nought to join them: 'Cum forth, Nought, behynde'. The unholy alliance clambers up and huddles together in consultation. New Gyse, the sharpest mind among the Vices, recalls that Mankynde believes Mercy to have been hanged; if Myscheff tells him that Mercy is seeking him out, he will think that a ghost has come for retribution and hang himself from fright. Myscheff agrees to do this, and departs after a fulsome compliment to New Gyse from Nowadays. This creates a fresh difficulty of interpretation since in the text the stage-direction '*Hic [here] exit* MYSCHEFF' is followed immediately by a line of dialogue spoken by this character to Mankynde:

How, Mankynde! Cumm and speke wyth Mercy, he is here fast by
   (799).

Wickham's solution is to have Myscheff encounter Mankynde coming in as he goes out,[14] but Myscheff's exit is very positively indicated, and it seems that he must disappear if only briefly, departing through the main curtains and then reappearing, dragging in the petrified Mankynde with the cheery line quoted above. The play's hero now terrified and in despair calls for a rope to hang himself, and Myscheff is happy to oblige: 'Anon, anon, anon! I have yt here redy' he announces, and New Gyse brings forth the rope while Nowadays and Nought collect a gallows from behind the back curtain and proceed to set up the 'tre' on stage. New Gyse, no stranger to the halter, obligingly offers to demonstrate what Mankynde must do. We have then a superb stage-picture: Nowadays and Nought steadying the gibbet, the halter invitingly around New Gyse's neck, and Mankynde fainting in Myscheff's grip, about to commit the deadly sin of suicide. The tableau is held for long enough to increase the tension by convincing the audience that their stage-proxy is doomed, when Mercy bursts through the booth curtain – there must be no congestion to impede this entry[15] – armed with a whip which he proceeds to wield to good effect. Every man shifts for himself, the gibbet falls, the Vices scatter, and New Gyse for the second time in the play is almost throttled by the hangman's rope: 'Alasse, my wesant [windpipe]! Ye were sumwhat to [too] nere', he splutters, the last remark being addressed to Mercy bending over the recumbent form of the panic-stricken Mankynde.

Then the Vices are gone, and with their departure the play moves into its final phase as the priest rejoices over the repentant sinner. At first Mankynde does not raise his eyes from the dust to look Mercy in the face, since he cannot conceive that he is worthy to ask mercy. But exhorted to arise and seek grace, he agrees to go to Mercy's 'deambulat-orye' or cloister, a reminder that a monastery church stood close by, the same one as the audience were to imagine Nowadays had robbed earlier in the action. Mercy warns Mankynde not to fall into a trap and assume that forgiveness follows automatically on repentance for sins committed – 'Be ware of weyn [vain] confidens of mercy' (853) – or to leave suppli-cating for mercy until too late. Of Mankynde's contrition there can be no doubt, nor of his awareness that he has allowed himself to be led astray by the devil Titivillus, the three Vices who represent the World, and his own sinful flesh, who combined to bring him to Myscheff. His watchword now must be vigilance, and thus forewarned and resolved to persevere he departs with Mercy's blessing, preferably down the front steps and out into the world.

Finally the priest, no longer a figure of fun whose sermonizing appears mere verbalizing, but a respected spiritual guide, addresses us as 'wyre-schepyll soferens' and urges us to learn from the moral lesson just taught to Mankynde if we wish to attain everlasting life. Mercy lifts his hand in blessing, then turns, walks up-stage and enters the curtained booth at the rear. His mission and that of his anonymous creator have been fulfilled.

★ ★ ★

In *Mankynde* we see just how skilfully a relatively unsophisticated style of staging may be employed to enhance the dramatic impact of a relatively sophisticated script. The fact that its action is not solely confined to the bare platform of the booth stage but is permitted to embrace many of the areas conventionally assigned to an audience means that the Vices can not only establish a swift rapport with spectators from the stage but also create a sense of identity with them by speaking from the public galleries or even the public privies, or by entering and leaving the premises just like ordinary patrons. The ease of passage between stage and auditorium induces a stronger faith in the characters' existence than if they appeared as make-believe figures of no substance posturing behind an invisible pane of glass illuminated by mysterious means. The players in *Mankynde* are all too clearly flesh-and-blood. They offer tangible evidence of their corporeal presence as they shove us aside to reach the stage, bellow in our ear to beware of Titivillus, attend to their most urgent bodily needs within a few yards of us. *Mankynde* may sometimes bring the reality of 'intimate theatre' too close for comfort, but it remains a superb example of the flexible immediacy of medieval theatre methods.

2 · Scenic Structures: the Croxton *Play of the Sacrament*

The Croxton *Play of the Sacrament* is still relatively unknown, yet it must rank as one of the most appealing and lively of medieval religious plays. Much of its interest springs from the fact that it is the only true miracle play (in the strictest sense of the term) which survives in the English language. The working of miracles is featured in other English plays, but the chief examples of genuine miracle plays, dramas which depend for their appeal on the sensational stage presentation of supernatural events, are all continental. Transformations of men into animals and water into wine; fire-breathing dragons, serpents, and monsters; torturing and beheading; floods, lightning, and tempest; all could be ingeniously devised to create the atmosphere of awe and surprise so needful to induce belief among unsophisticated spectators. But *The Play of the Sacrament* is the only medieval English play in which a miracle forms the doctrinal focus of attention as well as the pivot on which the dramatic action turns, and the physical staging of the amazing incidents lying at the play's core must have been given particularly careful treatment.

However, the most exciting stage-feature of the work lies outside its capacity to thrill or to inspire devotion, and rests in the possibility that performance may have taken place at two locations in sequence: the major portion of the action presented at one site in the open air, and its culmination staged *inside a church* close to or within the playing-area. An apparent invitation issued to the spectators that they should approach and witness the termination of the play at a separate site, poses a highly intriguing theatrical conundrum requiring considered examination.

The general inspiration for the play is found in events said to have taken place at Paris in 1290,[1] and Norman Davis in his edition of the text lists several dramatic treatments of this theme, indicating that the English version was part of a vigorous European tradition (see Plate 7). Yet the Croxton *Play* was either based on other sources than its analogues, or else represents the work of an author with a very developed capacity

53

7 Manuscript illustration depicting two Jews desecrating the Host (Harley MS 7026) (Photo: British Library)

8 Hubert Cailleau's miniature of the setting for a Passion Play at Valenciennes (1547) (Bibl. Nat. MS Rothschild I. 7.3) (Photo: Bibliothèque Nationale, Paris)

9 All Saints' Church, Croxton, from a nineteenth-century drawing (Photo: Jacqueline Tydeman)

for inventing variations on his inherited theme. The choice of scene for his drama – somewhere in the Spanish kingdom of Aragon,

In Eraclea [Heraclea?], that famous cyté (line 12) –

suggests he may have known that a Spanish location was employed in a presentation of the story before Leonore of Aragon in Rome during 1473, though the final rubric is very insistent that the events depicted are taken from recent historical events:

Thus endyth the Play of the Blyssyd Sacrament, whyche myracle was don in the forest of Aragon, in the famous cité Eraclea, the yere of owr Lord God M cccc.lxj [1461], to whom be honowr, Amen.

Any link therefore between the Croxton *Play*'s Aragon setting and the 1473 production before Leonore may have arisen from a shared source, though there is no reason to imagine that the English writer was incapable of working independently of one.

This impression is confirmed by the assured manner in which the dramatist handles his material. He matches his Jew Jonathas with an opposite of more weight than the mere indigent woman who steals the wafer in other versions: Aristorius is a merchant of substance and authority who agrees to steal the sacrament for ready money, and the commercial bargain struck carries more moral and spiritual condemnation than attaches to a poor woman's desire to retrieve a pledged gown from the Jew elsewhere. The Jew no longer appears in his domestic context with a wife and children, but is depicted as an independent contemporary businessman backed in his misdeeds by four underlings who assist him in torturing the Mass wafer, and who may well have been inspired by those teams of *Tortores* or *Tormentores* playing such a momentous part in the cycle versions of the Crucifixion, even if their number is governed in part by the need for them and Aristorius to inflict on the sacrament the five wounds traditionally bestowed on the crucified Christ. In addition, the piece may serve as a microcosm of medieval civic life: the merchant is served by a clerk and a private chaplain, a bishop appears at the crisis-point of the action, and a quack doctor and his brisk servant add a comic dimension to part of the proceedings. Even in its ideological preoccupations the play tends towards a more independently humane resolution than some of its prototypes; Jonathas the Jew is not put to death, but rather undergoes a conversion along with his accomplices, while the merchant is likewise allowed to seek for God's forgiveness and amend.

Yet, as David Bevington's valuable introduction to his edition of the play in *Medieval Drama* makes clear,[2] *The Play of the Sacrament* does more than paint a portrait of contemporary life or point up a doctrinal moral. Its action is skilfully and deliberately structured to parallel in lurid but sincere terms the events of Christ's Passion, notably through the torments perpetrated on the Host, which not only symbolizes Christ's body but by virtue of the doctrine of Transubstantiation literally becomes its substance. Aristorius in betraying his Christian beliefs and stealing the consecrated bread for gain echoes Judas who sold his master for silver; the Jews inflicting wounds on the Host mimic their counterparts at Calvary who wounded Christ's body in five places. The wafer bleeds in the same way that Christ bled on the Cross; it is nailed to a post and then taken down just as Christ was crucified and removed from the Cross, while wrapping the Host in a cloth and placing it in a heated cauldron signifies the burial and descent into Hell. Finally, when the sacrament is taken from the cauldron and cast into an oven, sealed up only to burst open suddenly with great force in order that Christ's image should arise from it, we perceive without difficulty the Entombment and the Resurrection symbolically re-enacted in a most effective manner.

★ ★ ★

A notable feature of the Croxton *Play* is the existence of an eighty-line 'trailer' known as the banns, which exists only in the case of a handful of English dramas, although it is reasonable to suppose that texts for many similar preliminary announcements have perished. The device of 'crying a play' is well attested to in contemporary documents, and in view of the low level of literacy and the dearth of mass communications media in the Middle Ages, this was doubtless one of the few effective methods of publicizing any significant local event. The most important sets of banns which survive are those relating to the plays of the N-Town Cycle, which contain the famous words which have given this sequence of biblical dramas one of its several not entirely satisfactory titles, and those used to introduce *The Castel of Perseveraunce* (see pp. 83–5 below). *The Play of the Sacrament* resembles both in its use of two *'vexillatores'* to cry the banns, these 'standard-bearers' being in all probability members of the playing company, since the degree of vocal skill and personal presence required to execute their task with the necessary authority and panache is unlikely to have been found other than among those accustomed to public appearances (unless they were regular 'town-criers'). It is clear that, as with *The Castel of Perseveraunce*, the *vexillatores* were accompanied on their mission to drum up custom by musicians, or at least by the trumpeter or other instrumentalist exhorted in the banns' final stirring lines:

Now, mynstrell, blow up with a mery stevyn [note, tune] (80)

At what interval from the performance proper the banns were 'called' is difficult to ascertain. It may at first sight appear significant that the Second Crier begins his share of the exposition with the words

Sovereyns, and yt lyke yow to here the purpoos of this play

That ys representyd now in yower syght (9–10)

– this tends to suggest that the play will follow immediately the banns are completed. But a later reference makes it obvious that this was not the case:

> And yt place [please] yow, thys gaderyng [crowd, company] that here
>   ys,
> At Croxston on Monday yt shall be sen;
> To see the conclusyon [outcome, resolution] of this lytell processe
>   [story]
> Hertely welcum shall yow bene. (73–6)

It may of course be the case that banns were adaptable, and could be employed to commence an actual presentation, but commonsense would suggest that a suitable interval would elapse for the news of the forthcoming attraction to spread. One other possibility is that the banns were accompanied by a brief 'dumb-show' 'represented' in the sight of those who came to hear what was afoot, rather as the mechanicals in Act V of *A Midsummer Night's Dream* parade before the court while Peter Quince introduces them. Yet for the players at Croxton to do so seems a waste of player-power, if the performance itself was not to be staged till the following Monday. Perhaps it is safest to assume that 'representyd now in yower syght' may have implied no more than 'will be presented before your very eyes in the near future' or possibly 'at this season of the year'.

The words of the banns follow a tested formula: firstly attention is attracted by the First Crier conferring a blessing on 'thes semely, bothe leste and moste', and the nature of the performance is swiftly established along with its plot's credentials. The bann-criers proceed to outline the story, highlighting the role of the chief protagonists and the most sensational details of the torments visited on the sacrament. The Jews' conversion is ascribed to God's mercy, the authenticity of the episode once more testified to, and the moral of the drama made plain, before the culminating piece of information is supplied, namely the place and the day of the presentation, a welcome being extended to 'more and lesse' to favour the actors with their presence. A final blessing is bestowed, and the musicians are ordered to play a tune to round off the whole, before the *vexillatores* with their eye-catching banners move on to a new sector of the region to repeat the banns. Some scholars have assumed that the performance at Croxton was only one of several given, and that the banns would have been delivered elsewhere announcing further presentations at centres other than Croxton on days other than Monday. Yet while the place of performance is left blank in *The Castel of Perseveraunce* text and the term 'N-Town' is employed in the manuscript of that cycle precisely to enable a choice of names to be inserted –

> A sunday next yf that we may
> At vj of the belle we gynne oure play
> In N. towne . . . (525–7) –

the name 'Croxston' alone is firmly embedded in the manuscript of *The Play of the Sacrament*. Even though scribal methods may have varied, it is significant that no provision is made to insert another name for that of Croxton in the script.

It has been argued[3] that the mere existence of banns implies that *The Play of the Sacrament* was part of the repertoire of a travelling company, but a company did not need to travel very far from its home base to find it worthwhile to announce its intention through the use of banns. The organizers of the New Romney Passion and Resurrection Play in 1560 included among the expenses for their non-itinerant production two significant items:[4]

Item payd to Dodd to proclayme o[r] playe at Heithe [Hythe]   ij[d]
ffyrst in beardes & heares [wigs] for the bane cryers & a here
& beard for the ffoole   x[s]

which suggest that, even to publicize a series of single-site performances in one locality (and Hythe is only nine miles from New Romney), banncriers and extraneous attractions such as a fool were deemed desirable. There is reason to assume that the players presenting the Croxton piece had their origins in Croxton and district.

The search for Croxton's precise geographical whereabouts has revealed a number of places with this name within the East Midlands, the region which the linguistic forms in the text indicate as the most likely area for the play's provenance. A valuable clue to the likeliest spot is provided by the identification of the Doctor's place of residence as announced by his servant Coll in lines 620–1:

Inquyre to the colkote [charcoal burner's hut?], for ther ys hys
    loggyng,
A lytyll besyde Babwell Myll . . .

Although the reference occurs in an episode which may well be an interpolation into the primary matter of the play – though this is not the view taken by the present writer – it was still vital that original audiences were able to grasp the local allusion, in much the same way that spectators at the Wakefield Cycle performances could pick up the reference to 'Horbery shrogys' in the *Second Shepherds' Play*. According to Norman Davis, Babwell Priory was a Franciscan establishment on the road between Bury St Edmunds in Suffolk and Thetford in Norfolk, and a village of Croxton does lie on the B 1110 two miles north of the latter, which places it roughly twelve miles from Babwell; by this token it seems that we may safely associate it with *The Play of the Sacrament*.

Although the unique copy of the play is unusually well endowed with stage directions, few of these actually supply positive evidence for the physical appearance of the stage-area on which the piece was originally set forth. However, during the course of the action three locations or structures are indicated: provision has to be made for the 'stage' which Jonathas the Jew occupies as his house and which must be large enough to hold the Jew himself, his four accomplices, and the table on which the Host is abused; it might also have contained the oven into which the Host is flung at the climax of its maltreatment. A church is also an important feature of the setting, with a font and an altar from which the sacred wafer is stolen. It is also obvious that Aristorius, the rich merchant, must be assigned his own scaffold to correspond to that of Jonathas, since on several occasions the action is located in his 'house'. It is additionally attractive from the point of symmetry in staging to postulate the existence of such a platform for the play's most important individual character after Jonathas, in that it balances the stage picture, leaving the central position for the church where the culminating scene of baptism and forgiveness takes place. Besides these three sites, a main playing-area in the form of the conventional 'place' or *platea* is required for unlocalized scenes and journeys between scaffolds; its existence is proved by a rubric which occurs on the entrance of the doctor's servant, Coll:

Here shall the lechys man come into the place . . . (S.D. 524)

A plausible setting thus consists of three main structures, two of them in the form of raised edifices or 'houses' of the type familiar from Cailleau's miniature (see Plate 8) of a Valenciennes production of 1547,[5] the third the church indicated either by a similar stylized framework, or by nothing more than the presence of an altar and a font, probably mounted on some type of platform. But what of the playing-site itself?

All Saints' Church, Croxton (see Plate 9), lies half-way down a fairly steep incline leading to the village centre;[6] now very much altered from its original appearance, its distinctive flint-faced round tower and the fifteenth-century windows of the southern clerestory are still in evidence. On its southern side the sloping nature of the terrain immediately suggests that the site of the present churchyard and the land to the west of it would make a highly suitable playing-site, with spectators accommodated conveniently on the slope and with the southern elevation of the church acting as a 'sounding-board'. However, it is difficult to say if platform-stages could have been satisfactorily set up around the church, since the road downhill now runs through a deep cutting close to the western tower. However, it is at least feasible that a sufficiently extensive open space once existed here to enable two scenic components to be erected alongside the church, with the 'place' extending like a grassy forestage in front of them, so that the play was presented on a long linear stage occupied by the scaffolds with the church as a general 'backdrop', rather on the lines shown in the miniature from Valenciennes. The 'church set' could then have consisted of a property altar and font placed on a simple platform somewhere in the centre of the south wall of the church itself.

3 A conjectural reconstruction of the *Play of the Sacrament* in Croxton churchyard

None the less, it may seem strange to some that a church-interior was represented on the actual *exterior* of a place of worship when an actual *interior* lay obviously to hand, and arguments as to whether or not the audience were invited to pass into the church to watch the play's conclusion have been advanced. For the present we may postulate that *The Play of the Sacrament* took place in the parish churchyard at Croxton, for which practice there is plenty of supporting evidence from all over Europe.[7]

The opening speech, nearly seventy lines long, is delivered by the merchant Aristorius, and it is by far the longest stretch of solo speaking in the entire piece. There is no indication in *The Play of the Sacrament* just how the opening phase of the action was handled. One is tempted to assume that some means was found of stilling the chattering audience with a trumpet-call or the beating of a drum, but Aristorius's initial words in themselves might have proved sufficient, if declaimed imposingly enough:

Now Cryst, that ys our Creatour, from shame he cure us;
He maynteyn us with myrth that meve upon the mold [earth] (81–2).

(The irony of the merchant's lines would not be lost on those who knew of his impending disgrace.) The merchant could either have already been installed (or else appeared) on his raised scaffold, ready to begin the play from that location, or possibly he entered through the audience or at any rate emerged on to the *platea* from 'offstage' and made his way across the 'place' to his edifice, speaking as he went. The former method could certainly give the opening a good deal of impact, especially if Aristorius's 'stage' were curtained all round in the style of a four-sided tent, and he assumed his position there unseen, so that he or one of his household such as his clerk could draw back the curtains with a flourish, a movement which would have the effect of commanding the requisite degree of attention and surprise to enable the play to start.

Yet I incline towards the other hypothesis. The first speech is a lengthy one, and it would be more satisfying to have Aristorius deliver his lines while striding about and across the *platea* rather than while confined to the inhibiting limits of his scaffold. There is an amplitude and a swagger about the merchant as a personality that a wise director would wish to exploit, and not restrict through tying up a dynamic actor in a narrow area, so that the notion of projecting lines of such obvious bravura other than from the liberating realm of the 'place' seems unnatural:

In Antyoche and in Almayn moch ys my myght,
In Braban and in Brytayn I am full bold,
In Calabre and in Coleyn ther rynge [travel] I full ryght,
In Dordrede and in Denmark be [by] the clyffys cold . . . (97–100)

Such lines immediately remind one of the pagan emperors and King Herods of the cycle plays, and the opportunities the *platea* offered for parading and 'pomping' to the player taking the part of Aristorius were surely not neglected. There is another slight hint that the merchant initially occupied the arena and not his scaffold, only arriving at his 'stage' towards the end of his speech. In line 120 he informs the spectators that

My curat wayteth upon me to knowe myn entent,

and it is at least plausible for Aristorius to sight the priest patiently waiting for his perambulations about the *platea* to cease, and to explain to the audience the meaning of the cleric's attendance as a further means of boosting his own reputation. 'Petyr Powle', the merchant's clerk, must be located on his master's scaffold throughout the opening lines, possibly engaged in totting up Aristorius's fortunes in a ledger, and that this demands a table or desk with a bench is borne out later in the action when a meal is served on the table and the Jew is invited to sit beside the merchant at line 271. Even if the notion that Aristorius starts his initial speech from the *platea* is rejected, one may still imagine that he begins the scene on the platform attended by clerk and curate, and then descends to ground level on the remark 'Syr Arystory ys my name' (line

89), which is an appropriate line on which to begin making that closer contact with the audience which the 'place' is apt to encourage.

The first phase of the play concludes with the merchant being instructed by the priest to thank God for his good fortune, and the clerk being told to enquire if any foreign merchants have arrived in Eraclea. In this way all three characters are given adequate motivation for withdrawing temporarily from the action: the stage directions only refer to the clerk – '*Now shall the merchantys man withdrawe hym*' – but it is clear that Aristorius and his chaplain must also take some appropriate action before the dramatic interest shifts to the Jew. It would be reasonable to assume that they descend and go to the church in order

To wourshyppe . . . God that dyed on the roode [cross] (135),

but since it is later made plain that they do not, they must either remain on the scaffold, or leave the playing-area altogether. Possibly the clerk draws the curtains around Aristorius's 'stage' to prevent the continued presence there of the chaplain and the merchant from distracting attention from the next episode, but it might be simpler for the characters to remain immobile, possibly miming a static tableau of private devotion. The clerk is easier to track: he takes off in another direction

Smertly to go serche at the waterys syde (142);

though he may not disappear completely from the audience's sight, since he announces his intention to

walke by thes pathes wyde,

And seke the haven both up and down . . . (145–6).

Almost at once, one may assume, the curtains on the Jew's 'stage', closed until now, are opened – possibly only a chink at first to allow Jonathas to thrust his face out and to survey the audience. Does a delighted shriek of mingled hatred and fear burst from the crowd? Possibly not. Certainly the stage direction '*the Jewe Jonathas shall make hys bost*' does not suggest a very sympathetic portrayal of the character, yet it is notable that a surprising degree of dignity and integrity clings to this frequently vilified figure, despite the rôle in which the play's source casts him. He is seen engaged in the worship of Mohammed, the deity venerated by such medieval theatrical tyrants as Herod, yet Jonathas's words of devotion are mild and lacking in paranoid aspirations; his ambitions are almost solely confined to material gain. Similarly, we discover later that his wicked designs on the symbols of Christian belief are motivated in large measure by intellectual curiosity: how can the faithful claim to 'beleve on a cake'? How can bread and wine become flesh and blood? The playwright is at pains to render the bogeyman of medieval Christian tradition a genuine seeker after enlightenment and mental satisfaction, even though a perverted one. Was Christopher Marlowe aware of this paradox when he created the not dissimilar figure of Dr Faustus? It is certainly possible that his Jew of Malta owes something to Jonathas, and the Jew's richly alliterating catalogue of exotic possessions, with which he introduces himself, tempts one to think that he must have been shown on stage counting or admiring some of them, much as Marlowe's Barabas is discovered reckoning up his fortunes at the opening of *The Jew of Malta*.[8] While the elaborate imagery may have had to serve as a substitute for the visual experience, sensuously luxurious references in the text are often accompanied by indications of a demonstrative gesture:

. . . saphyre semely, *I may show yow attonys* [straightaway];

. . . curyous carbunclys *here ye fynd mown* [may];

Synymone [cinnamon], suger, *as yow may sene*

(163, 172, 183; my italics).

Some token goods and precious stones no doubt lay to hand on the Jew's 'stage'; we know that the platform was furnished with a table at which they could be inspected.

Jonathas is not alone on his scaffold, for he not only informs us that

Jazon and Jazdon thei waytyn on my wyll,

Masfat and Malchus they do the same (190–1),

but in line 197 addresses the former pair by name, and they reply, to be followed by Masphat and Mazdon. The scenic structure was therefore of sufficient dimensions to hold five men and a table comfortably, probably in addition to a seat for Jonathas, to stress his superior state to his minions: space might be saved by grouping some of them on the steps of the platform, rather than on the 'stage' itself. After discussing the peculiarities of Christian worship, Jonathas commands the group to depart:

let us walke to see Arystories hall, (223).

A few lines later the stage direction reads:

Jonatas goo don [down] *of his stage*

(confirming incidentally that the scaffold had steps), and this evidently implies that the four retainers go with him, since a little further on we are told that 'the Jewes' meet with 'Petyr Powle' who may have been wandering somewhere in the 'place' during the scene laid at the Jew's house.

As the Jews quit Jonathas's scaffold, the action again shifts to that of Aristorius. His priest Sir Isidore (who has probably remained silently in view with his master) announces his intention of going to church and saying evensong; his master gives him leave, and promises a good supper on his return. This brief scene of eight lines gives the Jews time to descend to the *platea*, to cross it towards Aristorius's 'hall', and for the merchant's clerk to time his movement so that he can encounter them before they arrive. Having spoken with the Jews, the clerk ascends to Aristorius to inform him that his visitors are waiting below, and the merchant, delighted at the news that 'the grettest marchante in all Surré [Syria]' is attending on him, orders Peter to deck his hall with rich hangings in the Jew's honour:

I prey the rychely araye myn hall
As owyth for a marchant of the banke. (259–60)

The clerk undertakes the task with alacrity –

Styffly [vigorously] about I thynke to stere [bustle],
Hasterli to hange your parlowr with pall (264–5) –

and the emphasis on speed is clearly meant to justify the fact that whatever means of conveying 'rich array' was employed, the transformation had to be executed swiftly or the essential flow of the action would be broken, since by now Jonathas and his team are pacing about at the foot of Aristorius's scaffold. There would thus be little time to do more than throw an impressive cloth over the merchant's table, and draw the curtains at the sides of the scaffold a little (but not to prevent vision) to represent costly tapestries, before *'the Jewe merchaunt'*, invited by Aristorius, ascends the steps to greet *'the Cristen merchaunte'*. The stage direction suggests that the other Jews ascend behind him; but in view of the fact that the lines spoken are assigned to Aristorius and Jonathas alone, and of the latter's request:

I wold bartre wyth yow in pryvyté
On [one] lytell thyng, that ye wyll me yt take
Prevely in this stownd [moment] (276–8)

– the Jew's attendants would remain more appropriately in a huddle at the base of the scaffold, possibly miming conversation with 'Petyr Powle'.

Two other details from the Jonathas–Aristorius exchange add to our mental picture of what might occur on stage. Aristorius greets the Jew in an honourable manner:

Sir Jonathas, ye be wellcum unto myn hall!
I pray yow come up and *sit bi me*, (270–1; my italics)

which not only reaffirms the location where the bargaining is to be done, but also indicates that both merchants are to be regarded as being on the same social and professional level, through their occupation of the same bench or of a pair of chairs set side by side. We may now therefore firmly allocate a bench or two seats to Aristorius's platform.

Negotiation for possession of the Mass wafer now proceeds, one of the merchant's arguments for refusing to steal the Sacrament being that

For and [if] I unto the chyrche yede [went],
And preste or clerke myght me aspye,
To the bysshope thei wolde go tell that dede
And apeche [accuse] me of eresye. (299–302)

This remark would naturally direct the spectators' attention towards the church setting, and its impact would be considerably strengthened if

Aristorius's own chaplain were kneeling at the altar, saying Evensong. Indeed, Aristorius himself refers to the priest a few lines later;

Syr Isodyr he ys now at chyrch,
> There seyng hys evynsong (323–4).

If we assume that he is in view, it powerfully illustrates that capability for depicting several pieces of related dramatic activity pursued similtaneously within one playing-area which was one of the greatest assets enjoyed by the medieval theatre. But as far as the use of Croxton church itself is concerned, we may find it an advantage to keep an open mind until we reach the latter part of the script.

The bargain between Jew and merchant is shortly struck, and paid for by Jonathas with 'an hundder pownd . . . Of dokettys [ducats] good', Aristorius agreeing to steal the Host that very night when 'Syr Isodyr' has 'buskyd to hys bedde'. Jonathas descends, rejoins his men, and they depart for their own scaffold. As they do, the priest completes his observances seen or unseen, and 'commyth home' from the church, mounts the steps, and greets Aristorius. Supper is then served at the table, the hard-worked clerk being pressed into service now as a butler:

Now, Peter, gett us wyne of the best. (339)

Master and chaplain sit side by side drinking their 'drawte [draught] of Romney red', and by a nice symbolic irony in view of the future action, 'a lofe of lyght bred' is also supplied for the repast. The main purpose of this scene, however, only emerges later in the text, though its function is swiftly apparent on the stage. Aristorius has to obtain the key of the church from the chaplain who has charge of it, and the meal, although covered by a mere dozen lines of dialogue, enables him to ply the priest with wine, and to divert his attention long enough to detach the key in some way from his person. The Bishop is later to rebuke Sir Isidore for his slackness:

Also, thou preste, for thy neclygens,
> That thou were no wyser in thyn office,
Thou art worthy inpresunment for thyn offence . . .
> be ware of the key of Goddys temple. (920–2, 927)

Thus by some unspecified ruse Aristorius must gain the vital key; the meal is swiftly disposed of, and the 'Presbyter' takes his master's hint that

Thys Romney ys good to goo with to reste (345)

and retires to his chamber, presumably departing through the curtains at the rear of the scaffold. Aristorius then calls his clerk (from the rear-space also?) and explaining that

For a lytyll waye walkyn I must (358),

descends from the scaffold to the main playing-area. The clerk presumably remains on the platform long enough to clear away the supper. Since Aristorius's 'stage' will not be featured again for almost five hundred lines, Peter no doubt finishes by drawing the curtains together around this spot.

Eight lines of soliloquy cover Aristorius's stealthy movement across the *platea* to the church –

Now prevely wyll I preve my pace (360) –

and he then 'enters' the 'building' with the key and taking the Host from the altar, announces his intention of carrying it to Jonathas. Once again the lines indicate movement through the main playing-area and the Jew's descent must coincide with the merchant's strides across the *platea*:

But now wyll I passe by thes pathes playne;

To mete with Jonathas I wold fayne.

Ah! yonder he commytht in certayn;

  Me thynkyth I hym see. (373–6)

Like the swift succession of events which occurs, the blatant coincidence of the encounter which follows is easily accepted on the non-naturalistic stage, the vital matter being the delivery of the Host into Jonathas's hands. Aristorius returns to the 'halle and bowre' of his own scaffold, where, since he is not required for some 450 lines, he may well be permitted to retire from the playing-area via the back curtains, or to rest behind the front curtains drawn by the faithful Peter. The Jew, covering the sacred object in a cloth for fear of discovery, crosses the arena, and presumably encounters his household at the foot of his 'stage', since, after addressing them all, he instructs Jason to go ahead with the Host:

Into the forsayd parlowr prevely take thy pase:

  Sprede a clothe on the tabyll that ye shall ther fynd,

And we shall folow after to carpe [talk] of thys case [affair]. (390–2)

The Jew's scaffold can hardly have accommodated a separate 'parlowr' with a table and sending Jason up the steps ahead of the main party seems the neatest way of establishing the new identity which Jonathas's 'stage' is now required to serve; the spread cloth on the tables on *both* scaffolds forms another satisfying piece of visual parallelism.

There follows a passage of some 320 lines, including the interlude of the quack doctor, during which the Jews subject the Host to every kind of torture and insult. This forms the central portion of the play and is indeed in some measure its *raison d'être*. Arranging for the Host to spurt blood when stabbed was no difficult matter for those accustomed to making corpses bleed; it was doubtless effected by the aid of a concealed bladder of animal's blood which Jonathas could pierce with the fifth dagger blow delivered. A false hand hidden beneath the capacious sleeve of the Jew's gown could be used when the Host was nailed to a post and Jonathas's hand became miraculously attached to it, being 'torn' from his arm as his assistants tried to extricate him. The cauldron of oil required to boil over with blood was a more demanding effect to achieve on cue even if the welling blood presented no problems. The oven which had to break in pieces and bleed once the Host had been placed inside it would be simpler to contrive, especially as Jasdon while 'stopping' the oven with clay could no doubt surreptitiously set a spring or light a fuse contrived to make an explosion and apparently blast the oven apart. The 'image' of Christ, intended to 'appere owt with woundys bledyng', was presumably represented by a human actor, since the role of 'Jhesus' appears in the cast-list, though a pictorial or plastic image might have been employed, with the actor simply used as a 'voice off' speaking the forty lines which Christ addresses to the prostrated Jews. However, the appearance of a live player would undoubtedly produce a more telling effect on stage, especially if we take the figure suggested by line 804 as literally that of 'A chyld apperyng with wondys blody', though it is in fact more likely that the word 'chyld' here simply indicates 'a noble young man' which would facilitate casting the part. The final miracle which occurs when the bishop having arrived at the Jew's house calls on the figure of Christ to revert to bread again, was probably effected by having Jesus exit neatly through the rear curtains of Jonathas's scaffold, perhaps masked from view by the bishop's upraised arms and the width of his cope. The wafer might then be swiftly substituted by one of the other players, or by the bishop himself as he held it up to the view of the audience.

★　★　★

We may now return to the staging of the play. The Jews are first assembled on Jonathas's platform with the Host laid '*on the tabyll*' before them, and as they debate the veracity of the cardinal tenets of Christianity, they resolve to put to the test the belief that the sacramental bread is capable of becoming Christ's living body upon consecration, arguing that if it is truly his flesh, it will surely manifest some signs of human suffering when it is abused. They proceed therefore to repeat on the Mass wafer the actions wrought on the body of Christ at Calvary, only to discover that the apparently inanimate object *is* capable of feeling human pain, and that similar surprises await them as they continue to subject what they argue is mere bread to anguish and torment.

Some commentators locate the entire action on Jonathas's 'stage', but this area would soon be intolerably cramped if five Jews, a table, an oven, a furnace with a cauldron, a post symbolizing the Cross, and the figure of Christ were all to be housed there! This feeling is reinforced by the fact that the *platea* is otherwise unoccupied by any character or any object throughout the long series of indignities inflicted on the Host.

It seems reasonable to assume that rather than this constricted and congested arrangement, we should visualize the scene of activities extended away from Jonathas's scaffold into the vacant *platea* as often as possible. Thus, after the initial stabbing of the Host, Jason raises a cry for a fire and a cauldron, to which Jasdon responds with the offer to help throw the wafer into the boiling vessel, while Masphat announces from somewhere:

Ye, here is a furneys stowte and strong,
And a cawdron therin dothe hong (489–90),

then calls angrily to Malchus for assistance:

Malcus, wher art thow so long,
To helpe thys dede were dyght [carried out]? (491–2)

On the basis of this evidence it is likely that the Jews, apart from Jonathas, scatter at Jason's call for fire, and descend with a clatter down the steps into the main playing-area, where Masphat draws their attention to the presence of the furnace and the cauldron positioned above it. This would then make better sense of the latter's irritable request for Malchus's help than if both characters stood within a few feet of each other on the same platform. Malchus has possibly shot off in another direction within the *platea*, and takes his time to come over and inspect the furnace that Masphat is so proud of finding! He collects the four gallons of oil, possibly from the base of the Jew's scaffold, and then tells his master jocularly to 'bryng that ylke cake nere', an action which is again more striking if Jonathas has to descend and cross to the furnace *bringing* the Host to incinerate it, than if he simply steps across a narrow platform to do so. Moreover, the later movement would scarcely require Jonathas's statement of intent to cover its execution, if Jews, furnace, and cauldron are all safely packed into the same confined space. As it is, the words run:

And I shall *bryng* that ylke cak
And throwe yt in, I *undertake*. (497–8; my italics)

Even if this initial hypothesis is unaccepted, it is extremely unlikely that the next piece of action was confined to the scaffold. Jonathas, unable to shed the wafer from his hand, now 'renneth wood [runs mad]', yelling out his intention to drown himself, and crying:

. . . I lepe over this lond (503),

an odd phrase unless Jonathas is actually running and jumping about in the open space of the *platea* ('this lond') and not still occupying his 'stage'. Jason's response appears to support such a viewpoint:

Renne, felawes, renne, for Cokkys [God's] peyn,
Fast we had owr mayster ageyne!
Hold prestly [hard] on thys pleyn
    And faste bynd hyme to a poste. (504–7)

The stage picture seems obvious: Jonathas runs amuck in the 'place'; his menials chase after him, seize him, even holding him down to restrain him 'on thys pleyn', and then drag him to a post fixed into the ground to which they proceed to bind him. There can surely be no argument that the post to which the Jew and the Host are nailed must be set up in the main playing-area and not within Jonathas's house. This seems proved after Jonathas's hand has become detached and left stuck to the Host, and the Jew decides to go back to the privacy of his own home, telling his men:

Now hastely to owr chamber lete us gon. (521)

This may merely indicate that he withdraws from his scaffold where these incidents have occurred to the area behind the rear curtains, but although the term 'chamber' usually indicates a room for private use, it can simply mean 'a room' and the use of the plurals '*owr* chamber' and 'lete *us*' suggests that the party of Jews anxiously pilot their one-handed master across the *platea* and up the steps to his bench on the scaffold, where he sits down, whereupon the curtains can be drawn once more on the tableau of the shaken little band.

There follow almost 130 lines of low comedy in which the quack doctor 'Master Brundyche of Braban' and his servant Coll hold the centre of attention with a comic double-act addressed largely to the spectators in the style of pairs of contrasted comedians at work today, which culminates with the doctor's offer to cure Jonathas's severed hand. Doubts have been expressed as to the integrity of this scene within the total structure of *The Play of the Sacrament*, in that it differs considerably in tone, language, and form from the main body of the text. The doctor himself has clear affinities with the wonder-working physicians of the English Mummers' Plays, whose miraculous if expensive cures often permit the hero or sometimes his pagan antagonists to come back to life in order to continue the fight which forms the core of the combat-type of mumming ritual. At the same time his bickering relationship with his 'man' resembles the mutually hostile partnership between master and servant as exemplified in Cain and his boy Pikeharnes in the Wakefield *Mactatio Abel*. It is further argued that Coll's irreverent and often bawdy backchat and the doctor's farcical attempts to practise his dubious skills are totally incongruous in the context of manifestations of Christ's almighty power to work miracles and to convert the heathen.

But whatever the ultimate source of this material, it is not so completely out of keeping with its surroundings that we should hurry to reject it. As Stanley Kahrl has demonstrated,[9] there is a good deal of farcical comedy in the treatment of the Jews in the previous scene. Moreover, the contrast between the spurious powers of healing laid claim to by Master Brundyche and the genuinely restorative capabilities of Christ shortly to be demonstrated on the person of Jonathas cannot be ignored, and the doctor's boastful claims and loose morals provide a valid parallel with both Aristorius's guilty egocentricity and covetousness and Jonathas's spiritual blindness. Furthermore, in terms of the play's structure, it is not necessarily a defect to introduce an interlude which will both reduce the tensions inherent in those scenes in which the Sacrament is insulted and also eke out a sequence of torments which might otherwise become merely repetitive. Jonathas too is provided with a welcome breathing-space from having to 'run wood'. Though parallels with the Passion are admittedly broken for a short time, they become that much more effective when resumed after the doctor and Coll have gone away, and an audience can concentrate on the further acts of violence, their taste for some innocent amusement satisfyingly catered for. As for the contrast in verse-form, diction, and register, it is not beyond the bounds of possibility that the anonymous playwright deliberately contrived that these should form an interesting, refreshing change from the surrounding texture of the main body of the play.

The 'doctor scene' presents no problems of staging worthy of comment: 'the lechys man' comes 'into the place' and conducts his monologue using the audience familiarly and intimately, much as Cain's servant Pikeharnes does in the Wakefield Cycle and stand-up comics do today. He confides to the spectators his master's weakness for drink and women, complaining of his late arrival, and finally 'makes a cry' for him, during which scurrilous 'proclamacion' the doctor creeps up unseen by Coll but seen by the audience, and pounces on him in the midst of his declaration that when run to earth his master ought to be placed in the pillory! They squabble and discuss one of the doctor's trickier female patients; the doctor then becomes aware of the audience, immediately seeing in its members a source of supplementary income, and orders Coll to advertise his prowess by means of another proclamation full of insult and innuendo:

All manar off men that have any syknes,
To Master Brentberecly loke that yow redresse [resort].
What dysease or syknesse that ever ye have,
He wyll never leve yow tyll ye be in yowr grave. (608–11)

Brundyche is then informed by Coll of Jonathas's plight, and the dialogue runs:

MASTER BRUNDYCHE: Fast to hym I wold inquere.
COLL: For God, master, the gate ys hyre [here]
MASTER BRUNDYCHE: Than to hym I wyll go nere.
My master, wele mot yow be!
JONATHAS: What doost here, felawe? what woldest thu hanne? (630–4)

These exchanges indicate that when the remarks begin Coll and the doctor are standing close by Jonathas's 'stage', and on being told that he is at the Jew's 'gate', the doctor declares his intention of making a visit, and so mounts the steps to the platform. The curtains might be drawn back by the Jew's attendants to reveal Jonathas in his pain, but if it were the doctor himself who pulled back the curtains rudely and thrust himself cheerfully upon the suffering Jew, it would give added point to Jonathas's dignified outrage:

Syr, thu art ontawght [ill-bred] to come in thus homly [familiarly],
Or to pere [appear] in my presence thus malepertly. (638–9)

The doctor is joined by Coll, who, since there appears to be money to be gained from the deceit, vouches for his master's skill, offering the Jew the kindly suggestion that 'In a pott yf yt please yow to pysse', the doctor can get to work. This is the final insult for Jonathas to swallow, and he orders his men to 'Brushe them hens'. They eject doctor and servant from the scaffold, chasing them out across the 'place' and beating them until they run away and disappear from view.

The second phase in tormenting the Host now begins. Jonathas, unable to participate himself, orders his four accomplices to take down from the post the hand holding the bread, wrap it in a cloth, and throw it into the cauldron as was his original aim. They leave Jonathas watching from his 'stage', descend to ground level, and proceed to carry out his orders: the cauldron boils with blood when they make the fire burn up, and in a state of panic they return to the Jew for further instructions. That they have to make a quite definite movement from the cauldron to Jonathas on his platform seems clear from Jason's words of greeting:

Ah! master, master, what chere ys with yow? (677)

Jonathas now orders the 'ovyn' to be prepared and heated until red-hot, whereupon the Host is to be cast in and the opening sealed up. The location of the oven is again critical to the managing of the later stages of the action, since it is after the oven bursts that the 'image' of Christ appears with bleeding wounds, and it is to view this sight that Jonathas brings the bishop to his house, which as we have seen must be located at the scaffold designed for it. Therefore, if the cauldron and the post are positioned in the *platea*, the oven must be placed either on the Jew's 'stage' or else close enough to it to seem part of the furnishing of his house. The other Jews then bring 'fyryng' consisting of 'straw and thornys kene' (the latter almost certainly another allusion to the Passion), from the site of the cauldron in the main area, and thus kindle the oven. Malchus can also quite plausibly send Jason *back* to the cauldron to fetch the 'cake' in his 'pynsonys [pincers]' and bring it across to the oven:

Now, Jason, to the cawdron that ye stere [hurry]
And fast fetche hether that ylke cake.
Here shall Jason goo to the cawdron . . . (699–700)

This seems the only feasible beginning if one is to achieve the adequate staging of the apparition of Christ to the Jews, since on the open *platea* the necessarily sudden appearance of the bleeding form would be very hard to contrive, whereas on a curtained stage it could be rendered very strikingly, especially for an audience preoccupied with the process of incineration. There may be further confirmation that the oven should be sited on or near Jonathas's scaffold in the fact that when Christ advises the maimed Jew to plunge his arm into the cauldron to restore his hand, he specifically urges him to '*Go* to the cawdron' (line 776 – my italics), a somewhat pointless order unless the cauldron is at some distance from the Jew's house. Jonathas must descend and proceed to the cauldron within which he places his arm, recovering his hand by the simple expedient of bringing it out of his capacious sleeve once again. Such a movement across the playing-area increases the excitement of the miracle, lessened if Jonathas merely takes a few steps across a platform. No doubt the twenty-line speech of thanksgiving which ensues was partly delivered while the Jew moved back from the cauldron to the steps of his own scaffold. That he must thereby approach fairly close to the figure of Christ on the 'stage' is apparent from Jonathas's closing remarks:

But, Lord, I take my leve at thy hygh presens . . .

The bysshoppe wyll I goo fetche to se owr offens . . . (794, 796)

Leaving his men kneeling before Christ's image, the Jew makes his way to the bishop, who had probably entered the staging-area unobtrusively, taking up his position at the church-site between the two scaffolds, and tells him of the 'swemfull [pitiful] syght'

In my howse apperyng verely (801).

The bishop then consents to walk with Jonathas to witness the vision.

We must now resolve the most controversial crux in the staging of this play. Before departing the bishop addresses two remarks to an unspecified group of people, either his own attendants on stage, or the members of the audience themselves. His words are:

Now, all my pepull, with me ye dresse [prepare yourselves]

For to goo see that swymfull syght.

Now, all ye peple that here are,

    I commande yow, every man,

On yowr feet for to goo bare,

    In the devoutest wyse that ye can. (808–13)

This speech raises fascinating issues: is the instruction to be taken as a piece of pure dramatic licence not to be acted upon? Or are the spectators at the play being literally invited to participate in its action by crowding from their seats on to the playing-area and converging on the image of Christ at the Jew's house, in the way that eager children and unsuspecting adults are lured up on stage during pantomimes? If so, is it really expected that they will remove their footwear as a sign of reverence? Is it not more likely that only actual performers could be guaranteed to obey the bishop's commands, and that therefore his words are most plausibly addressed to members of the cast? Yet attendants on the bishops are not specified in the list of players, and if the attached rubric which says that 'IX [nine] may play yt at ease' is followed, there seem to be no characters who can be spared from a scene which incorporates all the listed players except Aristorius and his chaplain who must be on their scaffold ready to view the procession which the bishop is shortly to lead from the Jew's house to the church, where they will join the assembled company. Admittedly, there are Coll and the doctor (although they may be required to double roles) but the general visit to view Christ's image and the procession to the church must be made up of more than *two* listed players!

The ingenious solution to the puzzle which has been advanced by a number of commentators has already been touched on. It is that the play actually terminated *within* a place of worship, and that the spectators, after watching the greater part of the action at an open-air site, moved *en masse* first to the Jew's 'stage' and then into a church for the final sequence of baptism and confession, thus themselves forming the procession and witnessing the termination of the miraculous proceedings more as involved participants than as interested spectators. This is an attractive theory[10] and has much to commend it at first sight, as well as being perfectly feasible at the setting in Croxton churchyard so far assumed. The interior of the church does not have to form part of the basic setting, and could simply be reserved for the climax of the action. The audience could observe the merchant's chaplain entering the building to say Evensong without requiring to see him saying it; Aristorius's actual theft of the Host does not need to be made visible, since it is certainly not accompanied by any dialogue; his

I wyll nott abyde by dale nor hyll

Tyll yt be wrowght, by Saynt Mary! (366–7)

could well make an effective exit-line as he unlocks the church-door and sneaks inside, following the rubric '*Here shal he enter the chyrche and take the Hoost*', returning with the words.

Ah! now have I all myn entent (368)

The bishop too might emerge from the church and appear at the church-porch on his first entry, and from there encounter the repentant Jonathas, make his exhortation to the spectators to accompany him to the Jew's house, and from thence suggest that they should process with him to the church interior. Once Christ's body has returned to bread again, the bishop can take it from the Jew's scaffold

And beare yt to chyrche with solempne processyon (837),

exactly as was done at the Feast of Corpus Christi with the laity following dutifully behind the Sacrament:

Now folow me, all and summe,

    And all tho [those] that bene here, both more and lesse,

Thys holy song, *O sacrum Convivium* [O sacred feast]

    Lett us syng all with grett swetnesse. (838–40)

The ensuing procession must be of fair magnitude to command the attention of the priest on Aristorius's platform, for Sir Isidore informs the merchant

The bysshope commyth processyon [sic] with a gret meny [company]
   of Jewys (844),

and a conversation of some twenty lines follows in which Aristorius confesses his sin to his chaplain and receives the advice that he should make a full confession in church to the bishop:

Lett us hye us fast that we were hens (862).

In fact, the ensuing stage direction indicates that Aristorius and his chaplain arrive at the church before the bishop and the procession appear. The *dénouement* is effected thereupon, with the bishop preaching a sermon, Aristorius admitting his guilt in selling the sacrament for gain, the bishop imposing a penance on him that he should refrain from buying and selling for the rest of his days, while even Isidore is rebuked, as we have seen, for letting the church key out of his possession. Finally, the Jews kneel down to ask remission of their sins, and confessing their fault in tormenting Christ in the form of the sacramental bread, request baptism which the bishop bestows on them at the font. Jonathas speaks of their intention to travel the world and atone for their evil deeds, and the former Jews depart after blessing the concourse: Aristorius declares his resolve to leave for his own country where he will attempt to teach others the lesson he has so dearly learnt; priest and bishop round off proceedings with admonitions to serve Christ, and to keep his commandments, and with the pious hope that God will bring them all to everlasting bliss in heaven. The traditional singing of the *Te Deum* ends the play.

The notion that spectators joined in the final portion of the Croxton *Play* and that its action culminated *inside* a church building is not impossible, but on close examination loses some of its plausibility. Firstly, it is open to the objection that if the play *was* taken on tour, not every suitable performance-site within a particular region would contain a conveniently-placed church in sufficiently close proximity to accommodate the final actions. Few companies would risk dissipating the dramatic tension created by having an audience process even a hundred yards to witness the climax of a short play. It would also seem rather vital to have the church centrally positioned within the playing-area, and this might again be difficult to arrange at every site. Even if one rejects the notion of a touring production, and settles for Croxton as the sole venue for the play which bears its name, there are other problems. Although Croxton does offer a potential playing-site close to a church, something is lost if the altar with the cross and the reserved Sacrament upon it or adjacent to it is not visible as a central symbol of the presence of Christ through the early part of the action. A visible church 'interior' enables spectators actually to see Isidore at his prayers and to witness Aristorius's sacrilegious theft. Even if this seems too subjective an objection, it must still appear inconsistent with the theory of a church finale that the bishop should exhort spectators not only to process into the church interior but also to leave their seats in order to view the image of Christ as it has shown itself in the Jew's house, when they can see it perfectly well (presumably) from where they sit. More important there is the problem of coping with the dialogue between Aristorius and Sir Isidore which precedes their rapid excursion to the church; if the spectators have just risen up and joined in a procession to the church behind the bishop, a procession to which Isidore draws the merchant's attention, who is left behind in the auditorium to listen to the conversation between the two men?

It therefore seems much more feasible to re-create the conclusion to the Croxton *Play of the Sacrament* in a manner whereby the entire performance is staged out of doors, in an open space probably in the immediate vicinity of the parish church, with the Jew's house, Aristorius's house, and 'the church' as its three fixed scenic components. After the appearance of Christ to the Jews, the bishop urges the people to witness the miracle, and a dozen or so locally-recruited extras not mentioned in the cast-list, with feet already bared for the purpose, quit their seats in the auditorium and form a small token crowd at the foot of the steps of the Jew's 'stage', and afterwards process to the 'church' location. Possibly they are local choirboys or choristers with some known talent for singing Latin hymns 'with grett swetnesse' as they parade around the *platea*. The allusion by the bishop to 'all tho that bene here' then follows the usual stage convention of referring to those within the acting-area and not to the entire audience. Thus most of the spectators are still present to hear and see Aristorius's confession to Sir Isidore, while they are simultaneously aware of the singing procession crossing the 'place' to form up in the church setting. If it goes 'the long way round', it enables the merchant and his chaplain to arrive at the church before them as the stage direction demands. For the christening of the Jews to be effected, the 'church set' must contain a practicable font, but this need not obtrude on the rest of the location in any way; indeed its presence would emphasize the nature of the scenic location depicted. At all events, if the method of reconstruction suggested here is adopted, the provision of personnel for the procession need not rob the penultimate phase of the action of all its auditors, and the problem of the best way to shift a group of spectators successfully from playing-place to place of worship simply does not arise.

* * *

The cast-list appended to the text of *The Play of the Sacrament* lists eleven roles, but omits Aristorius's 'Presbiter', Isidore; the manuscript then states that 'IX [nine] may play yt at ease.' This can be effected in various

ways, but presumably the players of Aristorius, Isidore, Jonathas, and
the four Jews were not required to double by virtue of the frequency
with which they are required to perform, or because of the size of their
parts. This means that the roles of Jesus, the bishop, the clerk, the
doctor, and Coll have to be shared out between the company's remaining
pair of actors. It would be possible for 'Petyr Powle' the clerk to leave
the stage after clearing away the remains of supper on Aristorius's 'stage',
and to return as Coll, 'the lechys man', some 150 lines later – the age of
the characters is roughly compatible – and again for him to be chased
away as Coll at line 652, and swiftly to re-appear from the rear of the
Jew's scaffold as the Christ-figure (assuming that a live actor appeared in
the role) at line 712, an interval of sixty lines interspersed with a fair
amount of stage action sufficing to cover the change. The other player
involved in doubling had a less strenuous brief: he was not called upon
to appear until line 573 when he came on as the doctor, and after his
precipitate departure from the *platea* at line 652 had until line 797 before
he needed to present himself as the bishop.

These suggestions do not represent the only possible method of casting
the play for nine players. If we assume that the curtains on Aristorius's
scaffold were drawn shut on his retirement thence after passing the Host
to Jonathas, or that the stage direction after line 384 – *Here shall Arystory
goo hys waye* – denotes his total departure from the stage-area and not
retirement into his 'booth', the actor is freed to play the doctor (a part
better suited to the player of Aristorius than is that of Coll), and still has
the opportunity to return to his own 'stage' and change his costume in
time to open the curtains and witness the procession passing to the
church. This means that technically the bishop could also appear as the
clerk or Coll, but given the likely personality and 'weight' of the player
taking the part of the bishop, it seems improbable that he could double
convincingly as either the cheeky and scurrilous 'lechys man' or the
dutiful subordinate, 'Petyr Powle'.

*   *   *

The Croxton *Play of the Sacrament* demonstrates the extent to which a
cluster of stage structures and an open 'place' are sufficient to convey a
sense of continuity and scenic variety with very limited means. The
accomplished manner in which the playwright shifts the dramatic interest
from one stage location to another is masterly, and the use made of
simultaneous activity in different parts of the playing-area ensures that
an integrated impression of communal life is never lost sight of, while
reminding us of the medieval taste for parallelism and prefiguration. The
identification of certain locations with particular figures helps to render
their dramatic function clearer, and the interplay between one sphere and
another – the crossing and re-crossing of the *platea* for instance – not only

emphasizes the various phases of the plot, but enhances the dynamism of the characters in a highly dynamic play.

The Croxton piece depends far less upon audience contact than does *Mankynde*: the major players never establish such a close rapport with the audience or impinge on 'spectator territory' quite so brazenly, yet there can be little doubt that a deep sense of involvement results from the intensity of a theatrical experience rendered more telling by the attention devoted to the inventive use of scenic structures.

3 · Theatre in the Round: *The Castel of Perseveraunce*

One of the world's most prized theatre-drawings is the 'annotated diagram' contained in the Macro manuscript of the fifteenth-century morality play *The Castel of Perseveraunce*. Its fame is justified, for it offers almost all the meagre pictorial evidence we possess for an understanding of medieval staging-in-the-round, and its exact significance is the subject of lively debate. Indeed, so dominant a position has the plan now assumed, that performance 'in the round' has come to be regarded as the standard medieval form of staging, and to dominate too much thinking on the topic.[1] Arena-staging is only one of a variety of medieval presentational methods, and it is misguided to treat every medieval play-script as if there were only one feasible way of staging it.

Nevertheless the fascination of the *Castel* sketch is obvious enough. Whereas not a single authenticated picture of an English pageant-waggon exists, we do have one illustration which, taken with the data written on it and the plans in the manuscript of the Cornish *Ordinalia*, goes some way in assisting us to grasp the principles of medieval arena-staging. Such evidence, however ambiguous and imprecise, is simply not forthcoming when we seek to visualize processional performances during the same period.

The Castel of Perseveraunce is by far the longest medieval English morality play to survive, consisting as it does of some 3700 lines, roughly four times the length of *Everyman*. It is constructed on an ample scale, not only in its theatrical requirements, but also in the scope of its action which ranges 'from heaven to earth, from earth to heaven', comprehending the hierarchy of Vices and Virtues which influence Mankind's worldly decisions as well as his spiritual destiny, and culminating in the long traditional debate between the four daughters of God on the ultimate fate of the human soul.

The staging of the play attracted relatively little close scrutiny, until Richard Southern in his *Medieval Theatre in the Round* in 1957 not only demonstrated how the manuscript illustration might be used to reconstruct a 'theatre' for the performance, but described in detail how the play could be staged in such a setting. Supporting his conclusions from apparently analogous systems depicted in Fouquet's celebrated miniature of the Martyrdom of St Apollonia (see Plate 10), in the 'Terence des Ducs' manuscript from Paris, and extant in the amphitheatrical 'rounds' of Cornwall (see Plate 11), Southern conjured up a spacious circular arena with a single castle-tower on stilts at its centre and a bed below it, the amphitheatre completely surrounded by a water-filled ditch to exclude non-paying spectators. Those who paid were permitted to stand within the flat central area, the 'place' or *platea*, as well as sitting on the sloping banks formed from the loose soil excavated from the ditch. Set into these embankments were five 'scaffolds', raised versions of the Croxton 'stages' offering an even more versatile scenic arrangement. These platforms housed the World, the Flesh, Belyal the Devil, Avaricia or Covetousness, and God, together with their attendants: access to and from the ground was gained by ramps or steps. During the action characters could retire behind the curtains enclosing the scaffolds; these allowed for exits and entrances too, and facilitated doubling, since a figure could retreat at the rear of a curtained scaffold to reappear in a different rôle elsewhere. Such a facility might be invaluable for *The Castel of Perseveraunce* with its thirty-five parts, although a large number of players are in fact required to be visible simultaneously.

Southern's book is a brilliant and central contribution to any discussion of medieval theatre, but unfortunately its hypotheses are open to serious objections.[2] One major doubt arises from the sheer scale of the operation involved in removing quantities of soil to form the ditch around the playing-site. Did players really have the physical or financial resources to arrange for hundreds of tons of earth to be excavated and piled up around an arena which Southern himself estimates to have measured 110 feet (34 metres) across, and fill the ditch with five feet of water? This would be a prodigious undertaking even for a single performance at a single site, and if this were a travelling show (as its banns imply), the notion of constructing several 'theatres-in-the-round' across the East Anglian land-scape becomes profoundly unlikely. Such structures would scarcely be utilized other than occasionally, even if there existed a whole repertoire of pieces geared to the facilities offered. Possibly they could be adapted to other uses, but it seems far more plausible to think of naturally-occurring sites roughly resembling that of the diagram being employed, rather than of laboriously-constructed arenas.

The presentation of *Ane Satyre of the Thrie Estaitis* at Cupar in Fifeshire[3] in 1552 at a site where the channel of the Ladyburn flanked the stage-area, separating actors and audience suggests that Southern may be wrong in believing that a ditch was dug externally to keep out spectators disin-

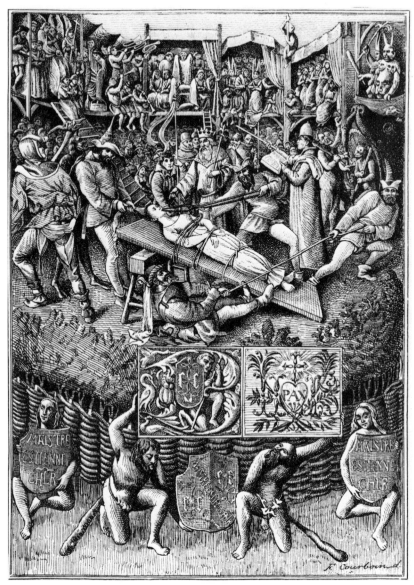

10 Jean Fouquet's miniature of the Martyrdom of St Apollonia (c. 1455), as engraved for Bapst's *Essai sur l'histoire du théâtre*, Paris, 1893.

11 A scene from Neville Denny's production of the Cornish *Passio* performed at the Perran Round, 1969. (Photo: University of Bristol Theatre Collection)

clined to pay. He himself admits that we cannot assume that an admission charge was made, and certainly many medieval plays were presented simply for public enjoyment and enlightenment.[4] If this were the case, there would be no purpose in a ditch or a fence keeping non-paying patrons out, but there might be added incentive to hold back over-enthusiastic or unruly customers who might disrupt or join in the proceedings. This would certainly be consistent with what is known of comparable stages on the Continent; at Autun in 1516 a water-filled ditch divided players and auditors, and at Doué in 1539 a low wall served the same purpose. At some French sites a brushwood or wattle fence as shown in Fouquet's miniature strengthened the sides of the ditch and held back the soil of a slightly elevated *platea*.[5] The image of an interior rather than an exterior ditch is also more consistent with the rubric on the *Castel* plan which reads: 'this is the watyr a-bowte the place [;] if any dyche may be mad ther it schal be played; or ellys that it be strongely barryd al a-bowt'. The fact that this legend occupies the two concentric rings surrounding the *platea*, with the scaffolds located *outside* the circle rather than within it, must strengthen this view.

Some have not accepted even this modification of Southern's theory,[6] arguing that the ditch is really intended to form part of the inner defences of the castle, so adding to its symbolic function as a place of protection and divine grace. When the Vices assault the castle's fortifications and Slawthe (Sloth) in lines 2326–37 attempts to divert the waters with a spade, this association of ditch and castle appears significant:

Ware, war, I delve wyth a spade.
Men calle me the lord Syr Slowe.
Gostly grace I spylle [destroy] and schade [pour away];
Fro [away from] the watyr of grace this dyche I fowe [clear].
Ye schulyn com ryth inowe
Be [by] this dyche drye, be bankys brede [broad].[7]

Certainly the notion of a modest moat-like ditch surrounding the castle-area is attractive: it clearly reduces the physical labour and expense involved in excavating a larger circle, but it also makes good sense theologically by acting as a symbol of purification through baptism, enhancing the castle as an image of protective fortification against evil.[8] At the same time, in order to accept this interpretation of the drawing, we have to explain the rubric 'this is the watyr *a-bowte the place*' (my italics), a phrase supporting the existence of an internal ditch between auditorium and *platea*. The only answer is to regard the castle as standing within the 'place' but separated off from the main *platea* by the ditch or fence which gives it a kind of 'inner bailey', or to assume that there were two ditches.

Equally important to an initial understanding of the plan is the location of the audience. Is Southern's loose earthen embankment really suitable for their accommodation? Again, the provision of such a mound of piled-up soil depends on the digging of an external ditch, yet if we reject this and settle for a natural site, a quarry or an earthwork or a hollow plain, audience-accommodation is not far to seek. But would spectators also have occupied the *platea* as Southern suggests? He bases his thesis primarily on the wording of the plan which runs: 'this is the castel of perseveraunse that stondyth in the myddys of the place, but lete no man sytte ther, for lettynge of syt [preventing people from seeing], for ther schal be the best of all', which Southern interprets as meaning that sitting or standing elsewhere in the *platea* was permitted. But, as I have argued elsewhere,[9] the rubric may mean that nobody is to occupy any portion of the *platea* whatever, since this will impede the view of those outside the arena, especially those on the 'terraces'. A body of milling spectators would certainly impede the performers, particularly in the battle-scenes vital to the play's success. The reliance which Southern places on Fouquet's miniature for this part of this theory is suspect, since there fore-shortening is probably responsible for the erroneous impression that the 'place' is filled with spectators. Nor does the plan's allusion to the presence of marshals – 'lete nowth [not] ovyr many stytelerys be wyth-inne the plase' – necessarily corroborate Southern's view that the audience stood 'within the place'. It is far more likely that the 'stytelerys' kept order by maintaining an inconspicuous presence on the perimeter of the *platea* ensuring that people occupied the edge of the circle in a well-regulated manner, and seeing that they did not make a nuisance of themselves while the play was in progress.

We have then a hypothetical setting for *The Castel of Perseveraunce*: a roughly circular amphitheatre with possibly raked sides, with platforms set within its circumference at the four main compass-points with a fifth to the North-East. Each has a ramp or ladder leading from it to the ground; each is supplied with curtains capable of hiding it from view on all sides. At the centre of the playing-area stands a 'castle', separated from the main *platea* by a shallow ditch of water or a fence, leaving a small 'inner bailey' free between the barrier and the castle. Beneath the castle a bed is placed with sufficient space below for an actor to be concealed, for the rubric tells us that 'Mankyndeis bed schal be undyr the castel and ther schal the sowle lye undyr the bed tyl he schal ryse and pleye'. We are also enigmatically informed by the plan that 'Coveytyse [Covetousness's] copbord be [by] the beddys feet schal be at the ende of the castel', but the significance of this statement may be deferred for the time being.

Like the Croxton *Play*, *The Castel of Perseveraunce* is preceded by a set of banns (probably later than the main text[10]) whose delivery was entrusted to two standard-bearers or heralds, armed with flags to attract

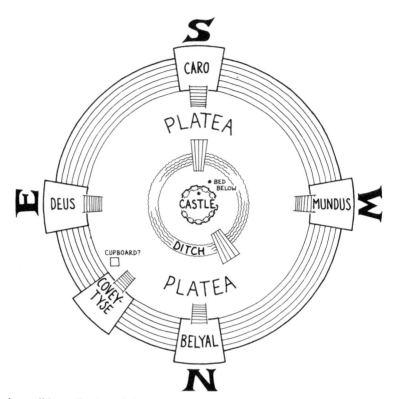

4 A possible realization of the *Castel* plan, with the ditch surrounding the castle structure

attention and accompanied by musicians, who visited the district where the play was next to be performed, to drum up trade. The banns occupy 156 lines, outline the plot and point up the moral for the benefit of 'all the goode comowns of this towne' (line 8). Despite the size of its cast, the evidence that a touring company handled this play is far stronger than at Croxton. The Croxton banns include the name of the village;[11] the gap in the *Castel* script, however, seems meant for a range of possible venues to be inserted, although it may again be pointed out that 'touring' in the fifteenth century was rarely a matter of covering vast distances:

These parcellys [parts] in propyrtes we purpose us to playe
This day sevenenyt [today week] before you in syth
At . . . on the grene in ryal aray. (132–4)

Further evidence that this play toured is found in the reference that 'we schul be onward be [by] underne of the day' (138) which Eccles takes to mean 'we must be moving on by afternoon', though Bevington reads it as 'we shall be ready to start performing by 9 a.m.'.[12]

The banns' allusion to 'the grene' is puzzling: is it an unequivocal indication that the play was staged on a level tract of grassland – Mundus's reference to a 'propyr pleyn place' in line 160 may confirm this – rather than in the amphitheatre proposed by Southern? He argues ingeniously that 'the grene' means no more than the flat space of the *platea*; Natalie Crohn Schmitt prefers the more obvious sense which survives in such terms as 'village green' or 'bowling green', using these to strengthen her notion that the *Castel* was presented at more flexible, less regularized performance-sites. But we should not ignore a third possibility that the words are nothing more than a convenient conventional tag, analogous to 'out on the grass' or 'in the open air', with no reference to actual playing conditions.

★ ★ ★

The opening phase, consisting of long bragging speeches from their respective platforms by Mundus (World), Belyal (Devil) and Caro (Flesch) who boast of their prowess and their enmity to Man, throws light on the function of the five scaffolds.[13] Since each 'King' is accompanied by three supporters, each scaffold can presumably accommodate at least four figures, the ancillary characters adding to the authority of their master, as well as being able to assist with such practical tasks as drawing and closing the front curtains. All three powers are discovered seated on thrones which accentuate their superior claims, Belyal categorically asserting 'Now I sytte, Satanas, in my sad [perpetual, irremediable] synne' (196). However, the energetic physicality of his speeches suggests that he, like Aristorius at Croxton, leaves his seat and parades about his stage or more probably down in the *platea*, a more spacious area for 'pomping'. Belyal's call to 'Gadyr you togedyr, ye boyis, on this grene!' (227) may indicate his presence in the *platea*, though he could simply be pointing to the ground before his scaffold. If he descends, however, by the end of his speech he has returned – 'On benche wyl I byde' (232) he affirms. By contrast Flesch is static:

I byde as a brod brustun-gutte [bust-guts] abovyn on these tourys
(235)

and the portrait of greedy self-indulgence is sustained by the image of this obese monarch slumped on his throne.

The opening speeches also extend our picture of the complete setting. The 'propyr pleyn place' Mundus refers to may not signify much, alluding simply to the fine open space of the *platea* rather than the auditorium as a whole, but his allusion to 'syrys semly, all same [together] syttyth on syde' (163) suggests that seating was reserved for the 'sirs' or better-off, just as in *Mankynde* and its 'soverens that sytt and . . . brothern that stonde ryght wppe [up]' (29). Perhaps the socially-elevated had a separate enclosure as in Fouquet's painting, while the plebs stood at the rear or in their own sector. Mundus's remark may link with Caro's final words:

therfor on hylle

Syttyth all stylle (271–2) –

although the 'hylle' may be no more than the sloping banks of the amphitheatre. Indeed, almost any elevation within the theatre's perimeter can be alluded to as a 'hill': Pryde alludes to Coveytyse's scaffold as a 'hill' in lines 906–7:

Wondyr hyghe howtys [shouts] on hyll herd I houte [ring out]

Koveytyse kryeth, hys karpynge I kenne [recognize].

Yet the word is again used to designate the centre of the *platea* beyond the ditch, since at line 1897 when he foresees his troops capturing the castle Mundus orders them to 'Howtyth [shout] hye upon yene [yon] hyll', an image reintroduced by Pryde almost thirty lines later:

On hye hyllys lete us howte [shout] (1926).

Given the symmetry of their occupants' verbal boasts, it would be strange if the scaffolds of the 'kyngys thre' did not bear a close resemblance to each other. Mundus mentions his banner, and it is thus likely that Belyal and Caro too were furnished with imposing standards, perhaps those used for the banns by the *vexillatores*. Caro informs us that his platform is adorned with costly drapes:

Wyth tapytys [hangings] of tafata I tymbyr [decorate] my towrys (239)

and doubtless the complementary scaffolds were also hung with silks, sufficiently differentiated to highlight World's preoccupation with wealth and conquest, Belyal's evil and cruelty, Coveytyse's avaricious rapacity, and the splendour and majesty of God. Parallelism and symmetry are essential ingredients in a play which might otherwise become a farrago of disparate elements, and scenic correspondences would almost certainly be brought out.

The appearance of the leading figure of Humanum Genus or Mankynde some lines into the play shifts attention away from the scaffolds to the bed beneath the castle from which the newly-born Humankind, naked or clad in no more than a loin-cloth, emerges with the 'sely crysme' or simple baptismal cloth about his head. Possibly a child took the rôle, though a medieval audience would see nothing incongruous in a grown man assuming the part of a new-born baby, and since the same actor would perform the role of Man in his old age, there is some consistency in having him play the child too. However, when Mankynde is taken to be dressed later, an opportunity does occur for an adult to take over from a child-player.

By line 301 Mankynde's Bad and Good Angels are beside him, for referring to the latter at his 'ryth syde' he adds 'ye may hym se'. At what point and from whence the angels appear is uncertain, but presumably they must be present with the hero before birth or arrive in the central area of the *platea* shortly afterwards. They might stand at either side of the bed throughout the opening phase of the action, but their presence might distract from the speeches on the scaffolds, and their arrival at Man's birth would add extra significance to the protagonist's first appearance. A clue to their manner of arrival is contained in line 317 when Mankynde beseeches Christ that he may follow

The aungyl that cam fro hevene trone.

If we take this literally, we may assume that the Good Angel descends from God's scaffold to the sound of 'heavenly' music while the Bad Angel simultaneously quits Belyal's platform, that they cross the *platea* in unison, ford the castle ditch and join Mankynde on the central 'grene'. Such harmonizing movement serves to focus attention on the opposing forces contending for mastery over a newly-formed human life, their synchronized behaviour stressing their common purpose.

As the angels seek to persuade Man to virtue or to vice, the Bad Angel strives to attract him towards World's scaffold by pointing out its rich appearance. This suggests that its curtains are not closed, but that Mundus, like Caro and Belyal, looks down with fervent interest on the struggle for Mankynde's allegiance. This undoubtedly adds a visual dimension to the Bad Angel's tempting words, and accounts for the way in which Man succumbs to the delights on offer. The character then steps over the ditch with its connotations of grace and protection, and leaving his Good Angel urging him to 'Cum agayn, be strete and style' (403), starts to circle the *platea*'s edge in company with the Bad Angel *en route* for the scaffold occupied by Mundus and his minions.

The slow circuit adds visual variety to the stage activity, and brings Man in particular into closer contact with the spectators than the castle area permits or even that achieved by the 'kyngys thre' from their scaffolds. Mankynde is after all the proxy representative of every individual spectator: it is vital that he should establish his identity as one of ourselves. The nature of the auditorium would also seem to be the chief factor behind the element of patterned repetition and recapitulation both in successive speeches as those of the kings, and within individual ones. A large audience dispersed around a circular area would need to be informed of the dramatic situation developing in a variety of locations and meant that the players had to move freely about the *platea* to be seen and heard by as many people as possible. In the same way circus-performers today take care to direct their acts and extend their bows to all parts of the Big Top. Expansive movements are mirrored in expansive speeches with their frequent use of rhetorical devices of amplification and duplication which confirm that audiences were accustomed to seeing and hearing only certain portions of a play at close quarters, but that those portions were emphatically stressed as vital to their understanding of the whole.

Mundus resumes his boasting at line 456: he presents himself to the crowd as a mighty Herod-like potentate, attended by 'comly knytys of renoun', and instructs Voluptas or Lust-lykyng and Foly (his page Garcio remains unregarded at present) to announce that he is willing to accept the vassalage of anyone who despises God and good men. Voluptas obediently descends, and using the common device of making a proclamation, much as Coll in the Croxton *Play* advertises the doctor's skills, involves the multitude in the action:

Pes, pepyl, of pes we you pray (491) –

offering riches and pleasure to anyone offering Mundus service and loyalty. Foly joins him in the *platea*, and emphasizes the importance of covetousness and foolishness in anyone who intends to serve World properly. Pat on cue there arrives before the scaffold the Bad Angel with Mankynde his recruit. Depositing Man a little way off, the angel confides in Mundus's henchmen:

I have browth, be downys drye [by barren uplands?]
To the Werld a gret present. (528–9)

(It is doubtful if any clue to the terrain of the site is contained in the phrase 'downys drye': the Bad Angel and his charge have simply travelled around the level perimeter of the 'place'.)

Suppressing their mirth, Foly and Lust-lykyng formally line up with Man between them at the steps of World's scaffold, and to the sound of trumpets present him to their master who makes him lavish promises before inviting him to mount:

Cum up, my serwaunt trew as stel (614).

He then details Lust-lykyng to take the scarcely-clad Mankynde off and clothe him, and the overawed neophyte is bowed out at the rear of the scaffold, while Mundus's accomplices, pausing only to assure him of their malicious intentions, slip out after Mankynde.

Bakbytere (Detractio), who runs into the arena now to the sound of music, is apparently the first figure not to have been present 'on the set' when the play began. Possibly he occupied a position on Mundus's scaffold alongside the silent Garcio, but as a messenger it makes sound sense to have him arrive as if he has just completed an errand, and to charge into the *platea* boasting of his slanderous talents. He appears to know of Mankynde's seduction by the World, but it is not therefore necessary to assume that he was present at the time in order to have learnt this. He abides silently until Mankynde returns, squatting at the foot of the scaffold to await the chance for further mischief. Scarcely has he done so than Lust-lykyng and Foly return to the platform above with a richly-dressed Mankynde between them. The clothing he wears is decorated with gold and silver coins, an excellent example of the symbolic use of costume, an aid also put to telling use in *Mankynde*.[14] Its importance is emphasized later in the play when the mantles or cloaks of the four daughters of God are on view, their colours being carefully specified on the plan. Mercy's is to be white, traditionally the hue of atonement and forgiveness, Rytwysnes's red to symbolize justice, Trewth's 'sad [dull or dark] grene', standing for constancy, while Pes's black indicates that she mourns for Mankynde.

The text suggests that Lust-lykyng and Foly are now able to address some remarks to their chief while Mankynde in his new finery stands far enough off for an audience to assume he cannot hear. This assumption is backed by the fact that Mundus after discussing matters in a low voice with his 'knights' has to *call* to Mankynde at line 731: 'Welcum, Mankynde! to the I call'. Hence the platform at which these four figures (plus presumably Garcio) congregate must permit at least the pretence that two groups of characters are out of earshot of each other.

The centre of attention now shifts to Mundus's treasurer 'Syr Covetouse' who is to make Mankynde 'the mastyr in hys house', and the World summons Bakbytere to 'teche hym the weye'. The messenger leaps up and commands:

Have don, Mankynde, and cum doun.
I am thyne owyn page. (779–80),

drawing to Mankynde's notice the scaffold to the north-east where Coveytyse is enthroned:

Lo, where Syr Coveytyse sytt
And bydith [awaits] us in his stage (783–4).

This alerts spectators for the first time to the 'stage' allocated to Covetousness, the fifth scaffold which breaks up the symmetry of the perimeter scaffolds and highlights thereby the dominant role Avarice is to play. By separating one of the Seven Deadly Sins of tradition from the others, the author of the *Castel* not only preserves the symmetrical groupings of the other six on Belyal's and Flesch's scaffolds, but also anticipates Coveytyse's superiority in triumphing over Mankynde after the siege of the castle.

By the time Bakbytere alludes to Coveytyse's 'stage' its curtains must be drawn back, though whether they have been open throughout the action so far is dubious. The advantages of having curtains at all would be lost if any scaffold were exposed to view for any length of time, unless for a dramatic purpose, and in the case of the structure allotted to God, it would mean that the actor would be forced to sit exposed in majesty for some 3200 lines before joining the action.[15] Bakbytere in this instance may be instrumental in drawing the curtains as he says 'Lo, where Syr Coveytyse sytt'.

The journey to Coveytyse's 'house' takes twenty-six lines, during which the Good and Bad Angels debate from the central area. Possibly Bakbytere and Mankynde make a circuit of the *platea*, and having arrived at the foot of the 'stage', Man is not only invited to ascend the steps but Covetousness even vacates his own seat to him:

Cum up and se my ryche aray . . .

Sit up ryth here in this se [seat] (831, 834).

Once sure of his man, he issues a loud summons to the remaining Deadly Sins to join them, and his directions suggest that the descent of the six Sins from their respective scaffolds and their movement across the *platea* is conceived in terms of a journey through a fictional landscape:

Dryveth [hasten] downne ovyr dalys drye [barren dales?]

Ovyr hyll and holtys ye you hyghe [hurry] (897, 899).

The frequent ascents and descents, the pattern of journeys to and fro between scaffolds across the *platea*, may seem repetitive, but they keep the action moving on a variety of levels, take the activity from one side of the arena to another, and help to transfer the audience's attention to different parts of the 'set' while the circle of the scaffolds about the central 'round' preserves pictorial unity.

The Sins' travels are not accompanied by any intervening dialogue, which suggests that either music covered their movements or that the three Sins with the shorter distance from Belyal's scaffold to span arrived first, and the first few lines of Pryde's speech sufficed to allow the three Sins from Caro's platform to join the rest. Yet these have the farthest to travel from the south scaffold, and their scene of leave-taking might precede more smoothly that of the Sins, who are closer at hand.

On their arrival Coveytyse informs the Sins that Mankynde has come to dwell with him in his 'hall', and since Man is actually on the scaffold, Coveytyse must come down off the scaffold to confide to the Sins that he and they will ultimately damn him. When Coveytyse remounts, each Sin in turn greets the errant man who responds with enthusiasm to their lavish promises. The patterned structure of the dialogue is matched by patterned movements: as each Sin finishes its speech of seduction it mounts to join the group on the platform above. Pryde is the first to ascend:

I [in] thi bowre to abyde

I com to dwelle be [by] thi syde (1084–5);

Envye's tag is perhaps the most significant for reconstructing the circular amphitheatre set with its scaffolds:

I clymbe fro this crofte [enclosed place]

Wyth Mankynde to syttyn on lofte (1144–5).

Whether we are to take the notion of 'sitting' literally is uncertain; Coveytyse's 'stage' will ultimately contain nine characters (Mankynde, the Sins, and Bakbytere) although as with the Croxton *Play* it may be possible to station some of them on the steps or at the foot of the scaffold, though a tableau of Man environed by the Deadly Sins is attractive. Mankynde invites Lechery to 'syt be [by] me' which, if we add Envye, means several seated characters, suggesting a bench of some width is used to parallel the thrones on other scaffolds. Space on Coveytyse's scaffold must surely be at a premium at this juncture.

★ ★ ★

This tableau of Man amid his enemies does not occupy the audience's attention long, for the play's tide is about to turn for the first time. The Good Angel's lamentations from the centre of the playing-area are heard by Confessio or Schryfte who appears accompanied by Penitentia or Penaunce, and offers to rescue Mankynde from the Sins. For Schryfte and Penaunce to enter like Bakbytere from the 'outside world' does not seem appropriate, and it provides a reinforcement of the symmetrical pattern so far noted if they, like the Good Angel, emanate from God's scaffold, parting the curtains of 'Heaven' in order to descend to the *platea* at the specified moment.

Inter-action between the scaffolds and the 'place' continues: Schryfte challenges Man from below as he dallies with Lechery and feasts with Gluttony above – 'We have etyn garlek everychone'[16] he says at line 1369 – and though Mankynde informs Schryfte that Slawthe 'that syttyth here' (can so many characters have been seated?) thinks Good Friday soon enough to confess one's sins, Penaunce mounts the steps and pierces Man with a lance, betokening 'swete sorwe [sorrow] of hert'. The mechanics of achieving this are dependent on the grouping on the platform, but afterwards Mankynde must rise and stagger free of the Sins, whom he repudiates from the front edge of the scaffold, which also enables him to address a larger portion of the spectators:

Lordyngys, ye se wel alle thys (1420).

Resolving to devote himself to penance, he cries to Christ for mercy, and encouraged by Schryfte, leaves Coveytyse's clutches for the safety of the *platea* where Penaunce and Schryfte receive him. Here a scene of contrition and absolution follows with Mankynde being led a little way out into the centre, not only stressing the fact that he has forsaken his evil advisers, but bringing him into more general view. The Sins on the scaffold look on in silent impotence.

The focal point of interest shifts at last to the titular castle at the literal and symbolic centre of the action, for Man must now be housed in a safe haven where his foes cannot assail him. In Schryfte's recommendation to Mankynde that he should

Goo to yone castel and kepe the therinne . . .

To yone castel I the seende [dispatch] (1552, 1554)

we again see how dialogue can stimulate an audience's imaginative powers, for 'yone castel' cannot be far off across the arena, even by Southern's expansive estimate. Although Mankynde will speak of it lying 'here but at honde' a few lines later, Schryfte's words lend its desirable towers distance. Mankynde sets off to reach it – 'thedyr rapely [swiftly] wyl I tee [go]' – and crossing the 'sad sonde [solid ground]' he makes his way to the central area, the Good and Bad Angels encountering him *en route* with contrary intentions. Go back to Mundus and enjoy yourself, advises the Bad Angel, but his good counterpart urges Mankynde on:

... spede now thy pace

Pertly [quickly] to yone precyouse place (1594–5),

'yone' indicating that the figure of Mankynde is relatively some way from the castle-area.

The precise mode of Man's approach to the castle can never be established for there now occurs another of those frustrating textual hiatuses depriving us of essential information. When the dialogue resumes, Mankynde is still outside the castle moat or fence, still attended by his Good Angel, and having been greeted by Meknes and Pacyens, is in the process of being saluted successively by the other Moral Virtues who make up the seven complements to the Deadly Sins. The presence of these traditionally female figures within the central ring below the castle seems to support the idea of an 'inner bailey', although they could theoretically be accommodated on the castle itself.

At Meknes's bidding 'Cum in here at thynne owyn wylle' (1694), Mankynde crosses the ditch and to the singing of verses from the scriptures either enters the castle or its 'bailey'. '*Tunc intrabit* [then he shall go in]' reads the rubric but this could refer equally to an entry to the castle's precincts rather than Mankynde's appearance inside the castle, on the battlements. Certainly Meknes's plea to Christ to 'kepe Mankynd in this castel clos' (1712) can easily mean that he is to be 'kept' within the ditch or fence rather than in the castle proper. Man must remain visible to the spectators for as long as plausible, although attention reverts at this point to the scaffolds on the periphery of the circle.

Till now the Deadly Sins have looked on in deserted dismay, and on their 'stages' Mundus, Caro, and Belyal have also watched proceedings with growing restiveness and anger. The Bad Angel triggers off the third phase of the action by reminding the audience of the presence in the ring of forces inimical to Man:

The synnys sevene, tho [those] kyngys thre,

To Mankynd have enmyte (1720–1).

Our interest thus secured in those who intend to break into the castle and win back Man in order to damn his soul, we forget temporarily the static group within the castle-ditch.

Theatrically speaking, what follows is the most exciting part of the play. To set it in motion a neglected figure is brought to the fore:

Bakbytere previously left lounging at the base of Coveytyse's scaffold is summoned to convey to World, Flesch, and Devil the news that Mankynde must be recovered from 'yene [yon] wenchys' who protect him. Bakbytere, in his true element, dashes around the *platea* performing his task with relish. There is scarcely enough dialogue to permit the Sins to remain on Coveytyse's scaffold until called for, even if Belyal and Caro descend to meet them in the *platea*. It seems that the tableau on the north-east scaffold must break up after Mankynde has arrived at the castle. No doubt as the Bad Angel begins to remind the audience of the evil forces looking on, the Deadly Sins descend and make their way to the foot of the appropriate potentate's platform. At Belyal's call Pryde, Envye and Wrathe immediately swarm up eager to obey him, only to receive a beating in a truly comic reversal of expectation, which Bakbytere enjoys along with the spectators. After Caro has also served Lechery, Glotoun and Slawthe so, the special status of Coveytyse is accentuated by Mundus summoning *him* with a blast on a horn. Although he too ascends and is beaten for his failure to secure Mankynde's person, in an abject speech of apology he promises to regain the lost ground. But Mundus is all for a direct confrontation with the Virtues:

Bylyve [swiftly] my baner up thou bere
And besege we the castel yerne [quickly]
    Mankynd for to stele. (1879–81)

Without doubt this is the moment most of the audience have eagerly awaited. The forces of evil are about to deploy the colour and ceremonial of medieval warfare and chivalry in an all-out assault on the castle: the verse quickens and the language exults. Banners are unfurled, trumpets sound off, and other devices increase the visual and aural excitement: drum-rolls, the roar of cannon, the sight and sound of smoke and fire-crackers are all orchestrated to one end. The characters don armour and helmets, producing a fine array of weapons – sling-shots, spears, lances, swords, cross-bows, and fire-brands – while Belyal is the subject of one of the most famous stage directions ever penned:

and he that schal pley Belyal loke that he have gunnepowdyr
brennynge [burning] In pypys in hys handys and in hys erys and in
hys ars whanne he gothe to batayl.

The first 'aray' on the move is that of Mundus, and consists of himself, Coveytyse who bears the banner, Foly, and presumably Lust-lykyng, although the script does not name him or Garcio, who to preserve symmetry is perhaps left behind on the scaffold. Belyal is the next tyrant to react:

I here trumpys trebelen [shrilling] al of tene [angrily].

The worthi Werld walkyth to werre [war] (1899–1900)

and summoning Pryde, Wrathe, and Envye, he sets forth for the castle,

Pryde carrying the flag and boasting of the damage he will inflict, particularly on Meknes. Last comes Flesch, aroused from his lethargy, and urges his force into the field, with Glotoun as its leading spokesman. They descend and join their fellows in the *platea*.

The whole stage-area is now in use: in the centre the castle and its inhabitants plus the Good Angel are enclosed within the defensive moat or barrier, some of the figures at least manning the castle itself. In the *platea* the three quartets of enemies prepare to encircle it. Some conference ensues as the Bad Angel assigns each Sin its contrasting Virtue for special attention, and the defenders of the castle prepare their strategy as they see their foes advance:

To batayle thei buskyn [hasten] hem bown [readily] (2013).

When Meknes alludes to the fact that they are all within 'this castel of ston', we again have to decide whether to take her literally or not, but the term may be figurative, like her later allusion to 'this halle' in line 2055, which obviously does not refer to an interior setting. The 'castel' may include its 'bailey'.

A verbal assault now follows, sparked off by Belyal who assumes the vanguard of the northern assault-force. Confronting Meknes across the barrier Pryde urges her to yield, to which she responds in spirited rather than meek fashion. Similar exchanges ensue between Wrathe and Pacyens, Envye and Charite. The principal point of stage interest to emerge comes in lines 2142–3 when Pacyens says to Wrathe:

If thou fonde [try] to comyn alofte

I schal the cacche [drive] fro [from] this crofte [enclosure]

'To comyn alofte' suggests that Pacyens is actually stationed in the castle tower, yet reference to a 'crofte' sounds as if she could be thinking of the space between castle and ditch. The best compromise is to imagine that a few of the Virtues guard the 'inner bailey' while others occupy the keep along with Mankynde: Pacyens above may then include the defenders below in her threat. Chastyte who warns her opposite number that

if thou com up to me,

Trewly thou schalt betyn [beaten] be . . . (2322–3)

also seems to retain a place alongside Pacyens and the hero. Mankynde is certainly 'alofte' for Chastyte confidently predicts:

For Mankynde getyst thou nowth (not) doun (2319).

Belyal tires of the war of words. Calling for music from 'claryouns' and 'brode baggys [bagpipes?]' he launches the first wave of the attack, a lengthy encounter in which the Virtues pelt their opponents with roses symbolizing Christ's Passion, a traditional and colourful touch confirmed by the complaints of Envye and of Wrathe who states:

I am al betyn blak and blo

> Wyth a rose that on rode [the cross] was rent . . .

Hyr [Pacyens's] rosys fel on me so scharpe . . . (2219–20, 2222)

So the first sortie is abandoned, much to the disgust of the Bad Angel who upbraids Belyal's division as they retreat to their scaffold. The Angel next incites Flesch's troops to breach the defences, and the pattern established by the first assault is repeated. Vice and Virtue exchange taunts and defiance: Glotoun armed with a flaming brand confronts Abstinence and Lechery may be similarly equipped, though her reference to making a fire 'in mans towte [buttocks]' may be merely metaphorical. She is opposed by Chastyte who, in alluding to 'Marye, well of grace' may have the water of the moat in mind.

Also associated with the water of the ditch is Slawthe, who rather than confront Besynesse (Industriousness) delves 'with a spade' in an attempt to divert the moat, and so allow the Vices to evade the power of the 'watyr of grace'. Besynesse points out the significance of what Slawthe is trying to accomplish:

Therfor he makyth this dyke drye

> To puttyn Mankynde to dystresse.

He makyth dedly synne a redy weye

> Into the Castel of Goodnesse. (2352–5).

If he can empty the moat, the Vices can enter dry-shod. The reference seems to strengthen the case for positioning a ditch at the centre of the *platea*, and for its partly-symbolic function in the morality, but there is no need to assume that it retains this function throughout the action, or that a literal ditch of water is imperative. A low fence which does not obscure the action is clearly viable, so long as Slawthe continues to mime the action of sabotage.

Caro is now impatient of delay, and his anger possibly distracts Slawthe from completing his breaching of the dyke; perhaps his efforts are in vain; perhaps he goes to sleep on the job. At all events, the second attack fares no better than the first: Gluttony slinks back to crouch in Flesch's 'gonge' or privy, Lechery has her fire put out, and Slawthe seems to suffer the fate of New Gyse in *Mankynde*, escaping in order that he may his 'ballokys bathe' (in the ditch?), although his head also appears to be injured.

The Bad Angel washes his hands of Caro's forces, and turns to Mundus, who instead of mounting another assault, summons Coveytyse to advance his banner, promising him pickings from the corpses on the gibbet at Canwick Hill just outside Lincoln for his services. The seventh Sin thereupon advances to the edge of the ditch, and the principal reversal of fortunes in the entire action is set in train. Avarice, abandoning a frontal attack, seeks to outwit the Virtues by approaching Mankynde as a friendly confidential adviser. 'I am sorry to find you a prisoner there' he blandly asserts:

Cum and speke wyth thi best frende,
Syr Coveytyse, thou knowyst me of olde. (2429–30).

It is a familiar theatrical device: several onslaughts having been repulsed, the hero relaxes confidently expecting the final assault to take the form of the others. When it does not, he is caught off-guard, and succumbs.

Man's ordeal by Avarice is skilfully built up: having insinuated himself into the hero's confidence, Coveytyse begins to prey on his fear of possessing nothing with which to counteract the graphic effects of ageing:

I gynne to waxyn hory and olde.
My bake gynnyth to bowe and bende,
I crulle [crawl?] and crepe and wax al colde (2482–4).

When a few lines later Mankynde refers to himself as 'arayed in a sloppe' and announces that 'Myn her [hair] waxit al hore', it is clear that some opportunity has been found for him to change the rich garments awarded him by the World for the long gown of an elderly man, and whiten his hair with flour or chalk-dust. No doubt while Mankynde and the castle's defenders relaxed after the defeat of Flesch's army and the Bad Angel rounded on the routed troops in a lavish display of bad temper, Mankynde kneeling down out of sight could be swiftly re-costumed and aged by two of the Virtues, much as in the *Mystère d'Adam* Adam bends down behind the wall of Paradise and changes his clothes after the Fall. An older man can then emerge, an obvious target for the blandishments of Coveytyse, to whom he rapidly succumbs. The Good Angel desperately enjoins the 'ladys, lovely in lace' to lock up their charge, but it is too late. Man descends from the protective tower, crosses the 'bailey' and the ditch (an old man would certainly need a bridge), and joins his tempter in the 'place'.

The Virtues excuse their inability to restrain Mankynde on the grounds that he has free will to choose his own pathway: Meknes's words perhaps stress that ditch and castle are conceived of as one unit, when she says:

As longe as he was wythinne this castel walle,
We kepte hym fro synne, ye sawe wel alle (2566–7),

since his final defection presumably only occurs when he has crossed the ditch. After departing, Mankynde remains within earshot of the castle, for Chastyte and Besynesse are able to remonstrate with him, while the Bad Angel, anxious to retain his victim, urges him to ignore the cackling 'quenys' and accompany him to his own scaffold. This is effected: the Good Angel mourns that

Man goth wyth Coveytyse away (2684)

and the Angel may even quit the *platea* entirely for a time if his 'Have me excusyd' is taken literally. The World back on his scaffold is filled with glee, though the parallel speeches we might expect from Belyal and Caro do not materialize as we might expect in this highly patterned play; it is World's forces who have prevailed over Man rather than theirs.

Coveytyse then proceeds to load Mankynde with riches to his spiritual endangerment, and we are faced with the difficult crux which involves the location of 'Coveytyse copboard' which the plan informs us is 'be [by] the beddys feet . . . at the ende of the castel'. Since this legend appears on the drawing at either side of the central castle, it has always been assumed that the 'castel' and 'bed' of the legend refer to those at the centre of the *platea*. But it is a curious place for Coveytyse to keep his cupboard, since its presence there conflicts with the associations of security, protection and divine grace, which the Castle has acquired. Mankynde has only just left its shelter, and is being conducted to Coveytyse's scaffold by the Sin who says:

Go we now knowe [to become acquainted with] my castel cage [stronghold].

In this boure I schal the blys [make happy]. (2703–4)

When Coveytyse gives Mankynde money some twenty lines later it should surely be at or near his own scaffold:

Have here, Mankynd, a thousand marke.

I, Coveytyse, have the this gote (2726–7),

and the obvious inference is that it comes from 'Coveytyse copboard'. Can this important piece of furniture be located 'be the beddys feet . . . at the ende of the castel' at the centre of the playing-area?

The answer must surely be that it cannot, but that it is in its logical position on or beside the scaffold assigned to Coveytyse. Yet it is unlikely that Coveytyse's reference in line 2703 to his platform as his 'castel cage' accounts for the diagram's reference to a castle, and this allusion remains an enigma. The suggestion that the cupboard lies 'be the beddys feet' may however be a scribal misreading: the word 'ladder', which can be variously spelt in Middle English as leddre, ledder, leddyr, laddre, etc., might easily be written in the genitive as 'leddyrs'. A scrivener conscious of the proximity of the all-important bed might then have mistaken 'leddyrs' for 'beddys', and written the rubric on the plan in the open space about the castle, without realizing the foot of the ladder leading up to the north-east scaffold was the intended location for the cupboard.

Whether or not this explanation is accepted, the cupboard must logically be placed at the base of Coveytyse's stage, adjacent to the ladder's foot, much as the Jew's oven might be similarly positioned in the Croxton *Play*. Coveytyse then has access to it on his arrival at the scaffold – its ostensible location would surely require an awkward doubling-back to the castle – indeed, it is vital that the cupboard should be nearby for as soon as Man receives his 'noblys rownde' from his new mentor he hastens to bury them 'undyr the grownde' which is obviously facilitated if the pair have not yet clambered up to the scaffold via the ladder. This is confirmed by the fact that when he has buried his gold and demanded greater possessions from his tempter, Man is urged to mount in order to view his new acquisitions from a height:

Clyffe and cost [coast], toure and toun (2755).

The ascent of Mankynde and Coveytyse is thus given dramatic motivation, but their departure from the *platea* also leaves it free for Dethe who can then enter an empty arena and deliver a speech of some sixty lines without distraction. Possibly Dethe descends from God's scaffold as if he were the Deity's servant like Dethe in *Everyman*: certainly no activity has occurred in the region of the eastern scaffold for most of the play, so that one is tempted to bring it into focus whenever possible. However, it is again more effective to have Dethe arrive (much as Bakbytere does) from the world outside, and to have him pace about the *platea*, an alarming skeletal figure for all his claim that 'Men of Deth holde no tale [care nothing]' (2818). Again the theatrical arrangement which arena-staging makes possible enables a universally recognized figure to make close contact with an audience. Dethe concludes his circuit before the scaffold of Coveytyse, and since like his counterpart in *Everyman* he is equipped with a spear, he is able, like Penaunce before him, to step a few steps up the ladder and thrust it into the body of the grasping old miser Mankynde has degenerated into.

As he did when pricked by Penaunce, Mankynde first has to distance himself from his immediate environment, which he achieves by simply stepping to the front of the platform, much as an Elizabethan actor separated himself from the scenic background in a public playhouse. From this vantage-point he mimes the infirmities of old age which now increase upon him, calling to the World for assistance and reminding him of his former promises. Mundus scornfully rejects Man's pleas, and summons his page Garcio, idle on his scaffold for so long, to 'aryse' and eject the aged hero 'oute of hys halle', since it is he who will now inherit all Mankynde owns. Garcio tumbles swiftly down the steps, and announces

I go glad upon this grounde (2910)

as he runs across the arena to the north-east scaffold where Man now slumps at the head of the ladder. Though Garcio brags that he will destroy the hero, his 'Into a lake I schal hym lyfte [throw]' (2913) is not a reference to the water of the ditch as some have argued, citing analogies from *Ane Satyre of the Thrie Estaitis*. Eccles's gloss for 'lake' as 'pit' or 'grave' resolves the matter: the water of the ditch may retain its connotations of grace and defence.

Garcio arrives at Coveytyse's scaffold and finds it hard to tell if Man is already dead or not, but the latter reacts vigorously enough to the news that 'I Wot Nevere who' is to inherit all his recently-acquired goods. Dispossessed and dying, Man reluctantly quits the platform, staggering down the ladder, not an easy assignment for a player pretending to be decrepit and clutching his wounded breast. It might be necessary for the now silent Coveytyse and Garcio to assist him, one from above, one from below. Mankynde then stumbles across the *platea* towards the bed where he is to die. A speech of two stanzas takes him to the centre, and he possibly delivers a single stanza from his death-bed.

Given the allegorical significance of so many occurrences in this play, it may seem odd that Mankynde has to die *within* the Castel of Perseveraunce, in the bed that 'schal be undyr the castel'. He has repudiated the castle's influence, yet he returns there to die. This can only be explained as theatrical necessity triumphing over doctrinal symbolism. Since Mankynde's death is crucial to the action, so crucial as to be at the centre of the play's *dénouement*, it must be placed at the centre of the stage so that it may be witnessed by all and its importance acknowledged. The medieval mind was far from inflexible: the castle has served its function as castle by this time. Presumably the Seven Virtues have long since departed, probably after Mankynde's defection; the central area is capable of being employed for a fresh purpose. Or can we claim that Man, despite his sinful nature, still enjoys a measure of divine protection, which will ultimately ensure his salvation?

With a last despairing cry for mercy, Mankynde dies, and in another amazing *coup de théâtre* the Soul or Anima emerges from 'undyr the bed' in accordance with the rubric on the plan. This startling action introduces the battle for its survival in the light of Mankynde's earthly conduct, but it also raises questions of stage procedure. Can we assume that the player was asked to remain hidden beneath the bed for 3007 lines plus the time taken to fill the auditorium with spectators? Merle Fifield suggests the use of an underground tunnel and a declivity in the ground to reduce the waiting period,[17] and the practice is certainly attested to on the Continent, but we must not lose sight of the fanatical dedication of medieval actors either.

The Soul laments its fate; the angels debate the Soul's ultimate destiny, but the text suffers from another lacuna at this point, and it must be assumed that some two hundred lines are missing. When the play resumes the Good Angel has accepted that the Bad Angel must bear the Soul off to Hell as justice demands. The Bad Angel taunts the Soul with its ignorance in listening to Coveytyse, beating it with his 'bat', and promising that it will now suffer the pangs of damnation, since 'In hye Helle schal be thyne hous' (3077), an oddly elevated location for Hell at first sight, which induces even Mark Eccles to gloss 'hye' as 'deep',[18] but which makes perfect sense if one remembers that Belyal rules from a raised scaffold. The Bad Angel repairs there with the Soul on his back and a jaunty farewell to the crowd:

Have good day! I goo to helle. (3128).

* * *

The last phase of a long play opens. No sooner has the Bad Angel lugged his burden up to Belyal's scaffold where the inhabitants form a grisly and gloating tableau with the Soul at its centre, than the four daughters of God, Mercy, Rytwysnes (Righteousness), Pes, and Trewth enter the arena. Since they go towards God's scaffold, they can scarcely appear from it, as one might otherwise wish to suggest, and the rubric that 'thei schul pleye in the place altogedyr' indicates that they congregate in the *platea*, having previously entered. Perhaps they take up their positions at the four points of the compass, below the scaffolds, a symmetrical arrangement well in keeping with the overall spirit of this drama. Lengthy speeches now ensue from each daughter in turn, which while slowing the pace down permit the audience to admire the symbolic colours stipulated for their costumes. Their speeches characterize their traditional positions in the debate over Man's soul, attitudes doubtless familiar to the average medieval spectator. At the end the ardent pleading of Pes persuades her severer sisters to submit the case to God who sits in 'yone hey [high] place'. The daughters then cross the *platea* and stand before God's scaffold. At long last the Father of Mankind is to enter the action.

At what point do God's curtains open and who opens them? One might feel that since the curtains have probably been drawn until this point, they should be flung wide as soon as possible, but there is a complicating factor. To the best of our knowledge, God, unlike Mundus, Belyal, and Caro, has no attendants on his scaffold to draw the curtains, and he can scarcely be expected to commit *lèse-majesté* by drawing them himself. If, however, the four daughters perform this task, the rubric that they shall 'pleye in the place altogedyr tyl they brynge up the sowle' suggests that they retire to the *platea* after opening the drapes, a superfluous move for in line 3228 we are told that they ascend to greet the Father and at line 3248 God invites them to come closer to his throne:

Cum forth and stand ye me nere.

If we set more store by the stage directions than the rubric on the diagram, we must accept that the daughters having drawn the curtains remain on the platform with God.

Here a further tableau is created akin to that in which the Sins surrounded Mankynde on Coveytyse's scaffold. Trewthe, Mercy, Rytwysnes, and Pes argue their cases in turn, a sequence of some 325 lines, constituting almost one-tenth of the entire play. For most members of a modern audience it is the least compelling or attractive portion of the action, as arguments for and against Man's salvation are expounded and recapitulated by four generally colourless characters. But to a fifteenth-century audience this was the doctrinal heart of the matter: on the result of the debate in Heaven depended the fate of Christians everywhere, and while it is unlikely that spectators ever followed the arguments with bated breath, the topic under review could hardly be said to be an academic matter of small personal relevance.

Pes finally reconciles the sisters and God pronounces the welcome tidings that Man's soul shall be saved from Hell's flames because of his last-second faith in Christ's power to redeem him. Moreover, God's love for Man revealed in dispatching his son to earth will be wasted if he does not now allow the sacrifice of Calvary to atone for Man's misdeeds. The conclusion of the debate represents a final vindication of God's beneficent purposes towards Mankynde.

God, who speaks less than thirty lines during the debate, now instructs his daughters to

Goo to yone fende [fiend]
And fro hym take Mankynd.

Brynge hym to me
And set hym here be [by] my kne,
In hevene to be . . . (3576–80).

Down from God's scaffold go the four sisters, and as the stage-direction makes clear, they ascend to Belyal's platform where the Bad Angel stands guard, and order him to release Mankynde's soul, Rytwysnes condemning the Angel himself to Hell for eternity, much as Christ chains Satan in Hell in the cycle-plays' *Harrowing* sequences. The Soul emerges from among the fiends, and accompanied by the daughters, descends to the *platea*, and crosses to God's scaffold to which it climbs. Almost certainly music, no doubt a feature of the whole action, would accompany the triumphant climax of the play, or at least greet the Soul's arrival in the 'blysse' of Heaven. The four daughters follow to join the final formal tableau on the scaffold, although they might group together on the steps, if the nature of the incline permits it. For this use of the steps of the heavenly scaffold, Fouquet's miniature offers a satisfactory precedent.

The Soul seats itself at the right hand of God, again suggesting that a bench rather than a throne might be employed here as on the other scaffolds, and then the Deity's last speech rings out across the arena, giving a foretaste of the day

Whanne Myhel [Michael] hys horn blowyth at my dred dom (3617),
a speech closely resembling those which conclude a number of the great cycles. At the close God seems to throw off his dramatic character and

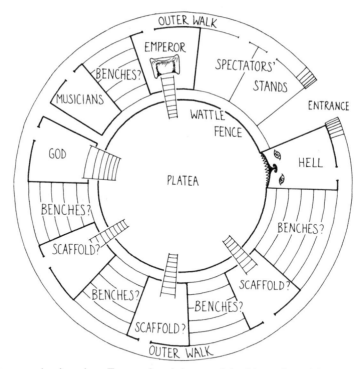

5 A stage-plan based on Fouquet's miniature of the *Martyrdom of St Appollonia*

speak as a flesh-and-blood actor, addressing the audience in his mortal
role, both as player and as fellow-human:

Thus endyth oure gamys.
To save you fro [from] synnynge
Evyr at the begynnynge
Thynke on youre last endynge!
Te Deum laudamus! (3645–8)

★ ★ ★

As the most elaborate and comprehensive of all surviving English morality
plays, *The Castel of Perseveraunce* exhibits most completely the complexity
and diversity of medieval theatrical logistics, and the manner in which
resources may be successfully deployed to create a spectacle at once
theatrically stimulating and theologically effective. The linguistic structure of the play, in which passages of declamation and debate alternate
with lively colloquial exchanges, is paralleled by its juxtaposition of
periods of dynamic stage activity with the creation of vivid but static
tableaux epitomizing and reinforcing moral and spiritual truths as well as
the prevalent stage situation. In this way ear and brain, eye and intellect,

are equally involved in the experience: movement up and down the steps, and across the *platea*, the opening and shutting of curtains, provide visual interest to match our concern as Mankynde's fallible nature is tugged this way and that by the forces opposing and protecting him. Yet symmetry and parallelism of speech and action help to prevent the play from becoming diffuse and sprawling. By setting its action within a formalized structure in which pattern and ceremony play central roles, the author has brought his cosmic theme within our reach. Similarly, the variety of staging areas within the circular arena offers a range of locations to be exploited both singly and in conjunction with one another, so that attention can be directed to wherever the action is taking place, while it can be withdrawn from areas where nothing of importance is occurring by keeping the performers silent and static, or by drawing the curtains on them. Yet the 'magic circle' of the total playing-area not only binds all these separate areas into one composite unit, but enables auditors to feel part of that unit, and hence to become participants in an action taking place all about them. The medieval theatre-in-the-round epitomizes the desire to make theatre a communal experience that welds all its adherents into a charmed circle.

4 · Processional Staging: the York Passion Sequence

The controversy surrounding the exact manner in which the biblical plays of the York Cycle were presented during their long lifespan as yet shows no sign of abating. When Lucy Toulmin Smith prepared her remarkably durable edition of the text for publication in 1885 she could speak confidently of the 'circle of performances through the city' and urge readers to bear in mind Archdeacon Rogers's well-known account of the processional manner of presenting the Chester plays, while they digested the York script.[1] On a subsequent page she printed a celebrated York memorandum of 7 June 1417 listing the twelve stations at which the pageants were staged in sequence, beginning at the gates of Holy Trinity Priory in Micklegate and terminating at the Pavement, the large open space in the city centre where public events often took place.[2]

The impression was thus given that in medieval York a long procession of pageant-waggons rolled in sequence through the narrow streets and then came to rest one after another at each of the twelve specified stations where the episode allocated to each cast was played before the convoy moved off to its next port-of-call. Many believed that a cycle of forty-eight or so individual plays could eventually be presented in this way at all twelve stations; the picture was not to be radically challenged for many decades. Admittedly, such men as M. L. Spencer and Hardin Craig felt that plays as parts of processions created severe organizational and logistical problems,[3] and H. F. Westlake wrote in 1919 that 'considerations of time would prevent any but the shortest of speeches by the players'.[4] Their strictures were partially endorsed by Neil C. Brooks in an important article describing German processional practices[5] which led its author to believe that

> spoken plays of groups marching in a procession were given, more
> often than has been usually assumed, all at one place and at one
> time, usually, it would seem, on the market place and at the end of
> the procession . . . This way of combining procession and play has
> been largely ignored by modern scholars and yet it has such obvious

advantages that it should surely be reckoned with as a possibility in cases of doubt. This usage made it possible to march without tedious delays; it adorned and enlivened the procession with the costumed and dramatically grouped players, and, by putting the play at the break-up of the procession, it gave all the participants an opportunity to see the play . . . If the plays were . . . to be given at various stations, they would soon, through the time required, be completely severed from the procession proper. This is again a difficulty that would be solved by giving the plays at the conclusion of the procession.[6]

While this suggestion was used to explain practices at certain English centres, few attempted to question the traditional interpretation of the York documents and Archdeacon Rogers's *Breviary* as applied to performances at Chester and York at least. Even A. C. Cawley in the necessarily terse introduction to his selection of cycle play texts for the Everyman Library only modified the opinions that 'the cycles at Chester, York, and Wakefield were acted processionally' and that 'each guild performed its pageant on a waggon which was moved from one station (or pre-arranged acting-place) to another' by reminding readers that many plays 'were not processional but stationary in type, i.e. acted in one place' and drawing attention to Newcastle where 'the crafts took part in the Corpus Christi procession and afterwards seem to have acted their pageants in a prearranged place or "stead".'[7]

However, in 1961 with the introduction to his translation of the Wakefield cycle Martial Rose became the first to voice serious doubts as to the accuracy of the familiar picture of processional performances at York.[8] Rose estimated that each of the plays of the York manuscript, if played at the twelve stations cited in 1417, would require to be played more or less continuously for fifteen hours. The result would be that if the first pageant were enacted at Station 1 at 4.30 a.m., the forty-eighth would be completed at the twelfth site just after midnight, if a tremendous pace were maintained from start to finish. Rose concluded:

> The processional street-pageant staging of the York cycle has been too readily accepted without due consideration given to the practical problems . . . Wakefield . . . shares with York the practical problem, indeed the practical impossibility, of performing the whole cycle at a number of stations in the compass of a day . . .[9]

Not far behind Rose came Alan H. Nelson, whose book *The Medieval English Stage* is the most sustained effort so far to revolutionize the orthodox approach to the genesis, function, nature, and staging of the English cycle plays. In a technically sophisticated manner Nelson provides convincing further evidence to endorse Rose's commonsense opinion that even the longest summer's day would supply insufficient daylight for the satisfactory presentation of the extant York Cycle at all twelve stations listed in the memorandum of 1417.[10] Nelson demonstrates that, because the York texts differ greatly in length one from another, considerable pauses in the smooth flow of dramatic activity would have been bound to occur in processional presentation, and so increase the duration of a performance of the extant text beyond measure. He and others are convinced that the plays could never have been presented satisfactorily in 'true-processional' manner, that is, sequentially to a series of audiences watching the plays in a fixed order.

However, Nelson's proposed solution only substitutes one set of problems for another. He advances the theory that a single private presentation was staged indoors after the procession exclusively for the civic hierarchy and their guests, while the general public had to be content with a glimpse of the plays in tableau-form passing through the streets. Martin Stevens's response is rather more plausible, and has precedents in German practices as outlined by Neil Brooks. He argues that while the traditional procession may have involved brief dramatic moments, the full presentation at York was reserved for a single public performance at the Pavement, perennially listed as the final station on the processional route but often not leased out to a private individual. Here the pageant-waggons could form up to supply the needful 'sets', and though a lengthy performance might still ensue, it would take nothing like so long to unfold as it would presented at twelve separate stations with intervals of varying lengths occurring between the different episodes.

However, there has been considerable resistance to the idea that full performances were not given *en route* during the cavalcade of vehicles, and a number of interesting explanations have been advanced to repair the damage caused to the traditional picture.[11] But there can never be the former certainty that the forty-eight extant York plays were all presented in procession on every occasion or that every individual episode was presented at every single station named in the memorandum of 1417. Some claim that only a 'hard core' of plays was invariably set forth, or that only those plays for which the guilds could command the resources were played in any one year, so that while some waggons contained an acted presentation, others carried merely a *tableau vivant*. Perhaps a mime or a brief extract from the script was delivered at each station – enough to be referred to as a 'pageant' – but the full performance only took place at the end of the route.

There is, however, a further possibility, argued for by Stanley Kahrl in 1974.[12] Kahrl suggests that, although all the plays were included in the procession of waggons every year, only a limited number of halts were made for the purpose of actually performing them. Thus all the pageants travelled past all the stations, but only stopped to enable a performance to be given at some of them. Kahrl perhaps weakens his case by arguing in favour of two stops only, which seems too few, given the widespread fame of the cycles, but by adopting a slightly more generous policy, one obtains quite a satisfactory compromise between an excessive number of separate performances and a dearth of them. Let us surmise that the waggons processed until the first *four* stations were occupied by a pageant; presentation of all four episodes could then take place at the relevant stations, after which the waggons could move on until the first eight stations were covered, whereupon the same process could occur. Thus by a series of 'shunted' starts and stops each of (say) forty-eight pageants could be played at three of the twelve York stations designated.

The procedure can best be illustrated with a table based on the concept of three stops *en route* per pageant and forty-eight pageants, which may be consulted in conjunction with the plan of the processional route at York.[13]

Phase	Pageants in transit	Stations occupied
1	Nos. 1–4	Nos. 4–1
2	Nos. 1–8	Nos. 8–1
3	Nos. 1–12	Nos. 12–1
4	Nos. 5–16	Nos. 12–1
5	Nos. 9–20	Nos. 12–1
6	Nos. 13–24	Nos. 12–1
7	Nos. 17–28	Nos. 12–1
8	Nos. 21–32	Nos. 12–1
9	Nos. 25–36	Nos. 12–1
10	Nos. 29–40	Nos. 12–1
11	Nos. 33–44	Nos. 12–1
12	Nos. 37–48	Nos. 12–1
13	Nos. 41–48	Nos. 12–5
14	Nos. 45–48	Nos. 12–9

Other solutions to the problems arising from the interpretation of the York evidence obviously exist. The suggestion that not every play was staged on every occasion has something to commend it, though certain episodes were vital if an adequate account of the scriptural narrative was to be rendered. It is still clear that all the episodes contained in the manuscript could not be accommodated without modifying either the script or the 'true-processional' procedure. While Martin Stevens's notion of a single-site presentation is attractive, it has to be reconciled with the references contained in the York documents which make it clear that performances of some kind were actually given as part of the procession. If Kahrl's basic theory is put to the test of imaginative reconstruction, and it then seems to satisfy the criteria of feasibility and dramatic effectiveness without violating the text or our knowledge of medieval staging in general, it will at least demonstrate the viability of one interpretation of the highly ambivalent data which relates to the staging of the York Cycle.

It seems wise to limit our investigation to a finite number of plays, and choice may appropriately fall on those plays which deal with the events of Christ's Passion from the Agony and Betrayal (Play 28) to the Death and Burial (Play 36), a group of nine plays which lie at the heart of the cycle as a spiritual and theatrical totality. It is typical of the York sequence that it devotes so many individual plays to this central Gospel event: four plays suffice at Chester, and the N-Town text contents itself with six, as does the Wakefield Cycle. York's largesse in this respect may of course have been due to the large number of separate trade-guilds wishing to participate, but even when this is borne in mind, the York writers clearly favoured leisuredly treatments of their subjects. No play of the Passion group is less than 300 lines long, three exceed 400 lines, and the Tapiters' and Couchers' play featuring Pilate's Wife reaches 548. The entire sequence considered as a whole involves almost four thousand lines of dialogue, without taking into account the lengthy dramatic business involved in such plays as the *Crucifixion*, the *Deposition from the Cross*, and *Christ's Burial*. The immense theological significance of the Passion obviously received ample emphasis through the theatrical impact achieved from its graphic and protracted presentation on the pageant-waggons.

★ ★ ★

The precise manner of the staging of the Passion plays as witnessed by the citizens of York during the annual performances at the time of Corpus Christi cannot be accurately ascertained. The choice of players and the responsibility for the productions varied from year to year, and we cannot guarantee that those guilds named in the *Ordo paginarum* of 1415 still continued to present the pageant assigned to them there. However, we may allow ourselves to imagine a typical performance as mounted in an average year, and explore such difficulties as an exemplary presentation confronts us with, remembering that no two performances of any play are absolutely identical.

Fortunately much excellent research has been undertaken on the processional route taken by the waggons.[13] It is now clear that the pageant-carts, having been taken from their 'garages' at Toft Green, set out from the gates of Holy Trinity Priory near Micklegate Bar on the south-western side of the medieval city, passed up Micklegate past the Church of St Martin-cum-Gregory and so over the River Ouse via Ouse Bridge. At St Michael's Church, Spurriergate, the floats turned left into the present Coney Street, and continued past Jubbergate and St Martin's Church to the junction with Stonegate where the Mansion House now stands, but where in the Middle Ages stood the Common Hall Gates. Here the processional route bore northwards into Stonegate until it reached Minster Gate where it swung east into Petergate (see Plate 12), which it followed along its length to the junction known as the Mercery (now King's Square), and then forked left into Colliergate, from whence, after passing St Saviour Gate, it turned south-west into the Pavement where the final station was situated. This route seems to have remained constant during the life of the plays.

During the fifteenth century there were usually twelve stations, although the number seems to have risen to thirteen, fourteen, and even sixteen during the following century. Obviously the number of stopping-places on the route varied from year to year, and so did the precise locations of the stations, although the range of variations cannot have been great, since certain sites suggested themselves automatically, and the route taken never varied. Most stations were located at strategic points

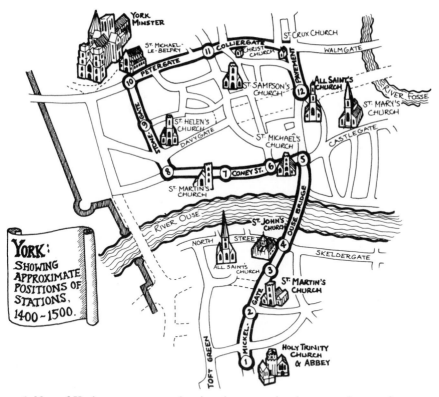

6 Map of York c. 1400–1500, showing the processional route and approximate positions for twelve stations (after Meg Twycross)

12 Petergate in York, part of the route taken
by the pageant-waggons (Photo: *Yorkshire
Evening Post*)

13 A pageant-waggon as reconstructed for the performances of the York Cycle at
the University of Toronto, 1977. (Photo: Records of Early English Drama)

along the processional way in accordance with the willingness of citizens to lease areas adjacent to properties they owned or rented, where viewing-points could be established. Sometimes pairs of citizens or even syndicates leased the stations, and charged the public for the privilege of occupying places, which enabled the lessee to make a profit, even after laying out money on refreshments and on building scaffolds to accommodate spectators. Thanks to the energetic researches of Meg Twycross, we know a good deal about the York lease-holders, their professions, their family connections, the factors governing the siting of the stations, and their relative popularity with paying spectators over the years. Twycross speculates on the apparent attraction of the Micklegate stations which feature early on in the processional route, and the apparent disfavour with which the Pavement location was regarded, one possible reason being that it was not always feasible to complete performances at this final station before nightfall, a speculation having profound bearing on the whole question of what was presented. She also makes the interesting observation that all the identifiable stations are located on the left-hand side of the processional route, which if universally valid must considerably affect our mental picture of the typical pageant-waggon, for if viewing were permitted only from one side, there would be less point in ensuring that the waggon-stage was visible from at least three sides.

The appearance and structure of the medieval pageant-cart have been a matter for animated discussion in recent years.[14] Most experts retain a general picture of a four- or six-wheeled waggon with a house-like frame erected on its base, a flat or sloping roof being supported on four corner-posts or pillars (see Plate 13). The stage-platform is reckoned to be either curtained on three sides or left open to view from every aspect, but more precise details are elusive, given the ambivalence of the evidence available. It is quite clear that the waggons and their superstructures would themselves differ from place to place, and from guild to guild. Some vehicles almost certainly needed to have lifting-gear concealed in their roofs, as the recently-discovered York indenture between the Guild of Mercers and the pageant-masters responsible for the Doomsday episode makes clear. It mentions

A brandreth [framework] of Iren that God sall sitte uppon when he sall fly uppe to Heven . . .[15]

indicating that a system of ropes and pulleys above the stage was a vital feature of this particular pageant-waggon. A sloping roof in this case would be virtually essential; in other episodes a flat roof or no roof at all might have sufficed, although some protection from the elements might be expected if expensive properties or costumes were displayed.

It has sometimes been thought that Archdeacon Rogers's description of the Chester pageant-waggons as being 'open on tope' signifies that only

roofless structures were used in that city, but it is equally likely that
Rogers intended to convey that the sides were uncurtained and so
permitted all-round visibility. If so, it hints that Chester differed in this
respect from York, given the evidence that at York the plays may have
been viewed from one side only. The Mercers' indenture positively refers
to

> A grete coster [hanging] of rede damaske payntid for the bakke syde
> of the pagent ij other lesse [smaller] costers for ij sydes of the Pagent
> iij other costers of lewent brede [broad-cloth of Louvain?] for the
> sydes of the Pagent . . .[16]

which suggests that on York waggons curtains masked three sides of the
platform, while the 'iij other costers' were used to drape the area below
the waggon-base from view. One possible reason for doing the latter is
suggested by Rogers's statement that the Chester waggon consisted of '2
rowmes beinge open on the tope, the lower rowme theie apparrelled and
dressed them selves and the higher rowme theie played', the lower room
being presumably formed by curtaining off the space beneath the waggon.
Some scepticism has been expressed as to the necessity or indeed the
viability of this arrangement,[17] but if the pageant-waggon stage were as
high as it appears to be from the few surviving pictorial representations
of analogous vehicles, there was a considerable space below the stage-base
which could have been used for swift exits and entrances, or quick-
changes of costume especially where the doubling of parts was involved,
and for green-room facilities in general. Rogers's testimony is not to be
dismissed lightly, as some commentators have tended to do; certainly it
is as easy to accept his 'lower rowme' as a likely area for retiring to, as
to adopt the far less likely suggestion that part of the limited stage-space
was curtained off, as on the booth-stage, to provide the same facilities.

What methods were employed to move and manoeuvre waggons
through the streets of medieval towns? Here again differing methods were
certainly used, and much scholarly energy has been deployed on the
technical problems of wheel-construction, of pivoted or fixed axles, of
manhandling as opposed to drawing the waggons by horsepower, of six
wheels as opposed to four, and so on. It is impossible to establish one
standard system for transporting the pageant-carts through the streets in
procession, but it does appear that in many centres the waggons were
propelled by human agency, no slight achievement if large vehicles with
fixed axles were employed. References in the records of various medieval
towns allude to 'berars of the pageaunt' and 'putters of the caryghe', and
probably a gang of at least ten men would have been required to haul
most of the waggons, particularly where the route included a steep incline
or two as at Lincoln, or an awkward corner to negotiate, such as that

occurring at York where the vehicles had to make a ninety-degree turn into Coney Street after crossing the Ouse Bridge.[18]

Naturally, not all the waggons carried an equally heavy load, and carts like the York Mercers' vehicle perhaps presented special problems because of their flying-gear, but the fact remains that considerable forces would need to be on hand to manoeuvre them through narrow streets and lanes thronged with people. Few medieval thoroughfares seem to have exceeded a width of 7½–9 metres (25–30 feet), so that the stage-areas offered by the waggon-bases could scarcely have been larger than 6 metres by 3 (20 × 10 feet). That these platforms could scarcely have been much smaller is apparent from the fact that on occasion they were required to hold large casts, scenic devices, and a number of vital items of furniture. Conditions were perhaps not as cramped as has sometimes been assumed, but attempts have none the less been made from time to time to argue that the waggons merely formed a background to street-performances, that supplementary platforms might have had to be wheeled up alongside the main vehicles, or that the roofs were extensively occupied for acting purposes. However, each of these suggestions is open to enough objections to force us back on the conclusion that the general medieval practice was to stage most processional performances entirely on the bases of pageant-waggons, even in those circumstances where the juxtaposition of two or more locations within the confines of one cart meant that space was at a premium. There seems to be no viable alternative method of presentation, given our present phase of knowledge about the medieval pageant-waggon and the type of performance it lent itself to.

★   ★   ★

We may now imagine that we are among the citizens of York preparing to witness the annual performance of the Corpus Christi Cycle sequence of that city on a summer's day around the middle of the fifteenth century. Let us select the year 1468, a year for which the names of the lease-holders of the various stations are known, and which also approximates to the date of the earliest staging of *Mankynde*. Our choice of station will depend on a variety of factors: the part of the city in which we ourselves reside may be important, although if we live on the processional route we shall probably watch from the upper windows of our own house or from the street outside it. Our social status and personal trade or craft possibly has a bearing on our position; do Nicholas Haliday and Adam Hudson who jointly lease the station at the gates of Holy Trinity Priory in 1468 favour those who like themselves are Cordwainers or Smiths, or is each member of the public who proffers the price of a seat treated in the same manner? The quality of the spectator accommodation offered is obviously an important factor, as is the accessibility of refreshments and what French records often refer to as *'lieux d'aissance'*. Family tradition may also play a part, and certainly if the performances may not be concluded before dark (and it is not impossible that playing can continue by torchlight), then a position early on the route may have much to commend it. Furthermore we must decide which of the many plays we wish to see performed in their entirety: here again personal interest will undoubtedly influence our decision as we weigh up the merits of a play presented under the auspices of our own guild against one known to include in its cast a virtuoso Herod or a good-looking Angel Gabriel. Not that we are necessarily forced to remain throughout at the station for which we have paid to be accommodated. The more energetic can probably follow a particular episode for some distance if they choose, rejoining their older or more sedate fellows to catch up with the intervening items; presumably we can even accompany a single play throughout its journey, although one interpretation of occasional remarks from characters in the York plays suggests that congested streets were common at the time of the performances. Satan in *The Temptation of Jesus* opens the play with the cry:

Make rome belyve [quickly], and late me gang!

Who makis here all this thrang [crowd]? (lines 1–2)

which since at this point the scene only contains Christ and himself must refer to the throng in the streets. More equivocal is the remark of a soldier in *The Dream of Pilate's Wife*:

Here, ye gomes [guys], gose [give us] a-rome, giffe us gate (229)

which could refer to either stage congestion or to players forcing a path through the crowds. At all events then the possibility of following the pageants along the streets might well appeal only to the very agile or the very aggressive.

Let us assume for the time being that we are neither, and that we have taken our positions at the fourth of the eleven stations allocated in 1468 (the Pavement franchise does not appear to have been taken up on this particular occasion). This station is positioned where North Street joins Micklegate at the Church of St John the Baptist, and has been assigned to a syndicate of which Thomas Barbour, Christopher Thomlynson, Richard Croklyn, and Richard Sawer [Sawyer?] are the leading figures, paying sixteen shillings for the rental. This sum suggests that the station is a lucrative one, like all the Micklegate positions, so no doubt it is a popular site offering comfortable seating. That seats rather than mere standing-room are provided is indicated from the 1417 memorandum which states that in that year the Mayor and Commons ordered a civic levy to be paid by those

who receive money for scaffolds which they may build in the aforesaid places before their doors on public property at the aforesaid sites from those sitting on them . . .[19]

Hence, having fortified ourselves for the long day ahead and taken our seats in the stands, we may comfortably contemplate the cycle sequence from its earliest episodes to the end.

This will no doubt involve being present on the scaffolds at the junction of North Street and Micklegate at an early hour, for the leading pageant-waggons will be leaving the departure-point at Holy Trinity Priory at first light. The clearest indication of this comes in the famous *Ordo paginarum* of 1415 which concludes with a proclamation regulating the conditions of performance, stipulating

> that every player that shall play be redy in his pagiaunt at convenyant tyme that is to say at the mydhowre betwix iiij[th] & v[th] of the cloke in the mornyng & then all oyer [other] pageantes fast folowyng ilkon after oyer as yer [their] course is without Tarieng.[20]

This regulation has puzzled some commentators who argue that if the pageants got off to some kind of staggered start, it was surely unnecessary to have *every* player present at 4.30 a.m., particularly those performing very late on in the cycle sequence. From this premise arguments supporting a non-dramatic procession and a single final performance have naturally arisen, but in view of the strong evidence against the notion of a procession without plays, possibly every pageant had to be checked before the first waggon began to roll. What seems clear and undeniable is that the programme of events in York on Corpus Christi Day got under way early.

From Station Four where we have chosen to take our seats, it would technically be impossible to see every episode of the York Cycle actually performed, but if Stanley Kahrl's plan as modified above is adopted, we shall be able to watch every fourth play, that is to say Plays 1, 5, 9, 13, and so forth, so that by the end, if we do not shift our ground, we shall have seen twelve of the forty-eight plays in the extant text. We shall also have seen all the other pageants pass by in tableau-form, but if we are prepared to desert our seats, we shall be able to watch several other episodes, particularly those at stations within easy reach of our own. For example, the graphic scene depicting Christ's crucifixion (Play 35) under the system adopted will be presented at Stations 2, 6, and 10, that is to say on the 1468 allocation at a site in Micklegate, at another in Coney Street (possibly at its junction with Jubbergate), and at the Minster Gates where Stonegate turns into Petergate. Thus, it will technically be feasible to double back after watching Jesus before Annas and Caiaphas (Play 29) at Station 4 and catch the Crucifixion at Station 2 in Micklegate, returning to our proper places for the Harrowing of Hell (Play 37). Or if we wish to witness the Judgement on Jesus which features in Play 33, then we can still view the Crucifixion by anticipating its arrival in Coney Street's Station 6 and speeding away (if such a thing is possible) as soon as the

Judgement is completed at our 'resident' station. In this way those of us who are sound in wind and limb can individually select to some extent which of the cycle episodes we can watch *in toto* from the comfortable vantage-point of our scaffold, which ones we shall have to track down elsewhere, and which we shall have to content ourselves with seeing pass by in tableau-form only.

The initial stages of our experiences at the 1468 presentation must be passed over fairly rapidly. From our station where we have assembled not long after the players formed up on their waggons at Holy Trinity Priory – one slight advantage offered by the later stations is that its occupants do not need to rise quite so early as those at the earlier ones – we have watched the first cart arrive containing the setting for the Barkers' play of the Creation of the World and the Fall of Lucifer, which probably consisted of an upper level with clouds and a throne to signify Heaven, with Hell represented by the floor of the stage-platform itself. Alternatively, the short sequence in Hell could be acted out at ground-level, with Heaven where most of the action takes place represented on the waggon-base. This would avoid the necessity of supporting an upper platform strong enough to bear a company of angels, as well as simplifying the physical fall of those actors playing the devils, who simply leap down to street-level. On the other hand, the amount of space available between the edge of the platform and the front row of spectators in the street is too problematic to make an absolute assertion on the point: descents to the ground may have been very exceptional, for the Coventry play of the Magi clearly makes a special feature of Herod's departure from the pageant-waggon stage:

Here Erode ragis in the pagond and in the strete also.[21]

The natural tendency would surely have been for spectators to press to the front of the waggon. Could players rely on being able to find landing-space among them at a moment's notice, even if in such cases a space would no doubt be cleared very quickly?

The Barkers move on, and past our station in sequence travel the Plasterers with their one-man play of the Creation, the Cardmakers with the Creation of Adam and Eve, and the Fullers with the disposition in the Garden of Eden, until the Coopers' waggon with the play of the Fall comes to a halt before us. There is no ostensible reason why we should not watch the Barkers' play again by visiting Station 8, except that this would mean following the waggon all the way to the Common Hall Gates at the far end of Coney Street, and then hurrying back to reclaim our seat at Station 4. Perhaps it is wiser to remain seated, and prepare to watch the Coopers.

Their play raises few staging queries: there are only five characters involved, and the only scenic requirements are for a Tree of Knowledge complete with an apple which can be picked and eaten, and a source from which the fig-leaves can be taken. One slight point of interest is the position of God in this play: is it possible for him to speak from some upper level such as the roof of the cart? It would certainly be effective if this were capable of being accomplished, as it clearly was in the case of the Mercers' Doomsday Play, but the play does not depend on it.

The procession continues to wind past Station 4 and there is no need to enumerate all the pageants passing our position. Those which stop to perform here do in fact provide us with a fairly adequate outline of Biblical events, one advantage of the generous number of individual plays included in the York Cycle. We can witness at this location both the Fall of Lucifer and that of Man; we can watch the story of Noah and the Flood, and the suspicions of Joseph concerning Mary, though not the Birth of Christ itself, although this episode will be presented at Station 3 at the same time as Joseph's Trouble over Mary is occupying Station 4, so that those able to move swiftly can exercise a choice as to which play they will watch without undue inconvenience. But even if we do not actually view the play itself, we shall certainly be able to see the waggon go by, complete with Joseph and Mary and the baby, the stable, the manger, and the 'beestis mylde' possibly represented by cut-out painted shapes as in the Chester version of the Flood, or by actors in skins as in the Chester Cappers' Play of Balaam, or even by real animals.

The next episode to halt at Station 4 is the Adoration of the Magi, and then come in sequence the Baptism of Christ, and the Entry into Jerusalem, both key-incidents in the Gospel narrative, providing further evidence that even merely witnessing from only one station performances of certain episodes of the entire sequence provides a satisfying entertainment in itself, given that the other pageants passing by in tableau 'fill in the blanks', and ensure that our appreciation of single episodes is assimilated into an understanding of the totality of which they form constituent parts.

★ ★ ★

The sequence of York plays dealing with Christ's Passion commences with Play 28, the Cordwainers' Play of the Agony and Betrayal, and goes on to deal with Peter's Denial of Christ and the Examination before Caiaphas (Play 29) staged by the Bowers and Fletchers; with the Dream of Pilate's Wife and Christ's Trial before Pilate which forms the subject of the Tapiters' offering; with the Litsters' [Lightsters'] Trial before Herod; with the return of Christ to Pilate, the Remorse of Judas, and the Purchase of the Field of Blood presented by the Cooks and Waterleaders as Play 32. The Tilemakers perform the second trial and the Judgment on Jesus; the Shearmen depict Christ led to Calvary; the Crucifixion is in the hands of the Pinners, and the Passion sequence ends with the thirty-sixth play showing the Death of Christ, which is the responsibility of the Butchers of York.

Of these only Plays 29 (the Examination before Annas and Caiaphas) and 33 (Christ's Judgement) can actually be watched as complete performances at Station 4 under the scheme proposed. Some readers may well feel this invalidates the projected system of processional performances advocated, since to perform at one station only two episodes out of the nine covering the vitally important incidents forming Christ's Passion may seem totally inadequate. But this may not have been how a medieval spectator viewed the matter. It is difficult for twentieth-century theatregoers to imagine that their medieval counterparts might have been prepared to forego seeing certain parts of a cyclic presentation, since we are accustomed to regard plays as complete units and expect to witness them as wholes, fearing that to miss a part is to fail to comprehend all. But cycle-play audiences were not looking for novelty nor comprehensive coverage; they already knew the familiar stories of Cain and Abel, the Doctors in the Temple, the encounter on the road to Emmaus. The episodic structure of the cycles themselves encouraged episodic viewing, however much the anonymous playwrights were motivated by a common purpose. Furthermore, a performance extending over a great many hours (or even several days as seems to have been the case at Chester) did not demand total attention throughout its span: it was impossible that it should. Medieval audiences are likely to have attended cycle-play performances more as modern pleasure-seekers visit a fairground or a carnival, an open day at an aerodrome or an agricultural show, not expecting to sample everything on offer or to watch every event staged for their enjoyment, but rather to 'be there' and to savour aspects of the whole with varying degrees of commitment, depending on their energies and interests.

Even so, we must remember that it was still possible for a medieval spectator to watch more than two of the Passion plays of the York Cycle if judicious use was made of the opportunity offered to leave one's scaffold and watch a play at a station other than that at which one had been assigned accommodation. As we shall see, by moving ahead of the play one had just seen, one could anticipate the arrival at a later station than one's 'home base' of an episode one would otherwise miss; by moving against the flow of the vehicles one could watch another play performed at a station prior to one's own along the processional route.

The sixth play to be viewed at Station 4 is that of the Baptism of Jesus, presented by the Barbers as Play 21 of the sequence. It is another relatively simple play with a cast of only four, the only point of interest in its staging being the possibility that the two angels who are present according to the script simply to sing the hymn *Veni creator spiritus* are also employed to represent the river Jordan by unrolling a length of blue cloth held between them. This certainly seems to be the inference to be drawn from expenditure such as that which occurs in the Coventry Smiths' records for 1569: 'halfe a yard of rede sea [i.e. say or serge]'[22] no doubt represented the Red Sea in which Pharaoh's troops drowned.

The Baptism is the sixth play we have witnessed from our seat on the stand erected at the open space before the Church of St John the Baptist. Let us assume that now we wish to watch more of the sequence in acted rather than tableau form than our allocated accommodation permits. So, leaving our less active fellows awaiting the arrival of Play 25 (*The Entry into Jerusalem*) which we decide to forego, we scramble down and hurry southwards along Micklegate, past Stations 3 and 2, until we reach the station opposite Holy Trinity Priory, the first along the route. As we push through the crowds, pageant-waggons are moving up in the opposite direction: they contain Play 22 (*The Temptation*), Play 23 (*The Transfiguration*), and Play 24 which includes in its contents the Raising of Lazarus. Next come the Skinners with Play 25 which will eventually end up at the station we have just left, but after a swift glance at their setting which incorporates both the Mount of Olives and the gates of Jerusalem, and at its attendant cast which includes the ass that Christ is to ride into the city, we hasten onwards to Holy Trinity Priory. *En route* we are passed by Plays 26 and 27 which deal with the Conspiracy and the Last Supper respectively, preparing to play at Stations 3 and 2, but our quest is Station 1, where we arrive in time to see Play 28, *The Agony and Betrayal*, the first of the Passion plays, presented by the Cordwainers. Squeezing in among the standing spectators who have to shift for themselves as best they can, not having paid to sit on the stands provided by Messrs Haliday and Hudson, we settle down in rather more cramped conditions than prevailed on the scaffold we have just left, to witness the play we have deserted our comfortable position to track down.

The Agony has a tripartite structure, over half the play being devoted to events in the Garden of Gethsemane involving Christ and the apostles. The action then shifts to the palace of the High Priest, and then after almost ninety lines moves back to the Garden where it concludes. The cast-list is extensive, including as it does Jesus and the eleven faithful apostles, an Angel, Caiaphas and Annas, Judas and Malchus, together with four soldiers and four Jews, an assembly of at least twenty-five players, all of whom appear to occupy the narrow confines of the pageant-waggon in the last section of the play, whose principal interest lies in its disposition of locations.

There is no need to assume the presence of much in the way of scenery or furnishings for this play. The Cordwainers could not expect to deck their waggon out as lavishly in this respect as could those guilds responsible for pageants requiring fewer actors or demanding less extensive stage activity, as was the case with plays emphasizing the static, majestic aspects of God's revelation of his role in human affairs, such as the Creation or the Day of Judgement episodes. These were no doubt felt to justify elaborate and spectacular effects, but in such plays comparable effects were always easier to achieve than in more dynamic scenes involving a good deal of physical activity. Even where scenery was acceptable, no scene was treated in a fastidiously realistic manner; even if space had permitted it, dramatic convention did not demand it.

Thus the opening phase of the play is unlikely to require a firm locale or to feature anything suggesting that this is the Garden of Gethsemane: a few plants may be used, but a simple backcloth is probably the only embellishment on the entire stage. Christ and the apostles doubtless enter from the rear of the waggon through this curtain much as the booth-stage performers employed such a rear hanging for exits and entrances in *Mankynde*, yet with such a large number appearing at once, entries can also be made up steps at the sides of the waggon, leaving Christ alone to appear in the centre, and so take up a commanding position at once. It is enough that Christ talks of his impending betrayal and capture to signify that this is the Mount of Olives, and to suggest his departure to pray in another part of the garden it is only necessary for him to cross to the far corner of the waggon to create the desired effect, with the apostles stretched out across the floor at the rear of the stage, conforming to St Peter's suggestion that they should

sittis us doune on every ilka side (line 19).

This very simple dramatic convention is sufficient to create the desired impression of separation between Jesus and his disciples. Christ in the foreground becomes comparable to a screen actor seen in close-up; when he steps back into the stage picture created by the forms of the sleeping apostles, he is viewed in 'long shot' by spectators who quite happily shift the focus of their attention to and fro as the play proceeds.

A more ambitious way of staging the Gethsemane scene would be to have Christ ascending to and descending from the pageant-roof, and certainly at least one line conveys such an impression, when the character says

Agayne to the mounte I will gang

Yitt eftesones [straightaway] where I was ere (84–5).

Can we assume that this reference can be squared with Christ's simply moving across the level stage to another spot, or does it argue for the use of an elevation? It would simplify matters if the angel who appears at line 113 could alight on the roof, yet it is not strictly necessary, and to have Christ actually climbing up or down on six occasions seems very wasteful of playing-time. The safest conclusion appears to be that the use of the roof is not essential but would be occasionally valuable, if not imperative to arrange.

There is no indication in the text as to what happens at the end of the action in the Garden. All that is clear is that the scene shifts to the High Priest's hall, where Annas and Caiaphas are planning the capture of Jesus, but there is no guidance as to the disposition of Christ and the disciples while this episode is being played. The effect is not unlike that of a 'dissolve' or a 'fade' in the cinema. Annas's first words come hard on the heels of Christ's rebuke to Peter, and the inference is that the Gethsemane party remains on stage; however, since a group of twelve actors occupies quite a large portion of a platform measuring no more than 6 metres by 3, it would seem preferable to remove the twelve players from the stage if possible. There seems to be at least one good reason for not having them retire through the rear curtain, since it is from here that the priests must emerge, and there is nothing for it but to have Christ and his followers leave the stage by means of steps at one side of the waggon where there would be sufficient space (especially if viewing were only possible from the front) to enable them to reach the ground and then move 'behind the scenes' to await their reappearance.

The scene between the High Priests and Judas is now played out on the stage; no scenic change or introduction of any furniture appears possible at this point. Although Malchus, the High Priest's servant, may bring on some kind of simple throne for Caiaphas, it seems likely that if he bears anything it is a torch or some other form of cresset-light, since he alludes to it later in the play; the advantage of such a property is that it can be carried off with ease and imported without incongruity into the next phase of the action. That the full stage is used for this episode seems clear from Caiaphas's request in line 169 that Judas on his entry should 'drawe nere us', which suggests that he stands waiting on the opposite side of the platform, for any entry from among the audience seems precluded by the playing conditions, and his rather hesitant approach would rule out a rumbustious eruption through the throng of the kind possible for the Vices in *Mankynde* or the servants in *Fulgens and Lucres*.

By the end of this phase the stage is filled with figures, four knights and four Jews having joined the priests and Judas to apprehend Jesus. The problem is to ascertain the most satisfactory way of managing the exit and re-entry of the conspirators together with the re-appearance of Christ and his followers. Allusions to a 'journay' and Caiaphas's 'late us spede A space' clearly indicate movement of some kind, and Lucy Toulmin Smith clearly felt justified in inserting '*Exeunt*' at the end of the episode, but more precision is called for in plotting this departure from the waggon. Consistency would argue for the exit being made through the rear curtain, but the resultant congestion would diminish the haste with which the party leaves, and the most simple method of facilitating the rapid departure of the conspirators is for Judas, since he is to 'wisse [teach] tham the way', to lead the soldiers and the Jews off down the steps to one side of the platform, and for only Caiaphas and Annas to exit through the hangings. On this cue it would be a simple matter for Jesus and his disciples to ascend the stage from the opposite side, and Christ's words

Now will this oure [hour] be neghand [approaching] full nere

That schall certefie all the soth [truth] that I have saide (245–6)

provide just long enough for the party headed by Judas to re-form at the foot of the steps before their leader crosses the platform to kiss and betray his master. The soldiers and Jews can wait at the side of the pageant-waggon until their prey is marked out by Judas's action, and then surge on to the stage to arrest Christ.

Two small technical problems occur in the last section of this play: the light which shines forth from Christ as his enemies assail him could have been created through the use of gold foil on Christ's face, but the speed of illumination (which parallels the light from the stable at the Nativity and that of the star which amazes the shepherds in Play 15) suggests that artificial means were employed, possibly in the form of a light suspended over Christ's head and lit with a fuse-wire soaked in an inflammable substance ignited to the rear. The severance of Malchus's ear raises problems only if verisimilitude is sought after; skilful miming by Peter and the servant himself can create the desired effect, though a bladder of pig's blood secreted on the body was a favoured medieval property when such incidents were featured, and Malchus may have held such a device in his hand.

The play concludes with the rapid departure of the Jews and the soldiers with the bound and captive Christ, at the side of the stage from which they appeared, with all the disciples apart from Peter and Judas withdrawing at the opposite side, Peter following the captive at a distance, and Judas being perhaps the last to leave, already indicating that he repents of what he has done. As spectators, we may have little opportunity to observe these subtleties, for we are now determined to watch Play 31 which depicts Christ's Trial before Herod, since it is rumoured that the Litsters have secured the services of an actor never seen before in York to play the role of Herod, and his fame has run before him to such an extent that we are prepared to take pains in order to watch his performance. We push our way through the crowd at Station 1 therefore, and make our way with the moving throng to Station 2 further down Micklegate. The pageant-waggons are making the same journey beside us: they contain Play 28 which we have just watched, with Plays 29 and 30 which are just beginning their circuit not far behind them. In fact, by arriving in good time at Station 2 we are able to see the tableaux on the two waggons succeeding the Cordwainers' pageant just witnessed, to observe the dumb show of Peter's denial, and the sight of Jesus confronting Pilate. So the time is happily filled in by watching the carts rumble on their way, and manoeuvring ourselves into a more secure and advantageous position for seeing the Litsters' Play when it arrives. When we view it, the guild (like the preceding pair of trade guilds) will be playing its pageant for the first time during this year's performance, another reason perhaps for watching the play as early as possible in its career, while the actors are still fresh and in good voice.

At length the Litsters' waggon pulls up opposite Station 2 where we have crammed ourselves in; the final touches are given to costumes and stage, and the play begins. Although a long episode of over 400 lines, *Christ before Herod* requires only a single setting throughout, so that it is possible to place on stage permanently the litter or couch on which the king attempts to take a rest early in the action. The central position of such a piece of furniture certainly accentuates the vital importance of Herod all through this play: it is he who dominates the scene both physically and histrionically, although ironically Christ's silence in the face of the king's jocularity and threats makes *him* the focal point of the spectator's attention. But it is Herod who is responsible for the dynamics of the play which bears his name; small wonder that this part can only be entrusted to an actor with real histrionic skill and power who, despite the part's reputation as one of rant and bluster, must exercise vocal and physical control and variation to realize its full potential.

Herod's opening harangue is a marvellous *tour de force*: he impresses himself on the crowd's consciousness right from the first with his raucous commands for silence as he brandishes his bright sword over them. Like many a comedian since his day, he insults us and we enjoy the experience partly because it is clear he is at least acknowledging our presence. He even accepts that as spectators we wish to view him in comfort if we can, though any unseemly scrambling for seats is strictly censured:

Plextis [squabble] for no plasis but platte you [flatten yourselves] to
    this playne (5).

The reference suggests a closely-packed mob swarming around the waggon, arguing over the 'plasis' – the seats on the raised scaffolds – and preferring not to have to squat on the cold cobbles. We ourselves may even be guilty of thus agitating for a better place; sheepishly at Herod's roar we subside among the unlucky ones on the 'playne'.

The king's irascibility is accentuated by the presence of his sycophantic 'Duces' or attendant lords who advise him to drink some wine and then retire for the night – 'youre bedde is new made' says one – and there is much mirth to be extracted from the gingerly way in which the king reposes himself:

laye me doune softely,

For thou wotte full wele that I am full tendirly hydid (48–9).

The ludicrous contrast between the bullying tyrant of the opening and the pampered valetudinarian is well taken. But the king's repose is of short duration, for no sooner has he commended his lackeys to Satan and Lucifer and bid them goodnight, than Pilate's 'knights' arrive calling for entry with Jesus, on whom they wish Herod to pass judgement. Some dialogue ensues before they are admitted. The action clearly shifts away from Herod on his couch with attendants hovering round him to some other area where the two soldiers who appear leading Christ exchange four lines of dialogue. It seems Christ and his captors first arrive at the side of the waggon at ground level, as if they have 'faren ferre' walking through the streets of Jerusalem, streets alluded to shortly by the king's attendant who says that unless the soldiers' message can contribute to Herod's happiness,

Stalkis furthe be yone stretis or stande stone still (62),

suggesting that at this point prisoner and escort are outside the royal chamber. This is conveyed by having the soldiers and Christ mount the steps to the height of the stage-platform, but not venture upon it during their conversation with the lord-in-waiting, who, advising them to keep Jesus under scrutiny, crosses to Herod for advice. Herod aroused in a vile temper consents to be dressed, and informed of Christ's capture, agrees to 'se of there sayng', and the knights then 'enter' by crossing the stage to stand in his presence with their prisoner. However, Herod at first ignores Christ. Inquiring 'what heynde' they have there and informed that Christ is a 'presente fro Pilate', the king is immediately suspicious and wishes to send Jesus back again, but is persuaded to hear the soldiers out. Learning of Christ's identity he is delighted; a new entertainment has been devised for his pleasure:

Nowe thes games was grathely [worthily] begonne (119).

Believing that the Roman Governor hereby acknowledges his authority, Herod's attitude to Pilate and his men changes radically, and there follows the semi-comic interrogation of Christ by the king, who ranges from cajolery and flattery to blustering and rage in his attempts to wring some kind of response from the adamantly dumb figure of Jesus. But the dramatic tension is not merely engineered between the garrulous Herod and the silent Christ. There is friction between Herod and his court when he is first wakened, and less pointedly between the king and the knights when he seems likely to allow Christ to go from him. These cross-currents unusual in medieval dramaturgy are reinforced by the action on stage: the soldiers' arrival disturbs the irate Herod from his slumbers, the king's suspicion of the Romans, his orchestration of the treatment of Jesus, all receive emphasis from the use made of the pageant-waggon stage, despite its limitations of space. Herod in insisting on complete independence from alien influence, makes Pilate's soldiers withdraw and his own men bring Jesus to him:

Wele sirs, drawes you adrygh [aside],
And bewscheris [*beaux sires*], bryngis ye hym nygh (159–60).

Herod, Jesus, and the Judean lords thus occupy the focal area where Herod's couch is placed. However, when Herod can make no impression on Christ, he allows the soldiers to come forward again in response to the exasperated sarcasm of 'Lo sirs, he deffis us with dynne' (189), and they step on to the 'king's half' of the platform, re-establishing the partly severed link between themselves and the monarch. Yet even among the Romans themselves there is wrangling, the First Soldier accusing his fellow of mumbling about Christ out of earshot of the king, and urging him to approach Herod himself –

Whe man, momelyng may nothyng avayle,
Go to the kyng and tell hyme fro toppe unto tayle (195–6) –

proving himself as the bolder spirit of the two. In the event, both lords and guards press closer, to inform the king of Christ's infamy in choric style; Herod is sceptical, and the First Soldier voices the pained query 'Why lorde, wene ye that wordis be wronge?' (224), but the king detects the underlying malice in his voice, and astutely enquires why the Romans are so anxious to see Jesus put to death. Such undercurrents of tension, such psychological complexity, such subtlety of motivation, such interplay of character, are not often encountered in the cycle plays, yet are a mark of the dramaturgical sophistication the best writers can achieve in this genre. Similarly, the contrast between the colourful, verbally-dynamic court and the pale silent figure of Christ indicates an exceptional talent for histrionic effect in this playwright's work.

Stage action and distinctions of dress play an important role in the closing stages of the play. Herod is amused to learn that Christ has called himself a king, and treating him like a visiting potentate, offers him a seat beside his own on the couch he occupies – 'Comes nerre, kyng, into courte' (236) he cordially coos – but Christ's continued refusal to kneel before him or to speak soon drives Herod into a blustering rage which contrasts with his former feline courtesy towards his prisoner. The text conveys a wide range of acting opportunities for the accomplished actor the part requires. His fawning councillors deduce that it is the king's powerful voice which has struck Christ dumb, or that his whirling 'fauchone' or light sword has frightened him. Herod's attendants, taking their cue from their master, mock Jesus, making obeisance to him, and it may be that the king lays aside his sword in order to 'softely with a septoure assaie', placing his own sceptre in Christ's reluctant grip, which would give added point to the mock-worship being accorded to the prisoner by the courtiers. The situation is further pointed up by the contrast in attire between the gaily-and opulently-dressed court and the shabbily-clad figure of Christ. The role played by costume in this episode is emphasized later when the three sons of Herod join in tormenting Christ, resorting to bellowing at him in unison until even their father is constrained to intervene, playing the tender-nerved valetudinarian once more:

O, ye make a foule noyse for the nonys (333).

The First Son now agrees that Christ must be a fool, and suggests that he ought to be dressed as one, and so an attendant lord brings forth, probably from a chest on stage or from the 'wings', a long white garment as worn by madmen, and Christ is arrayed in it, further stressing his alienation.

The final passage in which Christ is treated like a common criminal and 'cried' in the court increases his isolation, as well as adding to the dramatic subtlety of the entire play. We have already noted that there are undercurrents of tension on stage in this episode, which few of the other scenes aspire to. The dramatist appears at pains to show that God's enemies are far from being a unified force, and again his relative sophistication is demonstrated throughout this scene. Herod's antagonism, for example, is not all directed towards his victim: he falls to abusing the First Soldier who argues that if they return to Pilate with Jesus uncondemned, 'wise men will deme it we dote'. The king curses him for impertinence and commends him to the devil, for there is no law, he argues, which demands that an innocent should be slain. Herod even appears briefly as Christ's friend, ordering the soldiers to 'be not so bryme [fierce]' as they drag Jesus back to Pilate once more, and his final oath is directed not against their captive, but against his hated Roman escort:

Daunce on, in the devyll way (423).

This awareness of political nuance is well exploited in this piece, and forms the final irony in a fine play full of ironies, not least that the Judge of Mankind should be depicted here being judged by a monster of depravity like Herod. Eventually the soldiers march Jesus off the platform the way they came, while Herod and his entourage depart through the rear curtain. The Litsters' waggon is slowly drawn away from Station 2, and a play whose ironic complexities of psychology and situation make considerable demands on its actors and auditors comes to an end.

★ ★ ★

Station 2 now becomes the first port-of-call for the Pinners' Play of the Crucifixion, one of the highlights of the entire cycle, and if we stay where we are, we shall be well placed to view it. In the meantime we may take

7 Artist's impression of the York *Crucifixion* presented on a pageant-waggon

the opportunity to buy refreshments or answer a call of nature, shoving our way back into the throng assembled at Station 2 in time to catch the intervening pageants travelling past: the Cooks and Water-leaders miming the Remorse of Judas, the Tilemakers with the Judgement, and the Shearmen with the Procession to Calvary, all presenting in dumb-show the biblical incidents they will perform in dialogue later. And at last comes the play we have remained at Station 2 to witness.

The York *Crucifixio Christi* is a relatively simple play to discuss in terms of textual structure. Its chief dramatic features are dictated by the sheer practical mechanics of securing Christ to the cross and raising it into place. Unlike other playwrights tackling this episode, the York writer seems prepared, even eager, to emphasize the 'technical aspects' of the Crucifixion. The action is not set in some kind of cathartic framework as in the Wakefield sequence where Christ becomes the object of the Torturers' games, so that his bodily suffering is distanced. The author chooses to dwell on the precise mechanics of the operation, whereby the play is given a particular kind of actuality, an overriding concern with questions of technological precision which affects its overall pace and the acting style called forth from its players, and has a bearing on our response to its total impact as spectators.

One result is that as audience we become involved in and fascinated by the actual procedures employed to attach Jesus to the cross, to elevate it into the vertical position, and to stabilize it there once it has been levered into place. The episode's minimal cast – Jesus and the four soldiers – is partly dictated by the need to concentrate on the deed itself, and to ensure as clear a stage as possible for the physical exertions its successful accomplishment requires. The dialogue too is of the spare functional kind which conventionally accompanies physically-taxing activity, and that it is deliberately designed to this end seems clear from the contrast with the usually copious and diffuse style of the York Cycle as a whole. The scene is considerably briefer, too, than the lengthy Passion episodes which precede it: despite its centrality the York *Crucifixion* is only 300 lines long. Again the aim is partly to spare the players undue physical strain, partly to focus on that strain.

The play's setting is Calvary, but the soldiers speak as if they have only just received their instructions, so that we are kept informed of the point in the action which we have reached, so necessary with a fluctuating audience unsure of the prevailing dramatic situation. The First Soldier's address to his subordinates is directed towards us rather than them: his

Yee wootte youreselffe als wele as I
Howe lordis and leders of owre lawe
Has geven dome that this doote [dolt] schall dye (3–5)

places all spectators on equal terms. Yet the presence of the cross reveals all; at line 39 the Fourth Soldiers stresses that

The crosse on grounde is goodely graied [prepared].

The term 'grounde' may delay us a moment. Does it mean that the cross was placed at the foot of the cart on the same level as the street, or is it simply there to suggest that the floor of the waggon was taken to *represent* the ground? Although a greater degree of audience-involvement would clearly result for those sitting or standing nearby, in a narrow street few spectators could see a cross laid horizontally in front of the cart. Moreover, the increased effort required of the Soldiers lifting a cross plus Christ on to the cart from the street before hoisting it into the vertical position would seem to place a needless physical burden on performers whose task is quite taxing enough already, unless the feat was accomplished by having the mechanism for securing the cross placed at the outside frame of the waggon, and by lifting the cross from the street-level into its retaining socket in one movement. But given the likelihood of crowds in close proximity to the cart, it seems more probable that the scene was played on the waggon throughout.

Although the necessity for speed is stressed more than once in the opening exchanges, one senses that the Soldiers feel a certain reluctance to come to terms with the job in hand, for it is not until line 45 that Jesus is actually brought into the action, and he presumably must stand to one side while the Soldiers warm to their task by discussing it, by checking the tools which the Third Soldier has 'gone for' and no doubt carries, and by threatening the victim with dire torments. Firstly Christ is told to 'Come forthe' and 'Walkes oon' and prepare himself for death; while the Soldiers strip him of his white robe, he prays.

The general business of the Crucifixion is a relatively simple matter to grasp; less so the effect of its precise engineering in terms of stage action. The First Soldier tells us all we need to know of the actors' functions:

Lokis that the ladde on lenghe be layde

And made me thane [fixed] unto this tree (41–2),

he says, and Jesus is told at line 74 to 'bende thi bakke unto this tree', the Fourth Soldier expressing astonishment that Christ should be so willing to obey their orders:

Byhalde, hymselffe has laide hym doune

In lenghe and breede as he schulde bee (75–6).

Christ lies with his back on the cross, and the First Soldier then orders his three companions to 'Gose faste and fetter hym than ye thre', whereupon they go to the right and left hands and the feet respectively, and pretend to stretch them out until they reach holes previously bored to receive the nails. The fact that augur-holes have been pre-cut suggests that the soldiers use wooden dowels rather than metal nails to mime the securing of Christ's limbs later in the play: the terms employed are 'stubbe' (line 102) and 'nayle' (lines 120, 141), but the *Promptorium parvulorum* of c. 1440 distinguishes between 'Nayl of metalle' and 'Nayle of tymbyr', and given the presence of bore-holes, wooden pegs seem more appropriate in this context, particularly as the Pinners' craft was to fabricate such vital items.[23]

The First Soldier goes to Christ's head, partly for symmetry's sake, and the grisly work of stretching out the limbs begins; here the precise details are a little obscured by textual uncertainties. Soldiers 2 and 3 clearly tug the right and left arm respectively, and though each claims that he has brought it to the mark, later lines suggest that this is not achieved simultaneously by both men. However, there then occur in the manuscript two speeches in succession assigned to 'ii Miles', followed by another by 'i Miles'. However, 'Strike on than harde, for hym the boght' (line 101) sounds like a command from the leader of the group, Soldier One; it is analogous to his earlier orders such as 'Gose faste and fetter hym than ye thre', his position at Christ's head, and his enquiry 'Sir knyghtis, saie, howe wirke we nowe?' at line 97. It is then appropriate for Soldier Two who has Christ's right hand at the auger-hole to brag of the calibre of his hardware before hammering the peg home:

Yis, here is a stubbe will stiffely stande,
Thurgh bones and senous [sinews] it schall be soght – [*Hammers it home*]
This werke is wele, I will warande. (102–4; my insertion)

Soldier One as director of the operation may then be allowed his query as in the manuscript: 'Saie sir, howe do we thore [there] [?]' to which the Third crossly responds that 'It failis a foote and more', indicating that in tugging Christ's right hand to the mark, Soldier Two has shifted the position of the left, so that it lies a foot or so from the hole bored to take the dowel. But, as Soldier Three complains, the real fault lies with those who prepared the cross:

In faith, it was overe-skantely scored (111).

Once again the First Soldier demonstrates his N.C.O. status by deriding their lack of initiative:

Why carpe ye so? Faste on a corde
And tugge hym to, by toppe and taile (113–14).

The disgruntled Third tells him to 'helpe to haale', and a cord is tied about Christ's left arm and the offending limb dragged to the mark, where the Third is able to 'tacche hym too, Full nemely [swiftly] with a nayle', effected on stage by placing a peg between Christ's outspread fingers and striking carefully! Possibly the cords were also fastened round the wrists to assist the actor in keeping his arms in place:

I Miles: Ther [read 'thes'?] cordis have evill encressed his paynes,
        Or he wer tille [to] the booryngis brought.
II Miles: Yaa, assoundir are bothe synnous and veynis
        On ilke a [each] side, so have we soughte. (145–8)

In actuality the actor's feet would no doubt rest on a small step, enabling him to support himself.

Once the nails are home, the First Soldier again assumes charge, and a first attempt at the tricky task of hoisting the cross with its human burden 'on heghte' is made. The Second Soldier's reservations at the labour involved are made light of by Soldier One who again jeers at his detachment's feeble efforts – 'Thy liftyng was but light' – but rejects any protest that four men are inadequate to do the job, a view in which Soldier Three backs him. They bend again to their task – Soldier Four at the foot to 'tente his tase [toes]' – but it appears that they first must carry the cross horizontally across the stage, not simply lift it into the 'mortaise' immediately. Line 178 ('Late bere hym to yone hill') provides one reason for this, but this is probably not a literal instruction (for the floor of the cart is flat), but simply serves to remind the audience that the setting is Calvary. To some it may still suggest that the cross is raised from street-level to the waggon, but (as observed earlier) this seems an unnecessary labour, and the likeliest answer is that the cross has to be conveyed a little way across the stage to where the retaining device has been positioned.

The stage mechanism for erecting the cross is probably of the simplest: it may be sufficient to insert the shaft in a gap cut in the cart's floor. If the shaft is made to fit the space tightly, the weight of the waggon may be capable of counterbalancing that of the cross, although the text later states that chocks ['wegges'] are hammered home on four sides of the shaft to lock it in place. However, the reference in line 161 to a 'mortaise' suggests something more stable than a mere gap in the planking, perhaps some form of well-braced retaining socket solidly constructed to take the foot of the cross and extending well below the level of the stage. Into this 'box' the cross can then be guided and once there it will be held in position by wedges and the weight of the cart. In this situation the shaft of the cross may protrude some three feet below the waggon-base, and it is quite possible that if the 'mortice' is placed at the front of the cart, the entire length of the shaft plus the socket can be made visible to the spectators, thus extracting the maximum effect from the height of the cross above the ground (see Plate 14).[24] Alternatively, the same effect may be achieved by having the wooden 'mortice' mounted and bolted on a strong base which then becomes a portable foundation on which the cross may be erected in any area of the stage, where it can be secured with struts on all four sides (see Plate 15).

There follows the procedure of lifting the cross across the stage and into place. Soldier One takes the head of the cross while Four, who is to 'tente his tase', applies pressure to the foot to prevent it slipping – 'Thanne will I bere here doune' – and Two says that he and Three will 'see tille aythir side', which suggests they supply the power to lift the cross, along with one who 'walks' the cross up on end much as two men raise a ladder from the head. But the effort is still too great, and amid much complaining and puffing, the second attempt is abandoned, Soldier Four grumbling that they will never do the deed like this. However, Soldier One rallies his troops, and at last the cross is raised into the vertical position: 'The werste is paste' says Two thankfully. All that is needed now is for the upright cross to be dropped into the 'mortice' and secured, an act which the Soldiers gleefully acknowledge will cause their prisoner more pain than anything so far experienced. This is done, but there is a further piece of botched workmanship to contend with: the 'mortice' has been 'made overe-wyde' so that the cross now shackles about, and 'goode wegges' are required to secure it, a skilful way of justifying a technical necessity. Two and Three take it on themselves to

14 The York *Crucifixion* as staged at the University of Toronto, 1977, showing the cross braced to the cart. (Photo: Records of Early English Drama)

15 The Wakefield *Crucifixion* staged in Bangor Cathedral, 1962, showing the method of bracing the cross in position. (Photo: William Tydeman)

16 The Deposition from the author's production of a cycle sequence in Bangor Cathedral, 1972 (Photo: Emyr Roberts)

hammer them home. With a few gibes at Christ the four soldiers complete their appointed task.

The last phase of the play consists of Christ's words from the cross, and further jeers from his murderers, followed by the haggling over Christ's garments which features prominently in all the cycle versions, though it is not likely at York that the dicing for coat and kirtle actually takes place on stage, since there is no dialogue for it, and if it occurs, it must create a hiatus virtually at the end of the episode. Since no reference is made to which soldier obtains which garment, one can assume that the Soldiers withdraw as if to start their dice-play off-stage. Christ remains on the cross, although after the play ends he must presumably be helped down in full view of the spectators before the waggon moves on, thus weakening the dramatic impact of the final image of the Man of Sorrows deserted and alone. But the memory of his sufferings has been strikingly implanted.

The York *Crucifixion* forms a notable contrast to the *Trial before Herod* discussed earlier. Where the latter is copious, motivationally complex, and composed of multiple tensions, the former is economical of dialogue and personalities, reduces the interplay of character to a minimum, and concentrates our attention on a single agonizing operation. The stage is bare just as the dialogue is restricted to the functional, in order that the physical dimension can produce its maximum impact on an audience. The result is one of the outstanding plays of the series, but its dramatic virtues – theatrical austerity and stringent authorial control – are far removed from the psychological richness and verbal expansiveness of the *Trial before Herod*.

★ ★ ★

So far, as members of the medieval audience, we have been able to watch three plays from the Passion sequence, and by accompanying the *Crucifixion* waggon as it makes its laborious way through the streets we can witness one further play from the Passion, namely the Butchers' Play of the Death and Burial or the *Mortificacio*, which is thirty-sixth in the cycle. As the Pinners and Painters' cart moves up Micklegate, over Ouse Bridge, and into Coney Street, we move with it, past our 'base' at Station 4 until we reach Station 5 where we let *The Crucifixion* pass on its way to the sixth station opposite Jubbergate, and join the spectators at the east end of Coney Street, some of whom have been there throughout the proceedings, others of whom are peripatetic. As we settle into a vacant space, there arrives alongside the station the Butchers' waggon with its setting and its attendant cast who after a slight pause launch into their second rendition of their allotted play, the first having taken place at Station 1.

There are grounds for assuming that an extra large waggon may be needed for *The Death and Burial*, since several groups of characters appear on the stage simultaneously, formally positioned around the central figure of the crucified Christ who is flanked by the two thieves who also require crosses erected on either side of the main one; three crosses on a pageant stage must inevitably utilize a good deal of space. There is Pilate with the pair of High Priests and his entourage of soldiers to accommodate; there are Mary the mother of Jesus, Mary Cleophas, and the Apostle John; also apparently present are the blind Longeus or Longinus, a boy, and a Centurion, and room must later be found for Joseph of Arimathea and Nicodemus. However, not all these figures are on stage at once: Annas and Caiaphas do not speak after line 282 and Pilate not after line 342, so it is possible that they leave the stage shortly afterwards; certainly the group with the Virgin Mary departs at line 273, while Joseph and Nicodemus do not require to appear until lines 326 and 352 respectively. Thus, although stage conditions are occasionally cramped, they may not be impossibly constricted, the only figures who remain on stage throughout being Christ and the robbers. Nevertheless at the outset the platform must contain at least ten characters, namely Pilate, the priests, and those responsible for enforcing justice. There must be at least two soldiers apart from Longeus and the Centurion, and if one adds the boy who prepares the vinegar and gall for Christ's consumption, we have eleven figures including the crucified trio on stage at one and the same time. As we saw from *The Agony and Betrayal*, this is by no means an impossible number to accommodate, especially on an extra-large waggon.

The *Mortificacio* is not a particularly memorable or striking play. It is successful in the functional way that many of the cycle plays succeed, by advancing its narrative line simply and economically. Only the characterization of Pilate deviates from the 'two-dimensional', presenting the Roman as a dignified and rational upholder of the rule of law who regrets his weakness in allowing Caiaphas and Annas to persuade him to have Christ put to death. The priests' justification for their actions and their mockery of the dying man occupy the opening phase of the episode. Whether Mary, Mary Cleophas, and John are present through this section of the play is uncertain; if space allows, there is no reason why they should not be positioned on the opposite side of the waggon to the group surrounding Pilate. Indeed, the weeping huddled figures would contrast effectively with the disdainful Roman and the jeering priests. However, Jesus does not acknowledge their presence in his first speech (lines 118–30), and Mary's opening remarks could in fact be spoken on her entry from the side of the waggon, although in this form of drama it is not uncommon to have characters present on stage but silent until the attention of the audience is drawn to them, much as the cinema camera can select parts of a crowded scene for close scrutiny.

Christ's injunction that John should care for the Virgin Mary is followed by the apostle's suggestion that they should depart, but Mary refuses to leave until her son is dead, and the trio retire to a corner of the pageant waggon. The 'spotlight' then shifts to the crucified thieves left and right of Jesus, who after his promise to the penitent thief that he shall dwell with God in Paradise cries out in agony

My God, my God full free,
Lama zabatanye,
Wharto forsoke thou me . . .? (214–16)

and complains of thirst. His request is answered by the Boy, who until this time has perhaps knelt at Pilate's feet, assuming that the latter occupied some kind of chair or throne: he possibly has to leave the stage to fetch the vinegar and gall, for he says

Full faste schall I springe for to spede (224)

and it would clearly be more convenient if he leapt from the waggon to collect the vessel (or more probably the sponge) from a helper at the side or the rear of the cart. It certainly gives more point to the Boy's assertion that

A draughte here of drinke have I dreste [got ready] (240)

if he leaves the stage ostensibly to prepare it.

Christ's refusal of the drink forms the prelude to his death, and this is the cue for John and Mary Cleophas to lead his mother from the stage, their departure possibly revealing to view the Centurion and the blind Longeus who in the relatively congested conditions prevailing may have stood upstage of Mary and her supporters until this moment. Pilate now acts on Caiaphas's advice that the soldiers should finish off the prisoners with a knife, which is done; this then leaves Longeus free to pierce Christ in the side with his spear and so recover from his blindness, a stage trick doubtless effected by having a device in the head of the spear which could release a jet of blood onto Longeus's person. Speeches of praise and affirmation on the part of the cured Longeus and the attendant Centurion suggest that they now depart, and in order to effect a clearance, Annas and Caiaphas might also depart at this point, in a state of disgust.

The stage is now relatively clear: Pilate remains, with his soldiers still at the foot of the crosses containing the two robbers, so that Joseph of Arimathea can approach the Roman Governor and ask for permission to remove Jesus's corpse. It is a reasonable assumption that, having given permission, Pilate departs and that as Joseph crosses from Pilate's 'side', so Nicodemus enters opposite and they encounter each other in mid-stage with Nicodemus's 'Weill mette, ser'. Having realized their common intention, they approach the cross together and prepare to remove the body, one of the most arduous physical tasks in the whole cycle.

The problem is to keep the body of Christ in position while the 'nails' are removed from between the fingers and the more practically useful cords are undone from the wrists. The corpse must undoubtedly sag to such an extent that one man, especially if perched on a ladder, will hardly be able to retain the weight without the risk of letting the player fall. If Joseph were engaged in 'removing' the nails and Nicodemus in supporting Christ, a mishap might be a real possibility, and thus it seems likely that the soldiers remain, to help in the delicate operation by looping a cord around Christ's shoulders and back, and gradually paying out the rope, help to assist in lowering him to Nicodemus's shoulder (see Plate 16).[25]

Last comes the burial, which must have either been effected by utilizing some form of trapdoor in the floor of the cart, or by merely wrapping Christ's body in the 'sudarye' or winding-sheet brought by Joseph, and leaving it on stage. However, simpler as is the latter scheme, Nicodemus's words

In grounde late us grave hym and goo;
Do liffely latte us laie hym allone (391–2)

suggest a rather more literal interpretation of the notion of burying Christ's body. It would not be a particularly complicated task to provide the waggon-floor with a hinged flap which would fold back and enable the corpse to be lowered into it to be received by waiting hands. It would be undeniably more effective to do this rather than to leave the body lying on the stage.

*   *   *

We have now examined the feasibility of the notion that members of an audience at a single performance of the York Cycle were able to witness four of the nine plays which make up the Passion sequence, even given the 'shunting' method of processional presentation proposed earlier. We have also been able to analyse some of the differing modes and techniques required by the individual plays which make up a typical medieval play cycle, and how those needs could be catered for under the auspices of a single annual production. Such diversity within the framework of one unifying dramatic experience is to be expected of one of the greatest artistic flowerings of the Gothic tradition.

5 · Great Hall Theatre: *Fulgens and Lucres*

Dramatic entertainments presented in indoor places of communal assembly and activity are commonplace occurrences throughout the Middle Ages.[1] The banquet-halls and throne-rooms of European courts and castles supplied sites for eulogistic tributes to rulers, amateur *momeries* and disguisings, and professional pageants. Many pieces staged in such settings echo social pastimes of the aristocracy such as tournaments, dressing-up games, and competitive sports. A well-known reference in *Sir Gawayne and the Grene Knyght* likens the knight's startling appearance to the

Laykyng [performing] of enterludes, to laghe and to syng,

Among thise kynde caroles of knightes and ladies (lines 472–3)
which form part of the Christmas festivities. But it is impossible to say just what the frequently-used term 'interludes' indicates in this or other contexts: professional performances of plays with dialogue, 'party-games' (*ludi*) between (*inter*) two teams or between two courses of a feast, miniature pageants analogous to the French *entremet* or Spanish *entremés*, all constitute examples of 'interludes' in medieval times. In England the word covered a variety of dramatic kinds from the ribald *Interludium de Clerico et Puella* to the sort of 'play' which Robert Mannyng in his thirteenth-century poem *Handlyng Synne* linked with carols (i.e. dance-songs), wrestling, and summer-games as things to be deplored when performed in churchyards and hallowed places, and which the anonymous author of the *Tretise of Miraclis Pleyinge* condemned as unsuitable for priestly participation. Yet an *Interludium de Corpore Christi*, mentioned at Bury St Edmunds in 1389, is clearly religious in nature.[2]

Whatever its contents, the interlude in Britain was not noted for its intellectual sophistication, at least until the last decade of the fifteenth century. It is at this period that examples of the secular interlude begin to appear, none providing more interest and entertainment than Henry Medwall's *Fulgens and Lucres*, an excellent example of a play specifically written with performance in the dining-hall or Great Chamber of some noble house in mind. In fact, it is a reasonable assumption that this piece was first staged before Cardinal John Morton, former Bishop of Ely and then Henry VII's Archbishop of Canterbury, in his palace of Lambeth, probably during the winter of 1497.

Fulgens and Lucres was published c. 1513–19 by John Rastell, brother-in-law to Thomas More, in whose circle Medwall mixed, both as a member of Morton's household, and as a liberal Catholic humanist. Little is known of Medwall's life except that he derived from the Home Counties, was of 'a good family', served Morton as chaplain until 1500, and was the author of another interlude entitled *Nature*; his best-known play did not even surface in its entirety until March 1919, when a unique quarto copy was discovered among the contents of Lord Mostyn's library (see Plate 17).[3] Medwall as cleric and tutor would himself have been qualified to direct the 1497 performance of his play, which was probably presented before the Flemish and Spanish ambassadors who were in England negotiating the marriage of Catherine of Aragon to Henry VII's eldest son Arthur, which took place in 1501.

The banqueting-hall of the traditional English country-house or town-palace would not naturally commend itself to the potential theatre-director as the ideal playing-place, being virtually on one level (apart from a dais with its 'high table' at the far end), and bounded at one end by entrances through which the food had to be brought to table from the kitchens across the passage.[4] A wooden partition-screen, frequently erected across these openings, shielded the diners in the hall from the draughty transverse passageway or 'entry' which gave access to the rest of the building; long dinner-tables for the common-or-garden diners flanked the side walls of the room, leaving the central area between the tables virtually free, to facilitate ease of service and movement (see Plate 18). One might feel this to be an unpromising location for dramatic purposes, offering only a long T-shaped rectangle within which to perform, to which only limited access was offered through two openings in the screens at one end, and from which the spectators' attention might well be diverted by the food and drink before them. Yet the medieval Great Hall did provide playwrights and actors with some excellent features, particularly the degree of intimacy it encouraged between the players, the diners who sat on three sides of them, and the attendants and menials who almost certainly crowded into the space at the foot of the hall around the screen-entrances to watch the action, and who frequently had to be shouldered aside by characters entering and leaving the room. Players could thus utilize the servants' quarters off the entry-passage as a green-room, make their entrances from the 'entry' into the hall through one of the two gaps in the screen, and immediately find themselves in close contact with spectators on at least two of the three sides of them, commanding as they did the centre of the floor. If they chose, they could also aim some of their dialogue and

PD

17 Figures from the title-page of *Fulgens and Lucres*
(Reproduced by permission of the Henry E.
Huntington Library, San Marino, California)

18 The Great Hall, Penshurst Castle, Kent, showing
the screen-entrances (Photo: *Country Life*)

business at those congregated to the rear of them, treating the auditorium as a virtually unbroken square. Greater variety in choice of locations for exists and entrances might have been desirable; movements might have been less constricted in a less confined space. Plays chosen for presentation obviously had to employ a minimum of scenery and offer maximum opportunities for audience-contact and participation, since spectators had primarily assembled for social ends rather than for theatrical ones (see Plate 19). Yet overall the setting and circumstances suited a resourceful and ingenious company very well, whether in the case of *Fulgens and Lucres* the players were a specially-imported team of professionals, or, as seems slightly more likely, a cast drawn from Morton's own household. Certainly it is hard to envisage a play such as *Fulgens and Lucres* being more satisfactorily staged in any other kind of auditorium; it would clearly prove unsuited to the conventional proscenium-theatre of the later nineteenth and early twentieth centuries, whereas efforts to revive it in conditions approximating to those of its original milieu have proved highly successful.

In attempting a reconstruction of the earliest performance of *Fulgens and Lucres*, it might technically be possible to assemble historical and architectural evidence for the appearance of the Hall at Lambeth Palace in 1497 and proceed from there, but this would involve too pedantic a concern for antiquarian accuracy, whereas it is more important to convey the *spirit* in which a presentation of an early Tudor interlude might have been given in a typical hall of the period. However, this does not prevent us from visualizing the situation at Lambeth Palace: the candlelit Hall on a great diplomatic and social occasion; the Cardinal, the visiting ambassadors, and other dignitaries on the High Table, the lesser lights dining at ground level on the side-tables; a good fire burning on the hearth (a fact alluded to in line 1302 of Part One of the interlude); a gaggle of unofficial onlookers milling about the screens, and the bustle of serving and clearing away giving place to an air of anticipation as the players prepare to take over. As Richard Southern reminds us,[5] the light would not necessarily be bright, though extra candles or torches may have focused all eyes on the playing-area; the arrival of torch-bearers may indeed have arrested enough attention for the action to begin, or perhaps there was an announcement by the 'marshall' later referred to.

The play is in two parts, and this division is primarily introduced to allow part of a feast to be served between the halves, though it is clear that some feeding at least has already taken place before the play commences, since almost as soon as the scene opens, Servant A rudely demands of the company:

Have not ye etyn & your fill,
And payd no thinge therfore? (I. 3–4)[6]

19 A royal feast in progress in a
medieval hall, with musicians below
the dais (MS Royal 1 E IX) (Photo:
British Library)

20 Masked dancers entering a banqueting-hall (MS Add 18991) (Photo: British
Library)

Yet by line 1409 we find him remarking that a break in the action is not only justified by the exigencies of the plot, but also for practical purposes:

An other thing must be considred withall,
These folke that sitt here in the halle . . .
Thay have not fully dyned;
For and [if] this play where ones overe past
Some of them wolde falle to fedyng as fast
As thay had bene almost pyned [starved];
But no forse hardely [little harm truly] and they do,
Ussher gete them goode wyne therto,
Fyll them of the best [!] (I. 1412–13; 1417–23)

It is evident that, although *Fulgens and Lucres* was deliberately structured to meet the demands of the occasion of its performance, Medwall's theatrical confidence permitted him to draw an audience's attention to the reason for the interval without making some more covert excuse.

Indeed, this acknowledged and fully-developed exploitation of the presence of spectators remains one of the most remarkable features of *Fulgens and Lucres*, particularly the sub-plot. It is certainly reflected in the brash manner in which Servant A makes his first entrance, and by the tone in which he addresses the assembled company on his arrival. Assuming the assured approach of the skilled professional comedian and relying on an audacious and resilient wit to enable him to mount a direct assault on his auditors' sensibilities, he accuses them of feeding at someone else's expense, of hoping to see dancing-girls perform, even abuses them for maintaining the silence which has fallen on them since the entertainment began! Erupting into a hall full of expectant spectators and stalking up and down between the tables, he reacts to his audience's very attentiveness by proceeding to insult them for their quiescence, employing the perennial hectoring, teasing manner still current among comedians today:

For goddis will
What meane ye syrs to stond so still?
. . . I mervayle moche of one thinge,
That after this mery drynkynge
And good recreacyon
There is no wordes amonge this presse [crowd] . . .
But as it were men in sadnes [deep contemplation]
Here ye stonde musynge
Whereaboute [what about] I can not tell (I. 1–2, 14–17, 19–21).

One possible explanation of A's allusions to *standing* spectators is that he is addressing himself to the lesser fry, on their feet at the end of the hall, those he accuses of sponging on Morton's charity, who were perhaps of insufficient substance to be offered seats at the tables.

Richard Southern argues[7] that by line 20 or thereabouts, Servant A has probably worked himself round the available floor-space and down to the screen-entrances once more in order to address one of the press of people about the doors. Designating him 'what calt' [Whatyoucallit], A confides that he means to find out what is about to take place:

Tell me what calt, is it not so?
I am sure here shalbe somewhat ado [something going on],
And I wis I will know it or [ere] I go
Withoute I be dryven hens (I. 24–7).

This is the cue for Servant B to stand forth. The obvious inference is that like A he comes into the hall through the screens, but since A is confused a little later as to whether or not B is a stage-player –

I trowe your owyn selfe be oon
Of them that shall play (I. 44–5) –

it might be more effective, even though the text refers to B *entering*, to have him 'enter' from among the crowd already assembled, especially since he acts like a spectator in reassuring A that no one will eject him if he wishes to watch the forthcoming play. If B comes out of a mass of spectators, Southern's anxiety to get A near enough to the entrance-screens to encounter B at close quarters is unnecessary, since B could impinge on the action from any part of the hall. While it might weaken the impact of A's gag that he has mistaken B for an actor because gentlemen now dress as flashily as players –

Ther is so myche nyce [showy] aray
Amonges these galandis [gallants] now aday
That a man shall not lightly [easily]
Know a player from another man (I. 53–6) –

should B simply appear from the crowd rather than coming in through the screens like a player, B's emergence from among similarly-dressed spectators might, on the other hand, give extra satirical point to A's remarks on dress, and so raise a bigger laugh. Furthermore, although Richard Southern argues that A's question to 'what calt' in line 24 is directed at any innocent bystander, since A also refers to B as 'what calt' in line 195, it is at least plausible that it is *B* who is singled out among the onlookers for A's special attention in line 24. Again, this tends to strengthen the view that the text's '*Intrat B*' means no more than that B steps out on to the playing-area at this point.

A is delighted to learn that a play is afoot, and seeks enlightenment as to its content from B, who summarizes the ensuing action. This is a frequent occurence in medieval plays, which never seems to have called forth protests from audiences that the revelation of the plot had impaired their enjoyment. It has been pointed out on numerous occasions that under the disguise of a debate-drama Medwall succeeds in effectively publicizing the policy of the relatively novel monarch Henry VII towards a larger part of the feudal aristocracy of whom he was rightly suspicious, and towards the 'new men' of his own choosing and creation whom he envisaged running the country according to his instructions. Thus in the final discrediting of Publius Cornelius the patrician, and the success of the plebeian Gaius Flaminius in obtaining the love of Lucres, the daughter of a Roman senator, Henry's intention of preferring as his deputies commoners whose loyalties were ultimately to the person of the king rather than to their own class is not only symbolized but promulgated.

Not that Medwall is so naive or unscrupulous as to deliver such propaganda neat or unleavened by any touch of humour or note of opposition. Indeed, almost as soon as B reveals the play's conclusion as to the relative merits of Lucres's two suitors, A announces his intention of persuading the senators of Rome to reverse the verdict:

I wyll advyse them to change that conclusion.
What, wyll they afferme that a chorles son
Sholde be more noble than a gentilman born? (I. 129–31),

thus raising doubts among the spectators that the action will necessarily proceed in quite the way B has outlined, although eventually all does conclude as planned! However, the interaction between the two servants and the characters of the main plot is one of the most theatrically rewarding aspects of Medwall's play, involving familiar contact between A, B, and the spectators, which helps both to 'frame' the work's serious, more political content, and to distance the Roman scenes sufficiently for an audience to view them objectively (especially as the play's probable outcome is known in advance), and to retain its capacity to analyse and judge the issues at stake. Here the uninhibited comments of A and B, who of course shortly attach themselves to the two suitors, encourage the auditors to debate the relative merits of birth and ability, reminding them that the actions and conduct of Cornelius and Flaminius are not only offered here in Brechtian style for assessment rather than mere amusement, but are also employed to contrast the fictional world of ancient Rome with the factual world of Tudor England, even though A and B in reality are members of the same troupe as those portraying Lucres, Fulgens, and the suitors, rather than watchers at the feast as they pretend to be. In this way, by commenting freely on the serious action even after they have become incorporated within it, and acting as proxies for the audience, A and B make the fiction of the Roman world less remote, yet ensure that it is recognized for the dramatic device that it is.[8]

This is made evident by the debate that ensues between the two men, in which A and B disclaim any connection with, or any responsibility for, the proceedings about to follow. However, they do discuss their pleasure in watching plays, and B defends the genre from A's charge that the players intend to hold truth and reason up to ridicule, though A still vows not to withhold his opinion on the two suitors when the piece has been safely concluded! At this point B announces the arrival of the acknowledged players:

Pees, no moo wordes, for now they come,

The plears bene evyn here at hand (I. 188–9).

A, startled, asks where he should stand to be out of the way, and B reassures him that they can stand together among the crowd. However, they do not join those impeding the screen-openings since these are the very people on whom B rounds sharply, telling them that the actors cannot enter until they stand aside:

Geve rome there syrs, for [before] God avowe [I vow]

Thei wold cum in if thei myght for you (I. 193–4).

It would therefore appear that the arrival of the players announced by B only brings them to the entry-passage beyond the screens, where they have to wait until the actor playing Fulgens finds the abashed onlookers have cleared a path for him to enter the hall. B therefore requires some signal of their presence to be given, and Glynne Wickham makes the plausible suggestion that a drum or trumpet is heard prior to B's 'Pees, no moo wordes'.[9] Fulgens can then enter, compose himself, take a few steps about the playing-area to establish his presence, while the whispered conversation between A and B subsides on B's promise that the anxious A will see the 'feyr doughter Lucrece' before very long.

Lucres's father Fulgens now launches forth on his very leisuredly speech of exposition whose formal style contrasts strongly with the colloquial freedom of the exchanges between A and B. Like them Fulgens no doubt permitted himself full use of the open space before the High Table and between the side-tables in which to move about and from which to deliver his somewhat sententious lines. Some of his remarks seem addressed towards the great ones ensconced on the dais; discussing God's gifts he remarks that

To some he geveth the grace of pre-emynence

In honour and degre . . . (I. 213–14),

a flattering allusion certainly not lost of Morton and his guests. Fulgens also appeals directly to the general assembly as A and B have done:

Am not I gretly bound in this case

To God, as I rehersid you bifore? (I. 271–2),

and at the end of his ninety-line stint it is of all the spectators that he enquires as to Cornelius's whereabouts:

. . . cam ther non suche here? (I. 291).

Thus even the 'ancient Roman' characters are able to make use of the favourable opportunities for intimate contact with an audience which a Great Hall setting offers.

Cornelius then enters, and converses with his putative father-in-law for some fifty lines. They pay no further attention to the spectators, but when Fulgens exits to sound out his daughter's feelings, Cornelius takes the audience into his confidence, and admits that he now stands in need of an experienced adviser to serve him, asking if anyone among the gathering will undertake the office:

> So many gode felowes as byn in this hall,
> And is ther non syrs among you all
> That wyll enterprise this gere? (I. 354–6).

Receiving no response, he goes off to 'seche a man ellis where', leaving A and B to take the floor. B instantly sees a role for himself as Cornelius's servant, and airily brushes aside A's shocked reaction to what he sees as an intrusion upon the fiction set before them – 'Be God thou wyll distroy all the play'. B's confident retort is that 'the play began never till now', and his counsel is that A should get himself a part in the action too by offering his services to Flaminius who has yet to appear. The artistic audacity of this breaching of the dividing-line between supposed reality (the everyday world of the banquet which A and B have 'invaded') and the fictional realm of Lucres and her Roman suitors can be too readily taken for granted. Medwall plays with his audience's sense of illusion here: two characters who have pretended to be part of the world of Tudor Lambeth watching a play about ancient Rome are now proposing to enter the play-world, but to retain their Tudor identities! A few lines later the pretence is elaborated by a typical theatrical device. Shall we get any profit out of our service as advisers? asks A, and B tells him to keep his voice down, or everyone in the place will know what they are up to!

> Hold thy pece, speke not so hye!
> Leste any man of this company
> Know oure purpose openly
> And breke all oure daunce [ruin our chances]! (I. 387–90)

The audience's sense of privilege at knowing something which the actors are at pains to pretend they want kept secret is of course part of the traditional dramatic 'game' enjoyed by performers and spectators.

B departs to importune Cornelius and the assembly is again taken into the confidence of another figure, as A confesses that he and B are 'maysterles' so that employment, especially in the service of men who are going courting and are thus less likely to count the pennies, will be doubly welcome. He then stands aside with the *bona fide* spectators to allow a discussion of about fifty lines to take place between Fulgens and Lucres touching on her marriage and the fact that the choice must rest between Cornelius and Flaminius. Lucres is accompanied by Jone her maid as well as her father, and when the latter departs, leaving Lucres to ponder her decision – the stage direction *'facta aliqua pausatione'* reinforcing the short pause for contemplation required by the text – it is the maid who spies Flaminius himself entering the hall and interrupts Lucres's deliberations with her urgent

Peace, lady! ye must forbere,
Se ye not who cometh here? (I. 477–8).

The line suggests that, if Flaminius enters through the screen (as he must unless we postulate the use of those entrances at the dais-end of the hall almost certainly reserved for the party dining at the High Table), Lucres must be near the foot of the dais as far from the screen-entrances as possible. Jone however, wandering a little way down the playing-area, sees Flaminius enter, and dodges back to tell her mistress. This allows Flaminius to make his entry and Jone to spot him immediately, yet gives him time to advance slowly down the room to greet Lucres, catching her last remark and responding to it:

Ey gode lorde how wyste he
For to fynde me here? (I. 482–3)

Dramatic convention and the nature of the venue mitigate the slight implausibility of Lucres's unawareness of her suitor's presence from the first.

Flaminius now engages Lucres in conversation, urging his suit and protesting his ardour, to which she responds by telling him that her decision will shortly be made known. Hereupon she departs accompanied by her maid, which renders A free to approach the plebeian, crossing the hall to recommend himself as a trusty servant, although it is significant that one of his first acts is to inform Flaminius that he has a rival. It is perhaps odd that A should be eager to serve the lower-born suitor of the pair, and flatteringly allude to him as 'a gentylman of youre substaunce' when attempting to ingratiate himself, since at the outset it was A who reacted scornfully to the notion that 'a chorles son / Sholde be more noble than a gentilman born . . .' and stated that he hoped to persuade the Senate to change its opinion. There *is* some inconsistency about the psychology of both A and B, but here at least we may infer that A is a little like the parasite of classical Roman comedy, who serves a master purely for personal gain, an impression which the flattery of A's approach and the lie that he has overheard Lucres speaking to Cornelius tends to strengthen. Certainly at the conclusion of the whole play A seems highly put out that his master should have been selected to marry Lucres on the basis of his greater virtue, so it may be that we should see his intention in entering service with Flaminius as mere mischief-making, rather as the Vices make mischief in the moralities, though A's purpose is obviously not to ensnare Gaius Flaminius's immortal soul! His function is perhaps closely akin to that of Merygreeke, the mocking trickster of Roister Doister in Nicholas Udall's comedy. He certainly lies to his employer when he claims that they were once acquainted, and produces B (who at some previous point must have mingled with the audience again) as his 'character witness':

Here is a gentilman that wolde truste me
For as moche gode as he hase . . .
It is as honest a man as ony in the reall [realm].
I have no more acqueyntaunce within this hall . . . (I. 626–7, 630–1)

B supports A without reservation, and the latter is then engaged. On Flaminius's departure B reveals that Cornelius has likewise taken *him* into service, so both the rogues are now employed by the competing suitors, a situation which promises well dramatically, and indeed their rivalry is shortly to be extended in predictable but engaging fashion. B praises Cornelius's prodigality and his lavish wardrobe intended to impress Lucres, the first indication of the patrician's suspect nature, and a nice shaft of satire against the contemporary nobility: B himself only lacks fashionable livery because he has been taken on so recently! Some further satire on the miseries of marriage follows from A who, according to him, has several wives who earn their living in the local brothel, but the somewhat extraneous gossip is cut short by A recalling that he has a message to deliver to Lucres from Flaminius, and he is horrified to hear from his colleague that Cornelius is already with her. Cursing B for deliberately delaying him, A is about to rush off when B asks him to deliver a message on his behalf to Lucres's waiting-woman Jone, for whom he has conceived a fancy. A, lying again, retorts that B is too late; *he* has already gained Jone's consent to be her lover, yet he blandly assures B that he has not yet had sex with her! He shoots off to do his errand, while B falls to musing on Jone's somewhat dubious charms, which he hopes to enjoy at least before A does. The play's serious theme is thereby humorously echoed in the comic sub-plot, anticipating the same device in many of the great comedies of the Elizabethan age, notably Dromio of Syracuse's courtship of Luce in *The Comedy of Errors*. There is a further point of interest: when B speaks of watching for Jone 'this odyr nyght', we are apt to let the remark go unnoticed just as we do the dual time-scheme in *Othello* unless we recall that, strictly speaking, Lucres's maid inhabits ancient Rome and that A and B only just 'stepped into' the action from contemporary Britain a short while before. Yet already their existences are being extended backwards into the fictional world of the 'play within a play'.

While B is assessing his chances with Jone, the object of his desire appears but remains unseen by him for several lines. We must assume that his back is turned or that he stands in a part of the hall from which entries through the screen could not easily be viewed; surprised by her presence he exclaims 'Cockis body here she is' (line 858), but from her response it is clear that she does not plan to stop, and that B physically detains her against her will:

Tusshe I pray you let me go,
I have somewhat els to do;
For this howre I have soughte
A man that I sholde speke withall
Fro my maystres (I. 862–6).

The likeliest explanation is that Jone enters the hall initially looking about her for Flaminius or his serving-man, gradually closing in on B preoccupied with her mission and thus oblivious of him until he deliberately gets in her way and either grabs her or forces his attentions on her in some other manner. Jone's entry must be timed carefully not to coincide with A's departure to seek Lucres, yet the fact that all exits and entries were almost certainly made only through the screen-openings seems confirmed by B's remark to Jone that A

went evyn now frome me,
And I marvel gretly that ye
Met hym not by the way . . . (I. 874–6).

To achieve this effect Jone and A must have taken care not to use the same screen-entrance, assuming that two openings to enable hot dishes to be carried into, and empty plates to be carried out of, the hall, were obligatory. Discovering that she has had a lost journey, Jone proposes to depart, but B insists that she stay and talk, and a lively passage of sexual sparring ensues. B mocks Jone to the audience when she claims to be a virgin, and impresses on her the joys of being married to himself, the girl holding out for a handsome dowry, and sneering at his romantic notions. She does permit him one kiss, but at this point A returns and interrupts the proceedings much to B's annoyance, although A is suspicious that more than a kiss has been exchanged. Once more Medwall makes full dramatic use of the audience's presence: how could I have made love to Jone? protests B:

Nay nay, here be to many wytnes
For to make ony syche besynes [business]
As thou wenest hardely [truly]. (I. 1017–19)

Once again the worlds of fiction and of actuality are allowed to collide with no sense of incongruity or self-consciousness: how could B get down to 'besynes' with so many diners looking on?

A and B not surprisingly quarrel over Jone's favours, a clear comic parallel to the serious rivalry of Cornelius and Flaminius for the love of Lucres. Like the mistress the maid vows that she will only bestow herself on the worthiest suitor, although her test takes the form of a trial of manly accomplishments. Rejecting quoits as childish, A and B compete at singing, at wrestling (a sport found incorporated into more than one

8 Artist's impression of *Fulgens and Lucres* in a Tudor Great Hall setting

medieval play),[10] and finally at mock-jousting, B challenging A by flinging down a leather glove in parody of chivalric behaviour. (Indeed, the whole sequence may glance at the archaic traditions of the old feudal aristocrats.) B claims that they will not need horses if they joust at 'farte pryke in cule' (which might be rendered as 'stick-up-the-bum') which seems to involve each individual, having his arms or hands bound together, being trussed to a staff thrust behind the knees as he crouches down, and being provided with an improvized spear.[11] Clearly the traditional links between interludes and popular sports or party-games are very strong at this point, but the exact jousting procedure is hard to establish. The jousting analogy must mean that the two combatants charge each other in some way, and that A, who is the more nervous of the pair since he appeals to the spectators to

Fall to prayer syrs, it is nede,

As many of you as wolde me gode spede (I. 1201–2),

is 'speared' (in the buttocks?) by B and falls down crying out with assumed pain. As he does he breaks wind, much to B's disgust, yet neither helpless warrior is freed from his bonds by Jone who now calmly announces that she has another lover to whom she is engaged, and proceeds to batter both the trussed jousters before skipping triumphantly out. Gaius Flaminius enters swiftly and releases A and B from their fetters, but A, not daring to recount the true facts, manufactures a Falstaff-like story about being set on by Cornelius's servants who caused the gaping wound in his behind (no doubt much bawdy laughter greeted this remark), although B had valiantly come to his rescue. Flaminius sees through this fabrication, and at this point B, possibly fearing a further beating, may well dart to one side. However, the action does not require him to leave the hall entirely as Boas and Reed's interpolated stage direction at line 1286 implies; indeed, the text does not authorize such a significant exit. B simply nips out of trouble for some thirty lines while Flaminius talks to A.

Flaminius, however, is more anxious to pump A for news of Lucres's reactions to his suit than to punish his servant, and once informed that she will make her decision that evening or the next day, in the presence of her father, her suitors, and 'this honorable audyence', the plebeian leaves. Richard Southern argues sensibly that A accompanies him down the hall, which accounts for the direction in the text *'exeat Gaius & A'*, but that, having seen him out, A returns in time to catch the last part of B's speech.[12] Although the stage direction by which B is reintroduced reads *'Intrat B'*, B's opening words suggest that he has only to step forward to become part of the action once more. He bemoans his wounds which are still smarting from Jone's attentions, but A is all for forgetting their humiliation. B vows to get even with the girl who has ill-treated him, although he is also fearful of punishment from Cornelius for his long absence. A reassures him that Cornelius is unlikely to have missed him since he has other matters to consider: the audience is led to assume that when A 'went hens' to bring his master on his way, he encountered some of Lucres's household-servants around the screen-entry who told him that she had informed Cornelius that he was to meet her in the hall around supper-time and so receive the answer to his suit. A and B now debate as to whether the pleb or the patrician will prove the 'most noble' suitor, B favouring Cornelius with his blue blood and riches, but A warning him that the end of the piece may have a lesson to teach him, if he comes back to witness the *dénouement*. B is indignant that he should be put to the trouble of having to return to know the outcome of the courtship, and asks why the business cannot be cleared up then and there. A explains that Fulgens and Lucres are otherwise engaged at the moment and that time is still needed in order for Flaminius and Cornelius to prepare the best cases for themselves that they can: they will be worth hearing when they do dispute together! Moreover, another important consideration brings us back to the real world of Lambeth Palace and the feast: the diners are waiting patiently for their second course! The players must not outstay their welcome. And so with a blending of factual and fictional reasons for an intermission, A and B leave the hall, and the feasting gets under way once again.

★ ★ ★

The length of the interval which intervenes before the action recommences is impossible to gauge, but it is evidently of sufficient length for A's initial recapitulation of the situation in Part Two to seem justified, even if he compliments the audience on the fact that their 'wittis be not so short' as to have forgotten the subject at issue. By rushing in and pretending to be fearful lest he has arrived too late for the decision, A arrests the diners' attention as he did at the opening, although this time he is deferential, even apologetic, especially on the grounds that some spectators may have objected to the 'dyvers toyes mengled' with the serious 'matter principall' of the first half, but defending the horseplay as intended

To styre folke to myrthe and game (II. 23),

its purpose being to delight even 'the leste that stondyth here', another indication that the standing auditors were those of lower social status. Leaving his digression, A reminds his listeners of the dramatic context, marvels that the players (rather than the play's characters) have not yet arrived (thus freely admitting to the fiction of the drama), and is just contemplating the time, when a tremendous knocking is heard at the door, to which A responds:

A there commyth one, I here hym knoke,

He knokythe as he were wood [insane].

One of you go loke who it is (II. 73–5).

But B (for it is he) bounces in angrily and so forestalls any members of the audience unselfconscious or officious enough to rise to admit him. He is indignant at the tardiness of those who have left him to bruise his knuckles seeking entry. (No one thinks to question why he should need to knock for admission in the first place!) A chides him for his rudeness to the assembly, but B retorts that he little deserves abuse from A since he has only shown up at his fellow's suggestion that it might benefit him to do so. B seems on the point of withdrawing out of pique:

Now God be with you, so mote I the [thrive] (II. 96)

and probably begins to stalk off in a rage. However, A shames him into returning – 'Turne agayne, all be shrewyde [cursed by one and all]!' – and the quarrel is swiftly made up, so that the courtship of Lucres can be briefly mentioned, A declaring himself worried that the delay means that someone has got cold feet. B provides the additional information that Cornelius has hired 'certayne straungers fresshly disgisyd' to entertain Lucres, which not only brightens A's spirits –

A then I se well we shall have a mummynge (II. 126) –

but no doubt those of the spectators as well, at the thought of an extra spectacle.

A few lines later Cornelius himself arrives. Again the audience's attention is alerted to the arrival of one character by other figures some distance from the screen-entrances:

B: Mary here he commyth, I have hym aspyde.
    No more wordis, stonde thou asyde,
    For it is he playne (II. 131–3).

Cornelius is somewhat irritated by B's frequent absences from him, but the wily servant excuses himself by blandly assuring his employer that he has come to check whether Fulgens, Lucres, and Flaminius have arrived yet for the arbitration; he is told to go and find them. But B feels that his candidate for Lucres's favours is demeaning himself by appearing first and then being forced to await the pleasure of others; he advises his master to withdraw and when the rest of the company is assembled and everything is prepared, then the mighty Cornelius can be called forth!

The patrician accepts B's advice, provided that if Lucres appears first and alone, B will try to elicit from her some statement of her true feelings towards his master's suit. As a token of B's authority to execute such a delicate task, B is to recall to Lucres how Cornelius cast a ball into the hole in a hollow ash-tree to scare away a bird perched there. Cornelius departs to await his summons, while B confides to the audience that in his view the incident he has been told to cite as a 'token' suggests that his master is mad, but that he is merely the messenger and will speak as he has been told to. His reluctance intrigues the audience, and the seventy or so lines which follow painstakingly set up and exploit B's misunderstanding that, thanks to the ambiguities of Tudor pronunciation, he has been instructed to recall that his master (or Lucres) 'kissed' the other 'on the hole of th'arse'. Though the joke itself may be a poor one (even by early Tudor standards), its handling to create maximum amusement and comic tension is not without ingenuity. Medwall uses the familiar tactic of having B see Lucres in the distance before she makes her way to within playing-distance of him; he welcomes her and says that he has sought her two or three times within the hour, her queries as to his mission increasing the audience's curiosity too. As in the 'Carry On' films of the recent past, the obscene jest is then built up to by slow stages, agonizing if one knows the joke to come, intriguing if one does not. Again full value is extracted from the presence of the audience, for B, thinking to spare Lucres's reputation, offers to keep the details of her sexual activities to himself:

happely ye wold not have it declared
Byfore all this audience (II. 272–3),

Lucres unwittingly adding to the fun by innocently declaring that all the world may hear *her* deeds, though of course she is outraged when B delivers what he thinks is Cornelius's message! In fact, the laboured jest turns out to be the least part of this routine of misunderstanding: there is great humour in B's finer feelings for Lucres's honour, and in his desire to carry out his orders in spite of them, in his dogged attempt to get the message correct, in his anxiety to justify what he believes has occurred between the lovers – 'it was done for gode love / And for no synfull pleasure' he pronounces – and in his Costard-like concern for complete accuracy:

on the hole of thars I shulde say,
I wyst well it was one of the too,
The noke or the hole (II. 285–7).

When Lucres corrects his mistake, B suffused with shame at his misapprehension frames a confused apology and beats a hasty retreat, promising to learn his errand properly before he returns.

Lucres, not unduly shocked by the mistaken 'token', protests to the audience at the gross lewdness of the message. She is rapidly joined by A who says he has a letter from Flaminius, but immediately discovers that he has lost it on the way, possibly in the hall itself, an excellent excuse for once again involving the assembled spectators in the action:

Syrs is there none there among you
That toke up suche a wrytyng?
I pray you syrs, let me have it agayne (II. 326–8).

One can imagine much scrabbling under benches and searching under tables going on at this point; Wickham in his edition comments that it is not clear from the Quarto text whether the letter is found and returned or not, but the ensuing lines make it plain that no letter is handed over, for Lucres still remains ignorant of whom A serves. Furthermore, when she asks A his master's name, he has forgotten it or has possibly never known it, so Lucres sends him off to discover it, and indeed to find out his own name which also seems temporarily to have escaped him. (At this point one of the few explicit pieces of stage-business in the field of the Tudor Interlude occurs, for the text tells us that A, when trying to recall his own name, 'scratches his head for some short while'.) He promises to find it out from some of his company, which may refer either to the other members of Flaminius's household or the other members of the acting troupe. At all events, A goes out, leaving Lucres alone.

We are now over 350 lines into the second half, and so far the play has done little more than mark time. But the dramatic tension has been rising steadily, and now the serious action of the piece is about to build to its climax. Cornelius enters once more (although any stage direction to that effect is lacking) accompanied by B who has presumably fetched him as agreed, and begins to pay court to Lucres. She arrests him, however, saying that the contest must wait until Flaminius arrives, and warns him as well that violence and brawling are forbidden during the debate, which helps to colour Cornelius's character further. To pass the time, Cornelius offers her a diversion in the form of 'a bace daunce after the gyse / Of Spayne' which Lucres agrees to view: we may here recall the presence of the Spanish and Flemish ambassadors on the dais. Presumably it is B who is despatched to summon the musicians and dancers to perform, but the text is unhelpful at this point. B's news that one of the instrumentalists has a sore lip and cannot play may be intended to cover his re-entry to the hall along with the entertainers (see Plate 20), though he may simply remain where he is and obtain the information from the performers as they assemble. The dialogue at this juncture seems inadequate for the amount of activity going on, and possibly a vital stage direction and some lines of dialogue have dropped out. B urges the musicians to begin, addressing them in pidgin-Flemish, and the stately 'base dance' is now presented, the actors presumably tucking themselves out of the way while the dancers occupy the floor, though if Lucres is to retain her stage character, she needs to take a seat somewhere in view, with the ardent Cornelius hovering in attendance. At the close there is some discussion of the dancers' country of origin, B believing that they are 'wylde Irissh portyngales'; he is then instructed by Cornelius to stop chattering and to take the entertainers off to 'make them chere'. B ushers them to the kitchens to eat, dropping a comedian's perennial aside as he goes:

But one thing I promyse you faithfully,

They get no drynke therto [with it] (II. 403-4).

The danger of laying on 'drinks for the band' seems to have been recognized even in 1497!

At some point during the dancing, Flaminius, possibly accompanied by A, has arrived, for no sooner have the mummers been catered for than Lucres perceives him, and informs Cornelius. The decks are now cleared for the great debate, the only curious factor being that Fulgens is not present to hear it as had been the original intention. His absence cannot be explained by the necessity of doubling his part with another, since he has to appear on stage with every other character at some point, with the exception of Flaminius, though if Fulgens were to double with Flaminius, he would have a bare six lines in Part One to change both costume and appearance. His disappearance from the action is a mystery, as is that of Lucres's maid Jone, a prominent figure in Part One, unless she supports her mistress throughout the latter part of the piece and says nothing, which is unlikely given her sharp wits and pert tongue.

Lucres next agrees to adjudicate between the rival claims of her suitors, making it plain that her judgement in this case is not be taken as a universally valid precedent, not (as Southern claims[13]) that her verdict shall be made known to the two disputants alone. The central action of the play is thus initiated and it lasts some 330 lines; while it is clearly the doctrinal centre of the piece it raises few problems of staging or interpretation, each lover taking it in turn to make his case for being considered the more noble of the pair. The only moment of dramatic excitement comes about two-thirds of the way through Cornelius's speech when he starts to mount a personal assault on Flaminius's lowly birth and his present attempt to challenge the nobility on equal terms. Lucres intervenes and censures Cornelius's manner of proceeding (although Flaminius is more than prepared to answer the charges), and the patrician has to revert to a rehearsal of his ancestral virtues, his personal substance and liberality, and to stressing what a 'thredebare lyvynge' Lucres is likely to enjoy once married to the pleb. By making Cornelius a snob and a social bully, Medwall now begins to load the dice against him, and Flaminius, when it is his turn, is provided with an opportunity to address the assembled company as a whole before attempting to demolish his rival's pretensions to nobility of spirit. He not only claims that Cornelius and many of his ancestors have done little for the 'comon wele of this noble cytie', but accuses him of a variety of evil and disruptive deeds (reflecting Lucres's earlier strictures) and of leading a voluptuous and bestial life, arguing that

the title of noblenes wyll not ensue [be granted]
A man that is all gevyn to suche insolence,
But it groweth of longe continued vertu (II. 642-4).

Flaminius makes a spirited defence of the equality of all men, but argues that what makes one man excel another is virtue and godliness, not the accidents of blue blood and the possession of great wealth. When he has finished, Cornelius wishes to refute the charges, but Lucres (who has allowed Flaminius to attack the patrician far more freely than she allowed Cornelius to attack *him*) somewhat unfairly denies him the right of reply unless he can produce fresh arguments, and proceeds to ask if either suitor can summon witnesses to support his stated claims. Both say that they are content to be judged by public opinion in general, and at this point there occurs something of an anti-climax, at least in theatrical terms. Instead of announcing her verdict, Lucres says that she will now go and make enquiries and having done so, will then deliver her final decision *by letter*! Cornelius ardently desires to be kept in suspense no longer, but Flaminius is prepared to wait, a difference in response which some might regard as a testimony to Cornelius's deeper sincerity, but it is obvious that the burden of sympathy has now swung even more strongly in favour of Flaminius, although both suitors depart from the hall in a state of unknowing.

Yet it is not difficult to understand Medwall's dramatic strategy. The question of true nobility has been fully and plausibly set forth by the disputants, and the playwright has been at pains to keep the issues alive and fluid, despite his own quite unequivocal preferences. A crushingly total victory for one side or the other might have suggested that the debate was a mere formality; indeed, the heavily partisan treatment of the pleb late in the play comes dangerously near to diminishing one's interest in the *dénouement*, so blatantly is Flaminius's superiority engineered. Yet even here Lucres's firm but unstrident summary of her feelings in choosing Flaminius as the worthier man is deliberately contrived to mitigate any suggestion that hers is the definitive solution:

Now som mayde happely [possibly], & she were in my case,

Wolde not take that way that I do intend . . . (II. 752–3)

While she prefers her honest plebeian she does not despise all those of noble blood; however,

. . . unto the blode I wyll have lytyl respect

Where tho [those] condicyons [morals] be synfull and abject (II.
764–5).

But before she has completed her speech with an appeal to the audience not to think that she is advocating anarchy or the abolition of social hierarchy, B returns and, catching her drift, cannot help exploding with scornful horror to register that he has just heard a woman of gentle birth say

That by a chorles son she wolde set more

Than she wolde do by a gentylman bore [born] (II. 771–2)

This deliberately 'planted' speech gives Lucres the opportunity to expand on her judgement: virtue is to be praised in all men; noble blood is not to be revered purely for itself; *noblesse oblige*. She sums up the distinction:

. . . a man of excellent vertuouse condicions [moral conduct],

Allthough he be of a pore stoke bore [born],

Yet I wyll honour and commende hym more

Than one that is descendide of ryght noble kyn

Whose lyffe is all dissolute and rotyde [rooted] in syn (II. 789–93)

Her decision to marry Flaminius stems from this conviction; while she respects the aristocracy in general, she will not assent to wed Cornelius simply because of his blood. Then, suddenly pouncing on the unfortunate B, she tells *him* to convey her decision to his employer:

Ye be hys servaunt syr, go your way

And report to your mayster evyn as I say (II. 806–7)

Her promise to convey her judgement by letter after weighing the evidence forgotten, the masterful Lucres sweeps out of the hall. It may be that some of B's aggrieved reply is shouted after her as she goes:

Shall I do that erand? nay let be,

By the rode, ye shall do it yourselfe for me! (II. 808–9);

on the other hand, even from an outspoken servant anxious to avoid a beating from an irate Cornelius as the bearer of bad tidings, such a tone is a trifle brash, and 'Shall I do that erand?' may well be addressed to the audience as Wickham's edition suggests,[14] with B picking on a sufficiently docile-looking spectator as his substitute – 'ye shall do it yourselfe for me!' But B soon drops the idea, and grumbles about a decision which will drive Cornelius frantic, although B's personal response to his master's disappointment seems to be 'Good riddance to bad rubbish'!

The play is winding down now, but we naturally expect a final exchange between A and B who began the proceedings 2,000 lines and several courses ago, and have acted as our link with the main action throughout: we are not to be disappointed. A breezes in, asking the audience for news:

What now syrs how goth the game? (II. 830)

and B probably strides down the hall to inform him that Lucres has departed, and that Flaminius is preferred on account of his virtue. Even A as the victor's servant is baffled as to what kind of commodity virtue can be to be so highly prized, and asks the women among the spectators (indirectly informing us that ladies were present at this particular Tudor banquet) if that is the criterion they employ when choosing a husband? It is certainly not the basis on which men choose their *wives*, says B slily, no doubt nudging A in the ribs to point up the joke, and so some hoary satire follows on the subject of shrewish wives and how to treat them, although A breaks in and informs B that no one cares tuppence about his matrimonial advice. He is more concerned about their own fate now that their period of domestic service with Cornelius and Flaminius is at an end, and B has to tell him that they are free to go. A appears to be in a state of disappointed disbelief at this:

Why than is the play all do [done]? (II. 875)

We're the only people preventing it from coming to an end, says B, but A is reluctant to give over yet, rather as the duller Rosencrantz in Tom Stoppard's *Rosencrantz and Guildenstern Are Dead* is more unwilling than Guildenstern to let go his hold on life. I thought that matters would have ended in some other way, A says somewhat plaintively to B; what other conclusion could there be in the circumstances? asks his partner:

Is not the question
Of noblenes now fully defynde,
As it may be so [as far as it can be] by a womans mynde? (II. 883–5)

The diners have enjoyed a blend of instruction and amusement which B hopes, for all its deficiencies, has brought the company pleasure; if anything has offended them, they are to attribute it to the author's inadequacy, and perhaps a better man will take it upon himself to improve matters. As these traditional aspirations and apologies are being expressed, A and B move together through the hall to the screen-entrances where they turn so that B can deliver his final lines before these player-servants pass out through the screens to join their fellows assembled in the entry-passage, prior to returning to take their bow in among the audience with whom they have forged such an intimate bond during the staging of *Fulgens and Lucres*.

It is this intimacy between players and audience which forms the most notable feature of the action. Staged with no scenery, utilizing only the standard furnishings of a Tudor dining-hall, *Fulgens and Lucres* relies on the success with which its performers, especially the comedians, establish a *rapport* with the spectators surrounding them. That success seems reflected in the ready connivance accorded the frequent bawdry and horseplay imported into the serious matter by A and B, and to their ability to blend into the ancient Roman dimension while still retaining their Tudor identities. The theatrical sophistication and assurance of *Fulgens and Lucres* are a far cry from that 'tedious brief scene' performed in another great chamber for the entertainment of another noble company by Peter Quince and his friends.

Part Three

The English Medieval Theatre

I

Fortunately for our understanding of medieval theatre, playgoers of the western world in recent decades have become less hidebound by tradition. Perhaps, more accurately, we have rediscovered earlier habits of dramatic presentation than those prevailing since the Industrial Revolution. Since we no longer hold it an article of faith that stage-plays must be staged in custom-built playhouses or nowhere, we are prepared to sit on the hard floor of a drama studio or an equally hard pew in a place of worship, or to be squashed into a crowded pub. We are conditioned to accept that a theatrical experience can be created at any time and in any place where two or three are prepared to gather together in its name.

To the best of our knowledge, the Middle Ages possessed few if any permanent sites exclusively prepared and reserved for theatrical performances, although certain individuals may have understood the object for which the occasional surviving Roman amphitheatre was built, and used it for similar purposes from time to time.[2] But, in this, organizers of plays were merely following the predominant principle of utilizing whatever facilities came to hand, so that refectories in monasteries, audience-chambers in palaces, choirs of cathedrals, and halls of country-houses became eligible as playing-places. Nor did the principle cease to apply when outdoor presentation was called for. Village-greens, market-squares, churchyards, tavern-gardens, inn-yards, open spaces before ecclesiastical edifices or town-walls, areas of public recreation and assembly, were used whenever required. While specially-constructed sites were no doubt prepared occasionally it was far more common to adopt an existing location which could offer an adequate approximation to what could otherwise be achieved only by long hours of manual labour costing both time and money. It is known, for example, that at Shrewsbury 'the quarry outside the walls' provided an appropriate site for plays, since it supplied suitable spectator-accommodation on its sloping sides with a level base below for the erection of scaffolds. Goodybower Close adjoining what is now Wakefield Cathedral may well have been the venue for that town's mystery cycle performances, for this field too contained a convenient quarry-pit. At Norwich the lost cycle was probably staged at one of the open spaces (Chapel Field or Tombland) on the edge of the city, and Crockley Green, the site of the New Romney Passion play of 1560, could also have been employed in more or less its natural state. It has even been argued that the now well-known East Anglian 'game-places', allusions to which form a feature of local dramatic records, were rarely permanent structures, but rather open sites at which temporary scaffolds or 'stages' were set up.[3] Public assembly-areas sometimes offered themselves too, as at Clerkenwell Fields in North London, which supplied citizens with an open plain where they could pursue every type of recreational activity, including '*luctas* [wrestling] *et alios ludos*', the ambiguous final term probably incorporating the notion of stage-plays.[4] That such performance-sites were temporarily or permanently modified to assist players and spectators is certainly possible, though much would depend on the nature of the terrain to be adapted, and on the frequency of theatrical performances. Even if this were done, on many occasions drama would be only one of a number of attractions competing for attention in a public place, as Brueghel's 'The Fair of St George' makes plain. Mere players are unlikely to have been granted any very special favours.

Such naturally-occurring areas in town and country are likely to have formed the earliest performance-sites in Britain, though at this distance in time we cannot always point them out with confidence, or describe the form their theatrical offerings would have taken. But the perennial requirements were obviously an area to see from and an area to be seen in, and these could be met to a limited extent by nothing more than an accessible flat region in which people could foregather, provided that those wishing to view the spectacle on display did not exceed a certain number. Such a system can perhaps be seen in operation in the manuscript illustration of performers with a dancing bear in Harleian manuscript 603 (see Plate 6), or in Brueghel's 'The Procession to Calvary' where the crowd encircling the Crucifixion forms a ring no more than three or four deep (see Plate 21). Although Brueghel depicts a slight mound elevated above the plain as his 'playing area', there was little real need for the *platea* to be raised, or for scaffolds to be built to assist vision for only a few spectators, and modest presentations 'on the level' were no doubt common all through the period.

One of the earliest British references to the use of sites within towns and cities for drama is contained in a cartulary of King Edgar dated c. 960 where he complains of entertainers mocking the deficiencies of the monastic orders while performing *in triviis*, that is to say, in the public

21 Detail from 'The Procession to Calvary' by Pieter Brueghel the Elder (1564) (Photo: Kunsthistorisches Museum, Vienna)

squares and local marketplaces of his kingdom.[5] Such areas would doubt-less have remained viable for performances as long as they proved adequate to accommodate such spectators as wished to spectate. As the population expanded or performances became more widespread, sites within towns no doubt proved too congested, unless the community was fortunate enough to possess some spacious central space, such as the Pavement at York, which offered a convenient place of assembly for public announcements, civic gatherings, executions and other spectacles, and as stated earlier, possibly formed the 'theatre' for a single presentation of the city cycle at the end of the continuous procession of pageant-waggons.[6] A similar spot was no doubt the home of those semi-illicit entertainments at Exeter in the mid-fourteenth century complained of by Bishop John de Grandisson as taking place *in Theatro nostrae Civitatis*, a phrase which must mean a place of public resort rather than a playhouse.[7]

However, some playing-places do appear to have had a more exclusive function, even if they were not always devoted entirely to accommodating plays. Some relatively late documentation from Edinburgh is suggestive; in October 1552 James Henderson offered to construct a play-field between 'the Gray Freyr porte and the Kirk of Field' where 'interludis' as well as martial exercises could be carried out, but the site chosen was eventually 'in the Grenesyd', a stretch of low land to the north of Calton Hill, where on 12 August 1554 Sir David Lindsay's *Ane Satire of the Thrie Estaitis* was staged before the Queen Regent and 'ane greit part of the Nobilitie with an exceding great nowmer of pepill'.[8] In such instances suitable areas were merely adapted to make them more commodious, convenient, or accessible. However, a reference of 1577 to a 'game-place' at Walsham-le-Willows in Suffolk suggests that sometimes something more permanent, involving construction-work (and even landscape gard-ening) was set up:

> The sayd game place . . . is . . . a place compassed rownd with a
> fayer banke cast up on a good height & havinge many great trees
> called populers growynge about the same banke, in the myddest a
> fayre round place of earth wythe a stone wall about the same to the
> height of the earth made of purpose for the use of Stage playes . . .

Kenneth M. Dodd in his illuminating article on the Walsham site[9] draws parallels with the *plen-an-gwary* of Cornish tradition, in which a similar circular mound supported by a stone wall surrounded a level performance-area. Perhaps the only true surviving example is the celebrated Perran Round, near Perranporth (see Plate 11) although arguments have also been advanced in favour of regarding the remains of a circular arena at St Just-in-Penwith as a medieval playing-site, and clearly both structures are of the required type.[10] In general terms, however, we may assume that it was more usual for outdoor plays to be presented at natural places of public assembly and recreation rather than at specially-prepared ones.

One such natural assembly-area for medieval villagers and townsfolk was the local churchyard, at this period far freer of the densely-packed funeral monuments of today. Here fairs and markets were held, often to the detriment of Sunday worship, and numerous episcopal injunctions complain of wrestling-bouts, dancing, and ball-games on this piece of consecrated ground which also presented a tempting site for the staging of plays.[11] One of the most famous allusions to this practice comes from Beverley in Yorkshire in about 1220 when one summer 'within the enclosure formed by buttresses on the north side of the Church of Blessed John a representation of the Lord's Resurrection was set forth in dialogue and action by the customary masked players . . . the closely-packed populace standing around in a circle . . .'.[12] Whatever the auspices for such a performance (and they suggest the unofficial religious 'miraclis' frowned on by orthodox clergymen), the nature of the site and the encirclement of the action follow a familiar pattern. All such activities met with opposition from those framing diocesan statutes in the thirteenth century, and countless injunctions testify to ecclesiastical displeasure at the abuse of holy ground.[13] Among its early opponents were Archbishop Stephen Langton of Canterbury, Bishop Richard Poore of Salisbury and later Durham, and Robert Grosseteste, Bishop of Lincoln, but the essence of their attitudes is conveyed in the humbler but more engaging words of Robert Mannyng, author of the lengthy Middle English poem *Handlyng Synne* of 1303, which in addition to warning clerics what dramatic activities are permitted them and which not, proceeds to warn the laity against a sacrilegious attitude towards church premises, especially graveyards:

> Karolles [round-dances], wrestlynges, or somour games,
> Who-so ever haunteth any swyche shames
> Yn cherche, other yn chercheyerd,
> Of sacrylage he may be a-ferd;
> Or entyrludes, or syngynge,
> Or tabure bete, or other pypynge,
> Alle swyche thyng forbodyn es,
> Whyle the prest stondeth at messe (8987–94).

Mannyng goes on to recount the colourful legend of the dancers of Kölbigk punished for dancing round the church during the Christmas Mass by being forced to dance on for twelve further months inseparably linked hand to hand.[14]

Church performances also come under Mannyng's scrutiny, and he informs clerks in Holy Orders that while they should not 'make or se' 'myracles', plays in church are not forbidden entirely:

He may yn the cherche, thurgh thys resun,
Pley the resurreccyun, –
. . . And he may pleye, withoutyn plyght [danger, risk]
Howe God was bore [born] yn yole nyght,
. . . Yif thou do hyt yn weyys or grenys [streets or open spaces]
A syght of synne truly hyt semys . . . (4641–2, 47–8, 51–2)

Plays which are doctrinal in nature and purpose – perhaps Mannyng refers to liturgical pieces – are to be encouraged, but only if presented reverently in the church as part of the divine office, not informally and without sufficient reverence to amuse the passing stranger amid the hurly-burly of everyday secular life. Conversely, church-plays which contain scurrilous matter are indicted, notably by Bishop John Trillek of Hereford in 1348,[15] but these were probably of the type performed by clerics and choirboys during Christmas week, when the 'Feast of Fools' was celebrated accompanied by many forms of licence. Alluded to by Bishop de Grandisson in his prohibitions of 1360 as *'ludos ineptos et noxios'* these activities represented a rather special case. Certainly dramas continued to be played in churches throughout Britain late into the sixteenth century at least: as late as 1577 the churchwardens of West Ham were charged with allowing two plays to be staged in the parish church by 'comon players' on the Sunday before Lady Day, and on Lady Day itself, 'and the people were suffered to stand upon the communion table, diverse of them'.[16] However, church performances of a less secularized nature remain relatively common into the final quarter of the century.

For those in more privileged circumstances drama could be enjoyed at a variety of indoor sites. For the inhabitants of abbeys, priories, and monasteries, refectories supplied an obvious venue for travelling players and entertainers of all types to perform in, and the later records of Selby Abbey, for example, contain notable references to plays and players.[17] Durham Priory too numbered drama among its diversions, although E. K. Chambers's assertion that by 1465 one of its rooms designated 'le Playerchambre' was reserved for theatricals is viewed sceptically by a recent historian of the foundation.[18] Between 1422 and 1461 Maxstoke Priory in Warwickshire paid entertainers from neighbouring townships such as Daventry and Coventry to perform there, and although one cannot be certain that stage plays were always involved, it is reasonable to conclude that this often was the case. The great halls of castles and palaces fulfilled the same kind of function; possibly the miracle play of St Katherine staged c. 1100–10 by Geoffrey of Le Mans with boys from the choir-school at Dunstable was in fact presented before Henry I at Kingsbury Palace rather than in a place of worship.[19] Subsequent centuries offer plentiful examples of presentations taking place in minor and major palaces up and down the kingdom. The nobility, aristocracy, even the clergy, encouraged dramatics in their private houses, particularly significant being the possibility that *Wisdom* had its *première* in the Bishop of Ely's Holborn palace, and that Cardinal Morton sanctioned the playing of *Fulgens and Lucres* at Lambeth.[20]

Places of education could also accommodate plays. Winchester College played host to theatrical performers at various dates during the fifteenth century, rewarding 'the players of the city of Wynton [Winchester]' in 1400 and a 'summer king' twelve years later. In 1467 John Pontisberry and his partner performed in the college hall.[21] Records of similar functions at Eton extend almost as far back, and several Cambridge and Oxford colleges seem to have staged plays in their halls at least as early as the reign of Henry VII.

Perhaps the most important factor is that few of the sites selected were primarily intended for the exclusive purpose of staging plays. This has considerable bearing on the art of the playwright, performer, and director (if we may employ so recent a term for one whose medieval function is so shadowy). The variation in size between one site and another must also have had an effect on presentational styles, and the contrast between playing in the open air within a *plen-an-gwary* holding 2,000 people, and acting before a handful of nobles in the candlelit chamber of some private mansion must have been most marked. From the players it obviously required quite as broad a histrionic range as most modern actors display in switching between theatre, film, and television. There is of course no evidence that all medieval players were capable of meeting such a challenge, but it is something to be considered whenever we are tempted to dismiss medieval acting as lacking in technique, versatility, or method.

To what extent did choice of location leave its effect on the theatrical style of the works presented? As we have seen, plays presented in large auditoria such as those required for the Cornish cycle plays or performances of *The Castel of Perseveraunce* certainly had to dispense with extreme subtleties of visual and aural effect, and make their points boldly and graphically, often employing a deliberately repetitive, even incantatory, mode of address, and a demonstrative style of gesture. A text such as *The Castel of Perseveraunce* can be cut quite extensively without losing its essential elements, since verbal display is lavish and cumulative, as if a large, mainly non-literate audience stationed at some distance from the action demanded generous reiteration of the dialogue in order to absorb situations and sentiments. But the linguistic texture of plays reasonably certain to have been presented 'by weyys and grenys', in inn-yards and on market-squares, is less elaborately repetitive, and the action less formally structured. We need only contrast in this respect *Mankynde* with *The Castel*. Where an audience is mobile, thickly-thronged and close to the stage, response is quicker, points are taken more readily, dramaturgy is more subtle, than where spectators are dispersed over a wider area and enjoy a less intimate relationship with the players. Moreover, plays at custom-built or adapted sites can generally pursue a more leisuredly, expansive pace of development than can dramas staged in places of commercial activity or public resort. In the latter instance, after all, place and time are not entirely of the performers' own choosing, and the attendant pressures affect the presentational style adopted.

Besides which, at many medieval sites, a drama had to impose itself on the venue selected. One imagines that on numerous occasions citizens or villagers had to be persuaded to watch drama in spite of themselves, in situations where a theatrical experience offered itself only as one of a number of attractions competing on a holiday morning, to be sampled or rejected as fancy dictated. There was little formality about attending a play in the Middle Ages. The predominant tone of much medieval drama is thus public and imperative, as if the players required to make an impact on hurrying crowds and arrest them on their way somewhere else and force them like Everyman to 'stand still' and give attention. Hence follow the ringing tones of so much medieval dramatic rhetoric, the confident, even strident announcements with which so many leading figures introduce themselves in the cycle plays, or the Croxton *Play of the Sacrament*, or *The Castel*. Hence the strong probability that gesture too was flamboyant, arresting, and large. There is no need to decry such a style as primitive and uncouth: audiences were not decorous, captive, compliant middle-class souls who booked in advance and sat comfortably on sprung seats, clutching boxes of chocolates. As things were, squares, yards, banquet-halls, called for something more akin to the techniques of the modern fairground barker or circus ringmaster.

In some respects this was a handicap to the full development of medieval dramatic writing and medieval acting in that subtle nuance, delicacy of expression, psychological shading, went for too little, but at the same time the stage in the Middle Ages did have one inestimable benefit which arose from presenting its shows in fields and streets and houses and yards. By staging them in environments already familiar and unremarkable to their witnesses, organizers were able to present drama as an *extension* of everyday life, as something which grows naturally from the world of which men are aware even while it transcends it, rather than as a departure or an escape from it. They are to be envied rather than pitied by those of us today who are apt to neglect this vital aspect of the theatrical experience.

II

The art of the medieval stage was mainly one of improvisation and imagination, and this may be equally well applied to the furnishing and embellishment of the stage itself as to the visual style employed and the selection
of performance-sites. Scenic realism was never consciously cultivated as
an aesthetic principle in the Middle Ages, except perhaps in Italy whose
theatrical history is vastly different from that of the remainder of Western
Europe during this period, and in analysing *mise-en-scène*, we are again
fortunate in having passed beyond that phase in our contemporary theatre
which exalted verisimilitude as the only valid artistic criterion. Hence
we can once more contemplate early stagecraft without patronizing its
'primitive crudity' or 'peasant naivety'. Medieval theatre, like the art of
the Elizabethan public playhouse, depended for its impact on allusion
and suggestion, rather than illusion and representation, which does not
mean, of course, that it dispensed with grandeur, dignity, richness and
elegance when they were required.

To understand medieval conventions in such matters, attention may
now be concentrated on that handful of devices which took the place
occupied by scenery and setting in the modern theatre. Liturgical plays
would of course have been presented with a minimum of scenic aids and
most of the items employed would have been common pieces of church
furniture. Audiences for liturgical drama were well accustomed to
dramatic symbolism of the kind employed in the *Visitatio Sepulchri*, the
short ceremony re-enacting the Marys' visit to the sepulchre on Easter
morning, whereby the women's ointments were represented by censers,
Christ's tomb by the altar, and his body by a crucifix, and this familiarity
contributed to their willingness to accept other stage-objects at more than
face-value. In a similar manner side-chapels, steps, doors, choirs, and
upper levels could be employed where relevant, without requiring to be
disguised or modified in any way: an angelic chorus appearing in the
clouds could be located in a raised gallery; Joseph and Mary could flee
into Egypt down the length of the nave to the west door; the disciples
could search for Christ after his disappearance from Emmaus by scouring
the entire church.[22] Simple platforms and rostra, tables, benches, stools,
and a few basic fabricated structures appear to have been adequate to
cope with productions whose staging requirements were far less sophisticated than their theological content or their rhetorical structures.

More important than establishing the exact nature of every setting
constructed during the Middle Ages is to recognize some of the principles
which lay behind medieval *mise-en-scène*. One is the principle of simultan-
eity which lies behind Gothic art of every kind. To the medieval mind
there was nothing incongruous in placing in close physical juxtaposition

scenic locations widely separated from each other in the geographical sense. The three distinct structures called for in the Croxton *Play of the Sacrament* might happily be sited within easy reach of one another as forming parts of one town, but the Fleury *Filius Getronis* juxtaposes Getron's house in Excoranda with the far-off court of the heathen king who abducts his son, with no sense of incongruity. *La Seinte Resureccion* (c. 1175) requires seven '*maisuns*' to be simultaneously visible as well as the inn at Emmaus, along with eight '*lius*', probably simple platforms for such characters as the three Marys, Pilate, and Caiaphas to occupy. In the middle of the *platea* Galilee had to be sited, together with Emmaus, and if this play was indeed played indoors,[23] one wonders just how so many separate locations could be satisfactorily spaced out within the relatively limited confines of a church-building. Partly for this reason, some have indeed argued in favour of outdoor staging in the round, but whatever the truth, it should be noted that the 'scenery' was doubtless unelaborate, and that the 'sets' all occupied the available space at one and the same time; indeed, their very simplicity was no doubt dictated by this consideration.

The advantages of such conventions are everywhere apparent in medieval drama: literary and theatrical energy is not expended in attempting to make an audience believe that what it is watching is actually taking place in reality. Indeed, texts often deliberately remind spectators that they are merely viewing a play. Moreover, it becomes possible to weave locations and actions into a closer relationship than everyday time and space permit: while Christ eats the Last Supper with the disciples on one part of the stage, Judas plots with the High Priest in another; as Mankind's Soul is deposited on Belyal's scaffold by the Bad Angel, we are simultaneously aware of the daughters of God pleading for its redemption at the foot of the heavenly throne. Unhampered by aesthetic insistence on photographic fidelity to life, the medieval dramatist was able to exercise an authority over his material which a more naturalistic writer would have been forced to forego. He accepted that the theatre's primary function was not to offer its audience a carbon-copy of reality, but that if one condoned the inevitable make-believe and pretence of a stage performance and admitted the essential unreality of its artifice, one achieved a considerable gain in artistic freedom. Since the bare platform backed by a curtain, or the pageant-waggon stage with its two or three locations set up side by side could never be mistaken for any specific place at any specific time, but would always look like what it was, it could therefore be called upon to represent any place (or any number of places) at any time (or at several times in succession) provided spectators could be persuaded to use their imaginations to accept that what the author proposed as fact was so.

In this way a Tudor banquet-hall could be imagined to be a Senator's residence in ancient Rome; the *platea* and the scaffolds of *The Castel of Perseveraunce* were permitted to represent the symbolic bounds of man's life on earth and his spiritual destination beyond it. Indeed, such plays suggest that medieval audiences were less prone to enquire the precise siting of a particular piece of stage action than their twentieth-century counterparts: after all, it is impossible to state in cartographic terms where *Everyman* or *Mankynde are* located, nor is it essential for an appreciation of the impact of the Croxton *Play of the Sacrament* to create a geographically accurate reconstruction of 'Eraclea, that famous cyté'. Medieval writers seem singularly unconcerned to supply each piece of significant action with 'a local habitation and a name' and we should not be surprised to find far less emphasis in their plays on man's social and economic environment than in the work of Ibsen or Chekhov. Scenic illusion there could not be, in the generally understood sense of the term: no painted backdrops that might be mistaken for the 'real thing', no settings so lifelike that they could be stepped into without any sense of their being spurious. Apart from anything else, the medieval stage could rarely hide the real nature of its staging techniques from a public who could see exposed in full view virtually all that was going on.

Craftsmanship and ingenuity seem rather to have been devoted to producing small-scale illusions of reality, as when Cain deals Abel a deadly-looking blow in the *Mystère d'Adam*, or blood from the side of the stricken Christ appears to spurt out and cure the blind Centurion.[24] The appetite for vivid action was, after all, no less avid in the Middle Ages than at other periods of dramatic history, and the subject-matter of much medieval theatre was ideally suited to exploit a taste for striking and harrowing effects. Thus we confront the curious paradox of a predominantly non-representational stage which none the less was prepared to create realistic-looking situations for the gratification of an audience rarely concerned about verisimilitude as a larger artistic principle. But there is no necessity to believe that the two elements clashed, or that spectators only respond to dramatic situations they believe to be literally 'real'.

The Croxton *Play*, the cycle Passion sequences, and *The Castel* contain some of the best-known 'special effects' in medieval drama, but attention must be given to the more spectacular aspects of two of the so-called 'Digby Plays', *The Conversion of St Paul* and *Mary Magdalene*,[25] both dating from 1480–1520. There has been a good deal of discussion in recent years concerning the manner in which *The Conversion of St Paul* was presented, some favouring the notion of a peripatetic audience on similar lines to those advanced above for the Croxton *Play of the Sacrament*. Others argue that the piece was set amid a series of scaffolds arranged on the edge of a circular arena familiar from *The Castel of*

Perseveraunce, and that the Poet's invitation to follow the 'procession' (lines 155-7) simply indicates anxiety that the audience should keep up with the different phases of the action, which the narrator urges them to 'folow'. Some general arguments against mobile auditors have already been advanced in the discussion of the Croxton *Play* above,[26] and if *St Paul* was in fact staged before a moveable audience, it remains unusual, if not unique.

The play demands two major locations. One is the Temple at Jerusalem where the chief priests Annas and Caiaphas are housed, the other the 'house in the street called straight' in Damascus where Ananias meets Saul. These were no doubt represented by conventional 'houses' of the type depicted in the Valenciennes miniature. When Saul is struck down on the road to Damascus (represented by the space between the two cities) the stage-direction informs us that 'Godhed spekith in hevyn', and this probably implies some upper level, perhaps a building overlooking the playing-place. Some commentators suggest that the inn-yard where Saul's servant bandies words with the Ostler also requires its own apportionment of space, but it seems more typical of medieval staging simply to place this brief scene on the *platea*. 'The watery streme' where Saul is christened could be possibly but not necessarily an actual stream within the playing-area. It could however have been a conventional font, since one features in the Croxton *Play*.

The provision of a horse for Saul to ride on to Damascus is one of the simplest and commonest facilities medieval stage managers were asked to supply. Playwrights made frequent use of animals;[27] indeed, the Holy Spirit which appears above Saul at the home of Ananias and then descends may well have taken the traditional form of a live white dove, which often featured in church ceremonies for Pentecost. The most intriguing special effect is called for by the stage direction 'Here commith a fervent with gret tempest, and Saule faulith down of his horse.' The 'fervent' is evidently the 'light from heaven' of Acts 9.3, and the explosive burst of illumination required was probably obtained from some kind of fire-cracker lit and thrown at the appropriate moment.

Mary Magdalene also makes extensive use of sensational effects of this and other kinds. *Mary Magdalene* is panoramic in its sweep, and David Bevington has made out an excellent case for regarding its staging as analogous to that of *The Castel*, with Magdalene's father's castle as its central feature.[28] Bevington visualizes an arena-stage with eleven scaffolds grouped on its periphery, each formed of a basic scenic structure of the traditional type, with steps giving access to the *platea* where other more rarely-used locations such as a rock out to sea, the sepulchre, and Magdalene's arbour have their places, doubtless suggested by portable pieces of stylized scenery. *Mary Magdalene* is typical of the non-realistic orientation of the medieval theatre accommodating on the same stage-area diverse scenic components which remain in position throughout the action.

Much lively business is associated with the scaffold representing Hell, which appears to have been built on two levels, like the one depicted in Cailleau's drawings from Valenciennes, for a stage direction reads 'Here shal entyr the Prinse of Dylles [Devils] in a stage, and helle ondyrneth that stage', Satan later speaking of his 'tower'. Thunder and lightning are again accompaniments of the diabolic crew, and after Magdalene's repentance and conversion, the devils proceed to 'sett the howse on a fyere, and make a sowth [soot]'.

Heaven is also an important location in *Mary Magdalene*. Here angels are stationed as in the Fouquet miniature, and descend to earth from Heaven probably down a ramp. However, a system of ropes and cloud-platforms no doubt assisted Magdalene to make her ascent to heaven before the close, her slow gliding departure being suggested by the words '*Assumpta est Maria in nubibus* [Mary is taken up in the clouds]'.

Two of the most delightful moments in the play are purely secular in their appeal. One of Magdalene's adventures brings her to Marseilles where the king is a pagan worshipping idols, who denies the might of Christ. To teach the monarch the truth Mary prays for a miracle, which takes the form of a heavenly onslaught on the idols. First the 'mament' begins to 'tremill and quake' and then 'shall comme a clowd from heven and sett the tempyl on a fier', an effect possibly achieved by having a cloud travelling on an impregnated wire running from the Heaven scaffold to the Temple and ignited. Such an effect is described by a Russian visitor to a representation of the Annunciation in a Florentine church in 1439.[29] The other attractive device is the ship in which the saint twice undertakes sea-voyages across the *platea*, which takes on for the purpose the rôle of the ocean. 'Here shall entyr a ship with a mery song' we are told at line 1394, and an anchor is soon dropped in 'a fayer haven'. On its second appearance the Boy has to climb into the shrouds to spy out the land, and it takes 'on board' at least three passengers, the King and Queen of Marseilles, now converts to Christianity, and their little child. Later instructions are given to 'rere up the seyll', and the ship plays a vital role in the *dénouement* of the episode.

While we know that in certain circumstances it was possible to flood stage-arenas or construct a pool, the *Magdalene* play almost certainly featured a wheeled ship in a dry *platea*, or even one with legs which the 'seamen' propelled like a pantomime dragon.

As far as we can judge, in the majority of instances, scenery and setting were never permitted to dominate or overwhelm theatre productions in the Middle Ages to the detriment of dialogue, performers, or didactic purpose. Often sets and furniture had of necessity to remain functional and not over-intrusive, yet even when lavish expenditure and spectacular effects were permissible and possible, it is dubious whether medieval companies ever risked unbalancing the fine synthesis achieved in a theatrical milieu which accepted that drama did not require costly embellishments and elaborate machinery in order to achieve its ends. Something beyond 'truth to life' was striven for.

The same point may be made with regard to technical resources and equipment. It is quite clear that the best of medieval engineering science was often brought to bear on problems which arose from the staging of plays. Scholars have explored the mechanics behind, say, the York Mercers' *Play of the Last Judgement* with sufficient thoroughness for us to be aware that such matters were not left to chance or brute force or the inept bunglings of a handful of incompetent amateurs.[30] Nor can the manipulation of heavy pageant-waggons through crowded and often narrow streets and over hilly or uneven terrain be regarded as a task which could be safely delegated to willing but unskilled hands. Time, trouble, labour, and hard cash were all deployed to present plays worthily and satisfactorily, but they were not deployed to stage them accurately or realistically. Medieval 'directors' asked what the plays required to make their meaning effective, what audiences could be persuaded to accept as meaningful equivalents for the literal stuff of existence and the ideal stuff of the life to come, and how far with the material at their disposal an impact could be achieved that would be revealing and satisfying, given the employment of those perennial theatrical virtues of convention, suggestion, and imagination.

III

Despite the pains taken to mount performances skilfully and responsibly, the conception lingers that medieval dramas were acted out by clumsy and inadequate players whose abilities consisted of little more than 'out-Heroding Herod' or emulating the modern sergeant-major in vocal prowess. The notion that medieval play-acting was necessarily of the 'coarse' variety dies hard, but if we adopt such a dismissive attitude towards the player's craft in medieval times, it must prevent us from evaluating properly a central aspect of a considerable theatrical achievement.

At the same time it is not easy to find evidence with which to rebut those too-frequent assumptions that medieval actors were as incompetent or as ill-suited to their parts as the members of that homespun company who present the play of Pyramus and Thisbe in *A Midsummer Night's*

Dream.[31] The art of the stage performer has always been an ephemeral one, at least until our own day with its videotapes, gramophone recordings, and its verbatim accounts of performances by leading players, yet even these are no substitute for witnessing the actuality of a live actor making contact with a live audience. Certainly for all previous ages, the investigator is severely handicapped when seeking to recapture the skills of the great players of the past, let alone the minor ones; such is the dearth of even casual allusions that we rarely obtain even a glimpse of actual acting performances. Hence much of what we assert about medieval acting must be infused with conjecture, yet the effort to reconstruct even a shadowy picture of players in the Middle Ages is necessary, so vital must their contribution have been to the total presentation.

The earliest actors in Britain for whom we possess any repertoire are the clergy who participated in the liturgical performances sanctioned by the Church, but the ranks of the clerisy ranged widely, from very minor clerks in very minor orders to priors, abbots, bishops, and cardinals, so that we need not postulate that every medieval churchman was expected to appear in drama, or that high-ranking ecclesiastics invariably did so. One assumes that it was primarily junior and subordinate clergy who took leading roles in liturgical plays, if only because the more elaborate pieces required more rehearsal-time than busy senior ecclesiastics could be expected to give to them. European sources suggest that choristers, minor canons, priests and deacons were most frequently featured, and performances by nuns are recorded, notably for the Easter *Ludus Paschalis* from the abbey of Origny-Sainte-Benoîte of around 1284, and a fourteenth-century *Visitatio* from Barking, where the Marys were played by women, the disciples by male clerics.[32]

The earliest of these routines do not seem to have demanded great histrionic skill, but the notion that actors in liturgical pieces merely 'went through the motions' in a totally wooden manner seems wide of the mark. Even as early as the Winchester *Visitatio* (c. 965–75) rubrics instruct the three Marys to move 'hesitantly like those seeking something' although further acting opportunities are few enough. Similar instructions are found in a longer thirteenth-century *Visitatio* from Fleury where the Marys are told to behave 'as though sorrowful'; St Peter and St John are enjoined to approach the sepulchre 'as if running'; Christ draws back from Magdalene 'as if avoiding her touch'. The Fleury *Herod* requires the shepherds to act in a frightened manner on seeing the angelic choir, for Herod to fling his book of prophecies to the floor, and for him and his son to threaten the star with their swords; in *The Slaughter of the Innocents*, Herod 'as if demented' seizes a sword and attempts to stab himself.[33] More stereotyped behaviour *is* asked of performers in a fourteenth-century *Planctus Mariae* from Cividale del Friuli in Northern Italy, which carries almost eighty instructional rubrics, the large majority of which demand no more than the formal indication of grief by striking one's breast, pointing to one's tears, and indicating the presence of Christ's body on the cross.

The *Mystère d'Adam*[34] leaves a far more colourful impression of medieval acting. This amazing twelfth-century Anglo-Norman text is surprisingly detailed in its references to staging techniques, which include catering for Abel to protect himself from Cain's murdering blow by having an earthenware pot concealed on his person. This text suggests that the players needed to be given a good deal of elementary instruction in the basic elements of acting, but one reason for this may have been that the vernacular *Adam* was played to a more heterogeneous audience than most earlier pieces of this nature, and that standards had been less exacting where presentation was primarily for devotional consumption.[35] Possibly professional actors were now involved in religious performances, and their behaviour had to be carefully monitored. Whatever the reason for their presence, the rubrics are very insistent on convincing standards of performance, particularly in matters of diction and gesture.

Such instructions might appear to reveal fears as to the actors' competence, but further details contradict this by requiring performers to convey quite subtle facial and bodily expressions. The characters of Adam and Eve are implied in Adam's 'tranquil features' and the woman's 'slightly defiant' ones. At the Fall, they take up postures 'not completely upright, but bending over somewhat and extremely sorrowful, because of their shame for their sin'; on their expulsion they appear 'bowed down towards the ground, bent towards the ankles, as if sad and confused'. These clearly indicate that a little more than speaking the lines correctly was expected, an impression confirmed by a study of the dialogue, where there is subtlety in the flattery with which the disguised Satan slowly beguiles Eve, and in the murderous Cain's bland suggestion that he and Abel should walk in the meadows to refresh themselves after toil. The sexual psychology underlying Adam's long speech of self-justification and repentance is masterly. Moreover, while many of the rubrics governing gesture are conventional, they are occasionally orchestrated to great effect, as when the devil having come and planted thorns and thistles among their crops, Adam and Eve discover their loss, fling themselves to the ground, and strike their breasts and thighs, 'stricken with violent grief'.

Le Mystère d'Adam suggests that by at least 1200 medieval playwrights could count on the services of players capable of handling material far from elementary in its histrionic demands. While much stylization of gesture and posture is clearly present, a few less hieratic, more naturalistic touches are permitted to all the players apart from that of the Figura, or God, and even he, in turning a 'threatening face' on Eve and reacting to

Cain 'as though very angry', is conceived as expressing natural emotions on occasion. The pains taken to ensure that dialogue and action coalesce is a further sign of an awareness for the necessity of skilled playing, and that even in 1146–74 (the dates usually assumed for the composition of *Adam*) some measure of credibility was an important criterion in performance. It is doubtful if a bearded Eve would have been tolerated in quite the way that a bearded Mary might be in a *Visitatio Sepulchri*. Yet 'psychological identification' was far from being the medieval goal.

Unfortunately, too few plays of the *Adam* period have survived to allow us to confirm our impressions of its acting criteria: it may have been exceptional in its histrionic assumptions as well as in its literary and theatrical qualities. But we cannot rely solely on playtexts to tell us the full story of medieval acting. Certainly, when at the end of the twelfth century Giraldus Cambrensis compared the sign-language of the monks at the dinner-table in Christ Church, Canterbury, with that of players in '*ludos scenicos*',[36] he was presumably not thinking of gestures in plays such as *Adam*, which were not the type of drama against which bishops were to inveigh in their diocesan injunctions of the next century. The 'miracles' or 'steraclis' forbidden to clerics either as players or spectators were no doubt unauthorized religious plays of a popular nature, performed without the Church's approval, and involving more full-bodied, less restrained performance-styles, at which a Giraldus might well look askance. It is equally likely, however, that such '*inhonesti ludi*' 'inciting to licentiousness' (as one of the earliest sets of statutes describes them) were secular plays of the uninhibitedly bawdy popular tradition.[37] Whatever their nature, Giraldus disapproves quite unequivocally, and a similarly jaundiced view of players in general is taken by countless churchmen through the period under review, most notably by the thirteenth-century sub-dean of Salisbury, Thomas de Chabham, who in his *Summa de poenitentia* of c. 1230, had little good to say of *histriones* or entertainers, apart from those whose talent was that of the traditional minstrels 'who sing of the valiant acts of princes and of the lives of the saints'.[38] No doubt when de Chabham indicts those who distort their bodies in lascivious dances and poses, or repeat slanders about others, he was including players in ribald interludes of the *De Clerico et Puella* type, whose acting techniques could doubtless have been traced back to the art of the *mimus* and popular entertainers of the ancient world. Here repartee, clowning, improvization, slapstick, and broad comic burlesque all made a contribution, and there is little doubt that these ingredients remained an intrinsic factor in the appeal of those secular dramatic activities, which competed with more religious plays for public attention.

It might be argued that the two principal modes of medieval acting came to blend in the presentation of the vernacular Christian drama of the fourteenth and fifteenth centuries, the principal focus of the present work. There are grounds for doubting, however, whether the style employed in the officially approved mode of drama, and that of the secular interluders, were quite as distinct from each other as some commentators have argued.[39] Licensed horseplay such as that deployed at the Feast of Fools suggests that clerics could rapidly lose any inhibitions imposed by ecclesiastical circumstances, and perusal of such extroverted roles as Herod, the devils in *Adam*, the comic spice-seller in some versions of the *Visitatio Sepulchri*, lead one to the view that liturgical performances may not always have been the sedate affairs which some assume. However formal and stylized the acting techniques, performance of liturgical works was often infused with touches of colour and humour, as when the lions devour the wicked counsellors in the Beauvais *Play of Daniel* (c. 1180), and occasional semi-naturalistic gestures and actions form an artistic contrast to the more muted qualities of the whole.

But undoubtedly by transferring its main operation to the streets, to fields, market-places, and village-greens, medieval religious theatre assimilated something of the performance-style of those who had played there by tradition for centuries, and this included the craft and skills of performers in the broader, brasher, less formalized conventions of a secular mode, both interluders and folk-players. In much medieval drama two principal types of rôle feature, one which can be successfully accomplished within the limits of a predominantly formal and restrained style, the other demanding an extrovert, even extravagant, approach to the figure portrayed. So the Herod of the liturgical plays becomes an even more grossly exaggerated character in the vernacular cycles; an actor playing Joseph is able to draw on the comic portrayals of the *senex amans* in the *fabliau* tradition. The torture and execution of Christ derive some of their sadistic dimensions from ritual games and pastimes; battles between the forces of light and darkness in the morality owe a debt to similar combats inherited from folk-dramas. The way was opened to combining the generally unemphatic characterizations associated with church music-drama with those bolder personifications infused with the spirit of popular sport and entertainment. Thus the action of *The Conversion of St Paul* is enlivened by the appearance of disreputable figures such as the servant and the ostler, and the quack-doctor and his boy disrupt or reinforce (or more accurately, disrupt *in order* to reinforce) the doctrinal substance of the Croxton *Play of the Sacrament* with routines reminiscent of the Mumming Play. Most celebrated of all, the antics of Mak the stealer of sheep and folk-hero pave the way for the birth of the saviour of mankind in the *Second Shepherds' Pageant* of the Wakefield Cycle, and the confident swagger of the medieval entertainer becomes blended with the timeless humility of the shepherds at the manger.

Not that even the theologically respectable characters in medieval drama are called on to efface themselves abjectly from the scene by contrast with their more theatrically conspicuous fellows. Their stage was no place for shrinking violets or tongue-tied introverts. The attractive light in which the English cycle plays suffuse goodness and probity has won much comment; figures whose spiritual perfection has been hallowed by centuries of worship or approbation are still made uncloyingly appealing because of the sheer plausibility of their sincerity and integrity. Since goodness is therefore presented on the medieval stage as a positive human force, actors called to represent Christ, or Abel, or Mercy, or the Virgin Mary, are given sufficient humanity and individual dynamism to balance out their holiness and righteousness to make them not only watchable but credible. Those playing such rôles were thus given no encouragement to appear anaemic or withdrawn or priggish in their virtue. The York Mary at the Annunciation is typical in the naturalism of her sturdy lack of demure reverence for the Angel's message:

I knawe no man that shulde have fyled [defiled]
My maydenhode, the sothe to saye;
Withouten will of werkis wilde,
In chastité I have ben ay (lines 173–6).

Medieval acting, whatever its manifestation, rarely demanded a technique relying on nuance and half-tones, of things merely hinted at or unsaid (except occasionally from the silent figure of Christ before Herod as at York). Characters are unequivocally, unashamedly wicked or virtuous; their personalities are rarely complex or elusive to grasp. Because of the size or ambience of their auditoria, because of the social and educational background of the majority of their auditors, because of the general nature of medieval public spectacle, acting had perforce to be a presentational art, one in which players were not expected to identify with figures they portrayed, but instead were required to impress on an audience the nature of a character's personality. Characters great and small announce themselves publicly, or draw attention to themselves and their dramatic function through the use of formulae established long before the school of Stanislavski learnt to devise more ingenious methods of introduction and exposition. There is no subterfuge about such lines as:

I am gracyus and grete, God withoutyn begynnyng. (York *Creation*)

Mercy ys my name, that mornyth for yowr offence. (*Mankynde*)

Syr Arystory ys my name,
A merchaunte myghty of a royall araye. (The Croxton *Play*)

Few actors on the medieval stage are asked to play introspective or self-absorbed figures, for nearly all are required to deliver an account of their actions or intentions to the audience, even if not always on the unashamedly self-explanatory lines quoted here. There is little of the gradual revelation of character and purpose associated with naturalistic drama. As a result, outward appearance and behaviour count for a great deal in suggesting personality or moral and social worth, and blatant disguise plays a central role in plays of the period. It is overt dramatic significance that is emphasized rather than psychological motivation.

Even if this were not the case, naturalistic characterizations would have been hard to sustain in non-representational settings and on a non-illusionistic stage. Furthermore, many late medieval plays contain elements strongly reminiscent of the liturgical works which preceded them and perhaps influenced their more solemn moments, if only sub-consciously. Thus in the York Cycle Christ enters Jerusalem to the accompaniment of eight parallel speeches of acclamation delivered in sequence by eight Burghers; formalized exchanges of dialogue are encountered regularly as when the Virgin on her visit to St Elizabeth in the N-Town plays participates in an antiphonal duet. Other ritualized activities are also prescribed; hymns and anthems punctuate the speeches, processions are found space for, so that any impression of a credible picture of objectively-observed everyday life is rapidly dispelled. At the same time, we should not be deceived into believing that medieval acting was stiff, unconvincing, or lacking in subtlety.

In general, we seem to be confronted with a mixed presentational mode, which could range from the formalized and restrained (though still positive and direct) to the broad and even exaggerated (though still controlled and calculated). Obviously certain roles lent themselves more easily to one style rather than the other, and of course an actor's histrionic ability would have a bearing on how well or poorly a part was executed. But the acting opportunities provided by the extant texts (with all their limitations as a guide to theatrical realization) suggest that a wide range of talents could be catered for, from the virtuosi who undertook Satan and Herod, to the less dynamic player who could still create a memorable and moving Christ. Yet in plays such as the cycle dramas where a sequence of actors would often have appeared in the same role, consistency would have been impossible to achieve without some corporately-agreed method of acting. However, it is unlikely to have expelled utterly every vestige of individual interpretation from each performer. The plays themselves are too rich with a sense of pleasure in the resources of the human condition to support such a dogmatic and regimentalized view.

It would be tempting to assume that medieval actors received no organized instruction of any kind, but such were the pains taken with every other aspect of presentation that it seems inconceivable that performers were left to sink or swim unaided. It is not an area of production that receives much direct documentation: there is no means of knowing whether the authors were ever rewarded by seeing the histrionic effects visualized in their scripts achieved on the stage. But a skilful playwright will not ask the impossible or even the improbable of his cast, and certainly medieval English playtexts give the impression of being carefully constructed with enthusiastic, non-cerebral, amateur players in mind, a belief which the practical test of present-day production will often confirm.

One key to a better knowledge and understanding of medieval acting technique may be found in a reference contained in the York records for April 1476 where an ordinance decrees that

> . . . yerely in the tyme of lentyn [Lent] there shall be called afore the Maire for the tyme beyng iiij [four] of the moste Connyng discrete and able playeres within this Citie to serche here and examen all the plaiers and plaies and pagentes thrughoute all the artificeres belonging to Corpus Christi Plaie And all suche as thay shall fynde sufficant in personne and Connyng to the honour of the Citie and Worship of the saide Craftes for to admitte and able and all other insufficient personnes either in Connyng voice or personne to discharge ammove and avoide.[40]

If 'connyng', 'voice' and 'personne' were the three qualities felt to be essential for players in York in 1476, these may well be the criteria which were applied in the field of medieval acting as a whole. They correspond to what might be described today as 'talent or expertise', 'vocal prowess', and 'stage presence', and using these as our yardstick we may be able to formulate some notion of what medieval acting was like in the three areas of capability regarded as of primary importance by the devisers of the York document of 1476.

How skilful were actors expected to be? From the welter of instructions, injunctions, admonitions, and reprimands which survive, it is clear that competence at least was regarded as attainable. Although we have no means of knowing how trivial or heinous by today's standards were the errors for which they were punished, the fact that at Beverley in 1452 Henry Couper, a weaver, and Robert Thormskew were each fined 6s. 8d, the former 'because he did not know his play', the latter 'because the players of the Carpenters' craft did not know their play', suggests that serious inadequacies were heavily penalized.[41] In 1520 at the same centre the aldermen of the Painters' Guild suffered 'because their play of lez iij [three] Kynges of culleyn [Cologne, i.e. the Magi]' was badly and confusedly played, in contempt of the whole community, 'before many strangers', and Richard Gaynstang was also fined 'because his play of slepyng pylate was badly played' by the Tailors' Guild, the Beverley Drapers being penalized in the same year for a similar offence. In 1450 the Coventry authorities fined the actors playing Christ and St Anne, possibly for not committing their lines to memory, and the York ordinance of 1415 also makes it plain that incompetence of any kind would not be condoned:

> We command of the kynges be halve and the Mair & the shirefs of this Citee . . . that all maner of craftmen that bringeth furthe ther pageantez in order & course by good players well arayed & openly spekyng upon payn of lesyng of C [100] s to be paid to the chambre withoute any pardon . . .[42]

Some formal histrionic instruction might have been given, for the Middle Ages understood very well the important relationship which existed between word and gesture from their familiarity with celebrated classical treatises on rhetoric (which of course included its oratorical aspects) notably those of Cicero and Quintilian.[43] J. W. Robinson has pointed out how closely the direction in *Adam* stating that actors should make their gestures appropriate to what they are saying accords with the Ciceronian precept that gesture should accompany thought, and no doubt some medieval training for the stage consisted of learning how to 'suit the action to the word'. But when considering religious plays at least, we should recall the ecclesiastical background to the drama, for medieval preachers too had their own system of signs and postures, gestures and mannerisms, which contributed notably to their effectiveness in the pulpit. If, as seems highly likely, much of the coaching for the religious stage at this period was in the hands of the clergy, who certainly concerned themselves with dramatic activities well after religious plays became a popular outdoor attraction, then it is to medieval pulpit technique as well as to classical oratory that we must turn to obtain a glimpse of the medieval actor in performance (at least in one of his aspects, for no doubt the secular mime-players also passed on their techniques to those playing the Vices of the moralities and the devils of the cycles). The physical and verbal skills of Chaucer's Pardoner suggest a well-stocked repertoire of strategic devices which could be taught to a novice-actor directed by a clerical producer. His concern for 'an hauteyn [bold] speche' and eagerness to 'rynge it out as round as gooth a belle' are matched with an equally efficient 'demonstration-technique':

> Thanne peyne I me to strecche forth the nekke,
> And est and west upon the peple I bekke,
> As dooth a dowve sittynge on a berne.
> Myne handes and my tonge goon so yerne
> That it is joye to se my bisynesse.[44]

A fuller investigation of medieval preaching methods may well open the way to a profounder knowledge of the art of the medieval actor.

Vocal proficiency was obviously of great importance for players who were frequently asked to exercise their skills in large auditoria in the open-air, or in competition with other attractions. An ability at 'openly spekynge' was clearly prized at York, and a number of characters, notably Pilate and Herod, became proverbial for their capacity to rant and roar, as Chaucer's allusion to the Miller in his drunken state crying out 'in Pilates voys' makes clear. But volume in itself was not deemed all-sufficient; even as early as *Adam* we learn that correct *pace* and careful and accurate speaking were prized, as well as a capacity for speaking the lines as the author wrote them. J. W. Robinson finds confirmation of this in the first Prologue spoken by Contemplation in the N-Town sequence, where Christ is called upon to bless the performance, and to preserve

> . . . the personys here pleand [playing] that the pronunciacion
> Of here sentens to be seyd mote be sad and sure [may be firm and
>   confident]
> And that non oblocucyone [impediment or poor delivery] make this
>   matere obscure (*Play 8.* 3–5),

the suggestion being that clarity and confidence in speaking are deemed just as important as sheer vocal impact. We have a clear indication in the York *Passion* that the best of medieval Herods did not merely give rein to a powerful pair of lungs, but that his performance required to be not only intelligible, but subtle and flexible too.

That the playgoing public's awareness of vocal sophistication was well developed comes out in numerous ways when we read the plays of the period. Certainly we cannot claim that medieval players lacked any kind of expertise in this area of their craft. Actors must have been capable of responding to demands from authors that they should disguise their voices: Lucifer, for example, in the Cornish *Creation* has to adopt a female voice once he is metamorphosed as the serpent:

> Since I am close entered
> In thee, within,
> My voice lo! it is all changed,
> Like a maid in earnest.

Mak, the comic villain of the Wakefield *Second Shepherds' Pageant*, sees fit to adopt a Southern accent when trying to impress the shepherds that he is a messenger from a great king, and their response shows a true North-country contempt for his pretensions, a retort which could scarcely raise a response unless the dialectal joke were accessible to all:

> Bot, Mak, is that sothe [true]?
> Now take outt that sothren tothe [accent]
>   And sett in a torde!

As a final example of the subtlety required of medieval actors in the vocal dimension, we may instance the purely verbal humour of such a play as the Chester *Pastores* where in the darkness two of the shepherds attempt to make contact with their fellow, Tud, who is said to be too deaf to hear the feeble call of the Second Shepherd. The First, rightly scornful, urges his companion to greater efforts, and the direction then reads 'Secundus Pastor vocat submissa voce [the Second Shepherd calls in a weak voice]' so that the First waxes ironic:

Naye, faye; thy voyce is wonders dym.

In Harley MS 2124 the joke is repeated in the form of a second shout which still fails to arouse the absent Tud. This kind of effect could scarcely be achieved with stupid or inept casts, unable to produce the required contrasts in volume, or with audiences unable to relish them.

Vocal abilities of a very marked kind were required by those undertaking the flamboyant and boisterous roles in which medieval drama abounds, but for parts such as Herod, Pilate, Jonathas, Belyal, and so forth, 'persoune' or 'stage presence' was even more *de rigueur*. Acting in the Middle Ages appears to have been a far more *physical* activity than it often is today, or at least so many medieval stage directions indicate. Processional entries and sweeping movement about the *platea* are frequent, and so is the device of parading or 'pomping' about the arena which is particularly associated with characters in the *Passio* from the Cornish *Ordinalia*, where Caiaphas, Pilate, the doctors, Herod, and Lucifer all exercise themselves vigorously in this manner. Restless physical activity often denotes the villainous and aggressive characters of the cycles and moralities; it is the bad hats, too, who engage in wild bouts of fighting and squabbling as do the Vices of *Mankynde*, and brawling is certainly the trademark of the diabolic and depraved in *The Castel of Perseveraunce*. In the Wakefield Cycle it is significant that Cain and his boy are the first human figures to come to blows. Dancing too is another vigorous activity which often occurs, as when in the N-Town *Crucifixion* the Jews are instructed that

here xule [shall] thei leve of and dawncyn a-bowte the cros . . .

or when the script of *Mankynde* informs us that 'her thei daunce'.

Nearly all the actions legislated for on the medieval stage are robust and dynamic, and they serve to stress the necessity for 'persoune' (and not a little agility) on the part of those executing them. Thus we read:

Here rennyt owt from wndyr [under] the horrybyll mantyll of the SOULL seven small boys in the lyknes of dewyllys and so retorne ageyn. (*Wisdom*)

Heir sall Johne loup [leap] the stank [ditch] or els fall in it. (*Thrie Estaitis*)

here the jewys lede Cryst outh of the place with gret cry and noyse some drawyng Cryst forward and some bakwarde and so ledyng

forth with here [their] weponys A-lofte and lytys brennyng [burning].
(*N-Town Cycle*)

Discussion of the qualities desiderated in a medieval actor leads to the
question of amateur and professional status, and whether predominantly
amateur presentation such as the cycles involved professional actors also,
possibly in leading parts. The distinction between the two categories is
of course by no means as clear-cut in medieval times as it would be today,
and it is doubtful whether professionals would be trained any differently
from amateurs, although the former would obviously more rapidly acquire
experience. David Bevington has suggested that the guilds may often
have hired 'professionals' from troupes in regular employment to play
main roles, leaving guild-members to cope with the minor parts, but this
makes too artificial a division, and suggests that men who did not act for
a regular living were incapable of playing the more charismatic roles in
the medieval repertoire.[45] Some argue that any actor taking money for
performing is a 'professional', but we must be wary that in using this
term we do not make false assumptions about the player's trade at this
time. Many actors were paid who did not reckon to act for their livelihood.
We need only instance Robert Crow or Croo, a member of the Coventry
Cappers' company in the sixteenth century,[46] who, whether or not records
refer to one or several figures by this name, was a 'professional' actor in
that he received 3s 4d to play the part of God in the Coventry Cycle, but
it would be a rash assumption to claim that acting was his sole or principal
source of income. Similarly, a payment in 1553 refers to 'Vaughan tht
[that] shuld have played in Tompson sted', clearly an instance of a
payment to an actor (or in this case a non-actor), but there is no indication
that Vaughan was financially dependent on his salary as a stand-in. True,
Bevington finds significance in the fact that where the Lincoln Cordwainers provided three men to play the shepherds in their Nativity
sequence, they paid 'plaiers' to undertake the Magi, Joseph and Mary,[47]
but we have no means of knowing from whence such paid performers
were drawn. Some guilds, rich in acting resources, may have loaned
players to less fortunate guilds and charged them a fee: this was certainly
the practice with the Coventry Coopers who in 1572 recruited a tailor, a
barber-surgeon, and either a painter or a slater to their cast. The barber-
surgeon was in fact Thomas Marser (or Mercer) who in 1574 was paid
twopence 'to get him to pleay' for the Coopers once again, but his principal trade presumably remained that of barber-surgeon.[48]

When processional plays were presented, a large number of actors in
succession would obviously share the same role, whereas a single performance at a single location meant that one player could sustain the part
throughout. Such an actor would certainly have to possess considerable
stamina and the capacity to husband his resources, but it would not be

22 Minster Yard, Lincoln, prepared for Keith Ramsay's 1981 production of the N-Town Cycle (Photo: Gus de Cozar)

beyond the powers of an amateur actor to cope with these demands. Even where large payments are recorded in account-books, we should not immediately rush to the conclusion that 'professional' players were employed, nor forget that many talented medieval actors must have given their services free.

IV

The logistics of organizing dramatic presentations in the Middle Ages are perhaps better chronicled than any other aspect, for organization required expenditure, which lent itself readily to documentation. Thus there exists a large mass of documents regarding the control and organization of drama – permissions, prohibitions, injunctions, ordinances, regulations, balance-sheets, and memoranda – all of which shed essential light on the background to theatrical creativity from c. 1000 until the late 1500s. However, we know all too little of the organization of liturgical plays to be able to offer any very illuminating insights into this branch of theatre. Possibly Lady Katherine of Barking was only one of many church dignitaries who took an individual initiative in devising ceremonies 'to stimulate further the devotion of the faithful', but perhaps other institutions were reluctant to stage liturgical performances even in order to teach the rudiments of Christianity, to strengthen the faith of the fainter-hearted or more easily distracted, or to arouse devotion. Information on the precise circumstances in which the Latin music-drama of the church arose and was presented is difficult to obtain: such routines were perhaps regarded as part of the church's annual round of rites, requiring no special comment. Yet in such cases as the Beauvais *Daniel* or *Le Mystère d'Adam* one feels that special organizational problems must have occurred, and one would welcome details of them.

If information is sparse in the liturgical sphere, it is plentiful enough in the vernacular region, but chiefly for presentations of civic religious drama late in the period. Again, one would relish more data on secular performances, both those deriving from the traditional rituals and ceremonies executed by the people themselves, and those interludes and entertainments devised for their delight by itinerant troupes of specialized players, of which so few examples survive. More facts on organizing morality performances of such plays as *Mankynde* and *The Castel of Perseveraunce* would also be invaluable. As things stand, most of our knowledge of English medieval theatrical administration and presentation inevitably has to be extracted from records of civic and municipal performances of plays such as the cycle sequences. Such concentration must mean

that a far from balanced picture results, and one would gladly dispense
with some of the similar facts available from a half a dozen different
centres, in order to obtain data concerning, say, the staging of the Croxton
Play, or the preparations for *Fulgens and Lucres*.

There seems to have been no standard method of arranging productions
in the Middle Ages. A multiplicity of approaches to matters of financing,
casting, allocating plays to guilds, rehearsing, and so forth is only to be
expected, given the diversity of problems faced in a world where
professional theatre as we understand the term did not exist. Much of
the administration was undertaken by men whose life's work lay elsewhere, but this is not to say that an element of hopeful improvisation
infused all medieval productions. It has already been pointed out that
large-scale civic religious performances in particular were not mounted
casually or in a half-hearted manner, and the resultant care and efficiency
deployed on this type of theatrical event at least must not be underesti-
mated. Nor were less ambitious performances necessarily left to chance.

The general pattern of organization adopted in many towns and cities
was for an already-existing body such as the City Council or the Mayor
and Corporation or the masters of a religious or trade guild to take general
responsibility for presenting a play, and then to delegate to specific groups
or to individuals the task of actually preparing the production for public
scrutiny. In York, for example, the Guild of Corpus Christi, while it had
a central role in the civic procession, left the organization of that and of
the cycle play to the common council of the city. In Lincoln the religious
guild of St Anne was detailed by the corporation to take command of the
plays, and the craft guilds took their instructions from the religious
fraternity.[49] At many centres it was usual to elect or choose pageant-
masters to supervise proceedings personally, as an ordinance from York
dated 20 October 1475 indicates:

> . . . it is ordayned forthermore that all ande every maister of that
> occupacion [i.e. Armourers] Within this Cite for tyme beynge shall
> mete in A convenyent place Within this saide Cite yerely fro
> nowefurth the second sonday next aftre the feste of Corporis Christi
> And there and thanne to elect and chuse thair Sercheours [officials]
> ande Pagende maisters for the yere folowynge Ande who it be that
> fayleth to com Whan he is reasonably warned shall forfaite in that
> behalfe vj d [sixpence] in fourme beforesaide And the same day
> there the Sercheours ande pagend maisters to make there Rekenynges
> [render their accounts].

A document from Coventry of 1453 is also typical of the chain of
command involved in setting forth the civic religious performances:

> Thomas Colclow, skynner, fro this day forth shull have the rewle of

the pajaunt unto the end of xij [twelve] yers next folowing, he for
to find the pleyers and all that longeth therto all the seide terme [.]

It is uncertain whether there was any financial gain in taking responsibility for a cycle pageant, or whether it was more a matter of social prestige or business advantage. A similar undertaking to Colclow's from Beverley in 1391 is formulated in these terms:

John of Arras, hairer [haircloth-maker?] came in the Gild Hall before the twelve keepers of the town of Beverley, and undertook for himself and his fellows of the same craft to play a play called Paradise adequately, viz. every year on Corpus Christi day when the other craftsmen of the same town play, during the life of the said John Arras at his own proper cost, willing and granting that he will pay to the community of the town of Beverley for every default in the aforesaid play, 10s, Nicholas Falconer being his surety. And also he undertook to redeliver to the twelve keepers of the town, for the time being, at the end of his life all the necessaries in his possession belonging to the play aforesaid, under penalty of 20s, viz. j karre [one pageant-waggon?], viij hespis [eight hasps or clamps], xviij stapiloz [eighteen staples], ij visers [two masks] . . .[50]

At Beverley the city corporation was closely involved with the productions, and in other parts of the country towns and villages assumed parochial responsibility for raising money by sponsoring plays. Elsewhere it was more usual for the officers of the guilds to take charge, and to depute one or more of their members to 'find the pleyers and all that longeth therto'. Sometimes, as the York ordinance of April 1476 quoted above indicates, city and guilds combined to supervise the recruiting of actors, and at Lincoln, as has been suggested earlier, while some guilds found players among their own ranks and even loaned them to other guilds on occasion, some paid actors may have come in from outside the city.

The overall procedure for putting a play into production obviously differed slightly from place to place, but a typical schedule may be sketched in. Allocation of plays to individual guilds in the case of civic drama was at the discretion of the authorities 'to Alter or Assigne any of the occupacons . . . to any play or pagent',[51] and depended partly on tradition, partly on the willingness and ability of groups to undertake the responsibilities of presentation. When these decisions had been reached, the 'master copy' of the script was looked out and the official scrivener (or parish clerk in smaller communities) made from it copies of the individual players' parts which were distributed to those selected to perform. A document from York offers us a glimpse of this process, involving on this occasion the Creed Play which it was intended to stage in 1568. The entry is dated 13 February:

... first the Original or Regestre of the seyd Crede play to be goten
of the mastr & bretherne of St Thomas hospitall whoo have the
Custody therof And after expert & mete players found owte for the
conyng [skilful] handlyng of the seyd playe/than every of theym to
have ther partes fair wrytten & delyvered theym in tyme soo that they
may have leysure to kunne [con] every one his part And the seyd
Chambrelaynes [guild officials] furthr to see all . . . maner the
pageantes playeng geare & necessaries to be provided in a readynes /
. . .

Mention of 'Chambrelaynes' raises the question as to whether medieval
plays were 'produced' in the modern sense. Commonsense suggests that
there must have been some drawing-up of a master-plan on which presentation was based, and that someone – presumably a Thomas Colclow of
Coventry or a John of Arras of Beverley – must have tried to ensure that
the agreed bargain with the authorities was kept. Yet one hesitates to
suggest that such a person's powers resembled the virtual autonomy of
the modern director, a relative newcomer to the theatrical scene, and
definite traces of figures whose functions even *approximate* to those of a
production-controller do not appear in Britain until the sixteenth century.
One interesting reference occurs in the Lincoln records for 10 June 1517
when a chantry priest is appointed to the Guild of St Anne, provided that
'he help to the bringing forth and preparing of the pageants in St Anne
guild',[52] and it is probably to clerics that we should look for other instances
of early directors of English religious plays. Later occurs the name of
Robert Crow or Croo of Coventry, mentioned on a previous page: a man
of this name received 20s from the Drapers' company in 1557 'for makyng
the boke for the paggen' and in the same year received 2d for new gloves
presumably in his capacity as an actor in the spectacular pageant of
Doomsday. He almost certainly played the part of God, his role in 1562
and 1566. But Crow also made properties for the pageant, constructing
models of the world to be consumed by fire; he also appears as 'mendyng
the devells cotes' and in 1562 as being paid twelve pence 'for a hat for
the pharysye', so that it would not be a rash deduction to assume that
such a Jack-of-all-theatrical-trades exercised something of the function of
a modern play-director.

Certainly someone not unlike such an individual emerges at New
Romney in Kent in the shape of Gover Martyn who, in 1560, appears to
have been hired from London to take charge of the arrangements for the
Passion Play that Whitsun, and who is constantly referred to as the
'Devyser of our playe' in the municipal records. His authority was
considerable: he purchased stage materials in London, and received
several handsome payments for both 'servyce' and 'labor' in addition to
eight shillings and free suppers for himself and 'his men'. He also prepared

the script, either composing an original text or adapting one used on a previous occasion: for this he was 'lent' fourteen quires of paper. Whether he actually performed in the plays himself is uncertain, but there is a possible analogy in William Jordan, 'author' of the Cornish *Creation of the World*, whose duties comprised those of director, scriptwriter, and performer. Jordan is referred to in the playtext as 'the Conveyor' and on the strength of references among the stage directions Paula Neuss suggests that like Crow at Coventry he took the part of God. Thus it may be justifiable to argue that Gover Martyn probably played a rôle in the New Romney production, and since there is no record of who undertook the part of Christ in 1560, it may well be that this early actor-producer took the lead in his own presentation.

There is another instance of a 'director' at work in Chelmsford shortly after the New Romney performances. In the summer of 1562 'a propertie player' surnamed Burles was hired, no doubt from London, to direct a season of plays in Essex; his duties seem to have resembled those of Gover Martyn in Kent. He supervised the construction of the necessary sets and scaffolds, ordered and purchased properties, and conducted rehearsals of two of the pieces staged, which John Coldewey believes to have included *The Conversion of St Paul*, the Digby *Massacre of the Innocents*, and *Mary Magdalene*. The 'festival' season turned out badly, at least from a financial point-of-view, and Burles's contract appears to have been terminated, with local men directing the last two presentations (probably a two-part performance of *Mary Magdalene*), but he deserves recognition, along with Gover Martyn and William Jordan, as one of the earliest English theatre-directors whose name is known to us.

In the matter of the overall financing of medieval drama, methods encountered are as various as the types of stage used. Even when it was hoped that funds would be forthcoming either from making an admission charge to spectators or from taking up a collection or 'gathering' during the performance, financial support often had to be secured in advance in order to 'float' the production, and this was raised by a variety of means. In many instances the civic authorities would advance cash for the purpose, or at some centres guilds would levy a tally on their members, known as 'Pageant silver' or 'Pageant pence', in order to defray the expense of setting their waggon with its costly trappings in motion. The physical appearance and condition of the pageant-float, after all, could bring the craft either credit or opprobrium. Again, a York document is typical of many similar memoranda: in 1471 the city's Coopers decreed

> . . . that evere [every] hyred man of the same craft be it be [by] yere
> or be weyke [week] that has ben apprentez in the same craft within
> the said Cite shall yerely pay to the Serchiours [officials] of the same
> craft to the sustentacion of thair pagende iiij d [fourpence]. And yif

he were nat apprentez with in the saide Cite yerly he to paye to the
same Serchiours to the same entent vj d [sixpence].[53]

It was a further function of the pageant-masters or chamberlains to collect
the contributions from the individual guilds, as the York decree of 13
February 1568 makes plain:

> . . . all such the Craftes & occupacions of this Citie as are chardged
> with bryngyng forth of the pageantes of Corpus christi shall gather
> every of theym their accustomed pageant money and pay it to the
> Chambrelaynes handes towardes the chardges of bryngyng forth the
> sayd Crede playe . . .

This was one city's system, but pageant money does not appear to have
been levied from Coventry's guild members, yet as early as 1350 William
de Lenne and his wife paid half a mark on joining the religious Guild of
Corpus Christi in Cambridge 'in ludo filiorum Israelis [for a play of the
Children of Israel]' which probably depicted either Moses or the Massacre
of the Innocents.[54] This may have been a levy or merely private charity:
in 1979 Ian Lancashire drew attention to a bequest of money and a
velvet jacket to the wardens of the Corpus Christi plays at Tamworth in
Staffordshire in 1539.

But countless other arrangements pertained. Private individuals often
came forward to sponsor drama, as may have been the case with Thomas
Colclow and John of Arras, and those who loaned money included a local
schoolmaster at Louth in Lincolnshire in 1556–7, the tradesfolk of New
Romney in 1560, and the men of Chelmsford in 1562, not all of whom
recovered their outlay.[55] Sometimes several communities would pool their
monetary resources in order to stage drama, and the practice of mounting
ancillary events in order to raise funds for dramatic ones was common.
Church-ales, fund-raising quêtes on a house-to-house basis, sales of farm
produce, are all recorded, although one should never forget the frequent
occasions when plays themselves helped to subsidize other projects, such
as the restoration of the parish church at Pulloxhill, Bedfordshire, the
building of a new aisle at Braintree, and the construction of a bridge at
Sandon in Essex;[56] indeed, this must often have been the only reason
why some centres troubled to present plays at all. Conversely, a church
collection 'gaderett' at Holbeach in Lincolnshire went to meet the costs
of a pageant, and at Ipswich rents levied on grazing facilities near the
town were similarly apportioned. It is significant that the Epilogue in the
so-called 'Reynes Extracts' concludes with the announcement of an 'ale',
the proceeds from which were assigned to the church after production
costs had been met, so occasionally both church and players must have
been beneficiaries.[57]

Income was generated in other ways. In some parts of the country a
good wardrobe of costumes proved an invaluable asset, churches and

guilds being able to raise considerable sums from hiring garments to less fortunate companies and well into the seventeenth century the Coventry Weavers were leasing out 'playeres Aparell' for varying sums.[58] Garments could be acquired in a number of ways: in 1517 William Pisford left the Tanners' Company at Coventry two gowns for use when they staged their play, and in 1521 Lincoln City Council agreed to borrow a gown from 'Lady Powes' for one of the Marys, 'thother Mary To be Arayed in the cremysyng [crimson] gowne of velvet that longith to the Same gyld'. Church vestments were often loaned for dramatic purposes, and during the Vestiarian Controversy of the early years of Elizabeth I's reign, copes, albs, chasubles, and surplices were fashioned into theatrical clothing, at least in Essex, Suffolk, and Kent, although their popish connotations remained so strong that collections had to be sold off at Maldon in 1564, Chelmsford in 1574 (when it realized almost £7), and Braintree in 1579.[59] By 1574 Chelmsford had raised roughly £29 in hiring fees, while Tewkesbury Abbey also loaned out playing-gear between 1567 and 1585, as did the Somerset town of Yeovil in the 1560s.[60] Money could also be raised from the sale of costumes after a production, as at New Romney in 1560, and other items such as playbooks might be sold off to defray expenses. At Canterbury in 1542–3 the 'hole stage of the play' was purchased for forty shillings by 'master Batherst'.

Costumes were obviously a costly item in medieval staging since in the absence of scenery they (and the properties) had to provide the stage with much of its colour and splendour. Often they had to be made specially and frequently had to be gorgeous and imposing, but other components also made considerable inroads into the budget. Not only was there expenditure involved in the purchase of timber and metal parts for the scaffolds or waggons (Hell often requiring an iron structure to resist potential fire-damage), along with sundries such as nails, cords, pulleys, hasps and staples, but labour where not donated free had to be paid for, and food and drink for the performers and helpers often consumed a major portion of the budget, since refreshments were required not only during the performance but at rehearsals too. For example, at Whitsun 1550 the Chester Cordwainers and Shoemakers spent a total of £3. 15. 5d in staging their pageant of 'Jerusalem' which incorporated Christ's visit to Simon the Leper and his encounter with Magdalene, his ejection of the moneylenders from the Temple, and Judas's plot against him, but of this sum no less than £1. 12. 7d went on catering for the digestive needs of cast, musicians and stage staff. Beef consumed at the 'generall Reyherse' cost 3s 3d, while the players' pre-performance breakfast ran through 8s 4d; they and the 'potters of the carych' who heaved and steered the heavy cart through the streets put away 4s 8d worth of drink, but another 5s was also authorized for expenditure on liquor during the production period as a whole, as well as a mysterious sum of 20d paid to the Barkers (the guild or a family?) 'ffor wyne', possibly to be consumed on stage during the feast at Simon the Leper's house.[61]

By contrast, mounting the play only cost the company officially £1. 2s. od, even though this included such major items as a dozen boards for the waggon (presumably to repair its floor), the 'bakyng of godes brede' at 4s 8d, and 5s spent on the most expensive single item, 'payntyng & gyldyng of the pleyeng geyre', a further reminder that sumptuousness was a vital artistic criterion in civic religious performances. Wages only accounted for 17s 4d, God (i.e. Christ) receiving 2s, and the Jailor and Judas 16d each; the Jailor's Man got 14d while Mary Magdalene and Caiaphas were each content with fourpence less. By contrast, the 'potters of the carych' received 18d in addition to their generous allowance for 'drenke', while the 'Reygenall beyrer', whose role may have combined that of prompter with that of director or stage-manager, was paid only 12d. Minstrels, whose importance on the occasion of a medieval dramatic performance should never be overlooked, shared the sum of 2s 4d; the boy who led the ass features in the accounts although his wage was a mere penny, the same amount as was spent on 'soupe', probably soap to grease the waggon-wheels to ensure that they ran smoothly and quietly.

It will be no surprise to learn that both actors and stage crews often bound themselves by contract to appear or to carry out the construction work allocated to them. Actors agreed to attend rehearsals, to learn their parts, and to be ready to play them when the time came; failure to do so was penalized by the exaction of a stiff fine. But disciplinary action was also imposed on groups: typical is the ten-shilling charge levied from the York Girdlers in 1554 for not maintaining the smooth flow of waggons through the streets, thereby delaying all the subsequent pageants in the procession. Responsibility for ensuring that companies honoured their commitments rested with the 'management committee', but rehearsals can only have been conducted by individuals, and the division of blame for failure may not always have been easy to achieve. It would be helpful to know just how much power was vested in those cited as keepers or bearers of the 'regynall' or prompt-copy; the St Apollonia miniature suggests that such a figure was also the director on the occasion shown, but we have no means of knowing as yet just what his English equivalent's duties were. Frequency of rehearsals varies between individual guilds and at different centres. At Chester, where the mayor himself seems to have inspected each pageant personally,[62] rehearsal practice varied. The Smiths, Cutlers, and Plumbers held three recorded rehearsals in 1571, the last a 'genrall rehearse' which cost 7s 8d in beef and 10s in ale; whether this was a final rehearsal for all the guilds together, or simply for the Smiths and their colleagues is unrecorded; in a processional performance there would seem little point in a corporate rehearsal unless timing was being checked on. In 1575 the Chester Coopers held three practices before the 'generall rehearse'. Such sessions were rarely held in the place of performance: the Smiths and their allies conducted their first rehearsal of 1561 in 'Io Huntingtons howse'; the previous year had seen the New Romney players practising their parts in the parish church, and in 1567 the Chester Smiths rehearsed 'under St Johns' as well as 'before Mr Major [mayor]'.[63] In the same year the Painters, Glaziers, and others held their first 'Rehearse' at the home of an Alderman of their company. But doubtless almost any vacant space was pressed into service where other accommodation could not be found.

While the players busied themselves with their moves and their lines, other preparations went steadily forward. In the case of a processional performance, the pageant-carts had to be taken from their storehouses and assembled, the main superstructures being placed on the undercarriages, and such parts as were no longer in working order being replaced by new ones. In the case of a static presentation at a single site, scaffolds or stages needed to be built, their construction sometimes being assigned to different groups of individuals, as at New Romney in 1560. Audience accommodation also had to be arranged at many centres, particularly where a mobile method of presentation was envisaged, although at places such as York where viewing-stations were leased out, the problem was in the hands of the lessees where it caused pageant-masters no additional headache to contend with. Elsewhere, it was one further difficulty encountered by medieval organizers from which modern production committees are mercifully freed by the existence of custom-built theatres, subsidized village halls and community centres, and the invention of portable seating.

The communal aspect of medieval play-making must surely be one of its most compelling and attractive features. Drama was most often conceived of as a corporate activity into which a local community was expected to sink its available resources of time, talent, money and manpower, and even when a touring company arrived to present such a play as *Mankynde* or the Croxton *Play*, its members were frequently viewed not as imported strangers who sped from the district as soon as their play was done, but (given the limited range of such troupes' itineraries) as friendly denizens of the region where they played.

The spirit of medieval theatre too was different from that of today. The performance of a play invariably accompanied a holiday, and a holiday mood invariably accompanied a play; thus the spirit of 'play' in its broader sense attached itself to a medieval production, however arduous the preparations to bring it to fruition. Moreover, as has already been asserted, drama staged in the everyday settings of street and market-place, village green and private house, must have seemed to spring more directly from the world of men's and women's daily lives than does drama confined to buildings specially set aside for its use. If theatre is manifestly an extension of the social and working life of a community, this too helps to make it seem, not a rarefied or specialized activity whose mysteries are the exclusive preserve of a handful of specially-trained initiates, but the natural expression of a common quest for relaxation, mutual contact, and the enhancement of a drab and laborious existence.

V

Just how vital a place drama occupied in the lives of medieval English men and women it is impossible to discover. Even though allusions to theatrical events exist, references to audience response, average attendances, or crowd behaviour are not sufficiently plentiful to convey more than a shadowy impression of the popular view of dramatic activities during the period. One of the more memorable and graphic accounts extant is of that performance at Beverley in about 1220, in which the action proved so enthralling that a number of frustrated youths climbed to the triforium of the Minster to gain a better view, but one incident does not constitute a global reaction. We may also gain some insight into attitudes towards drama from such polemics as the Wycliffite *Tretise of Miraclis Pleyinge* of *c*. 1400 which, in aiming to demonstrate the essential sinfulness of Biblical plays by maintaining that people derive less spiritual enlightenment than diversion from them,[64] gives the impression that the folk were flocking to witness such performances, but it scarcely supplies us with hard and fast evidence. Hence, though it is still possible to discover some of the ways in which dramatics were regarded in the Middle Ages, we must exercise caution in interpreting such data, and avoid basing bold assertions on flimsy premisses.

It may be as well to dispose of that unsubtle argument that the medieval church disapproved of all forms of dramatic activity, since it is still encountered occasionally, even today. It is clear that the Church disapproved of *certain types* of stage entertainment especially if they were presented in certain places and at certain times, and it had little sympathy with drama if it was diverted from what the authorities considered its true purpose as an aid to worship or belief. Yet, despite having inherited a legacy of condemnation from the early Fathers, the Church did not refuse to sanction every form of theatre, and it is important to establish what was unacceptable, and why. The chief kinds of performance censured were those linked with the pagan past, those unofficial religious plays which tempted clerics to participate in them, or those which encroached on church premises or property, those which contained heretical, obscene or scurrilous matter, those which diverted folk from attending divine service, especially the Mass, and those which mingled sacred truths with frivolous material. The Church adopted a strict attitude towards the excesses of the Feast of Fools, as a celebrated letter of January 1207 from Pope Innocent III makes clear,[65] but the orthodox attitude towards drama in general is summarized in the distinction drawn by the anonymous author of *Dives and Pauper*, a long prose work composed between 1405 and 1410, during which a rich neophyte receives spiritual guidance from a mendicant priest. In reply to a question concerning the legitimacy of 'steraclis, pleyys, and dauncis', Pauper has this to say:

> Steraclis, pleyys, & dauncis that arn don principaly for devocioun & honest merthe to teche men to love God the more & for no rybaudye ne medelyd [mixed] with no rybaudye ne lesyngis arn leful, so that the peple be nout lettyd therby fro Godys servyce ne fro Godis word herynge and that ther be non errour medelyd in swyche steraclis & pleyys ayens the feyth of holy chirche ne ayenys the statys of holy chirche ne ayenys good lyvynge. Alle other arn defendyd [forbidden] bothin halyday & warke day . . . for to representyn in pleyynge at Cristemesse Heroudis & the thre kyngis & other proces of the gospel bothin than & at Estryn [Easter] and in othir tymes also it is leful and comendable . . .[66]

The speaker goes on to defend the making of mirth on the Sabbath, provided that the pastimes chosen do not conduce 'to lecherie & to othir synnys'; hence 'honest dauncis & honest playys don in dew tyme & in good maner in the halyday' are deemed permissible. This is one of the many issues, however, on which the Lollards and the ecclesiastical establishment were at odds, in that the Wycliffite *Floretum* firmly condemns both watching and participating in plays of every kind. Yet, as has been shown elsewhere,[67] some medieval clerics felt no shame in taking a leading part in drama, nor did they incur the wrath of their superiors for doing so.

None the less, some clergy may have felt uneasy with the notion of those in Holy Orders mounting plays, even outside churches, and one solution to the dilemma could have been to permit lay performers to appear in the newly-emergent vernacular plays under the joint sponsorship of church and city, or church and guild.[68] This, combined with the new humanistic spirit which infuses the drama of medieval Christianity in the twelfth and thirteenth centuries, undoubtedly contributed to the popular appeal of religious plays, and it is possibly because Christian drama was now in direct competition with secular entertainments for the attention of the populace, that the writers and performers of the cycle plays and moralities were persuaded to carry the war into the enemy's

camp and incorporate elements of secular comedy or traditional folk
drama into their work, although (as we have seen in these pages)
invariably moulding the secular and archetypal to serve doctrinal ends.
If guilds did indeed employ 'professionals' for certain important parts in
the cycle plays, then the appeal of religious drama would be greatly
increased, but even if this were not the case, the sight of members of the
local lay community participating in theatre might well prove equally
irresistible, as it can often do today. Nor were playwrights slow to exploit
this intimate relationship between stage and audience by inserting local
or topical allusions into their scripts, as we find in *Mankynde* or in the
pageants of Cain or the Shepherds in the Wakefield Cycle. The use of
anachronism and topographical references in plays of the time is an
implicit tribute to the presence of spectators eager to have the gospel's
story brought home to them in their own sphere. Such elements are a
reflection of the manner in which Biblical events and incidents in the life
of the spirit were regarded as having permanent relevance, and might be
regarded as taking place both within human time and yet outside it.
Events in first-century Palestine were not viewed as occurring exclusively
at one historical period and in one geographical location. The struggle of
Everyman to make ready his account-book or Mankynde's battle to sow
his crops were not to be weighed down with an oppressively over-
developed sense of the here and now, since they were presented as relevant
for all times and places, and applicable to all sorts and conditions of men.

How should we assess the audience's influence on medieval theatre and
its response to drama in the Middle Ages? That stage-plays represented
one of its favourite forms of entertainment is difficult to prove, if only
because the ambiguity of the Latin term '*ludus*', the French '*jeu*' and the
English 'play' or 'game' makes extant records hard to interpret. Yet we
may still suspect that widespread enthusiasm for the theatre did exist, an
enthusiasm which at times bordered on the disruptive and disturbing if
statements contained in prologues, epilogues, and direct addresses to
spectators are taken at face-value. Duk Morawd opens the play which
bears his name with advice which, for all its stock elements of tyrannical
rant, suggests that he is confronting an unruly mob or one quite capable
of becoming so:

I prey yow, lordyngys so hende [courteous],
No yangelyngys ye mak in this folde*
    To-day;
Als ye are lovely in fas,
Set yow alle semly in plas . . .
And therfor I warne yow infere [all together]
That ye mak neyther criyng ne bere [clamour]. (lines 7–11, 23–4)
(*Probably not 'in this yard or enclosure', but a tag: 'no rumpus at all')

The Durham Prologue is more direct in its appeal:

Pes, lordyngs, I prai yow pes,
And of your noys ye stynt and ses,
Oure gamen to lett [hinder] ne cry in pres [together]
    For your courtasy. (1–4)[69]

Clearly medieval theatre like any other popular entertainment attracted its hooligans and rowdies, but such hints that undesirable elements were present increases the likelihood that play-performances were highly attractive to the more orderly-minded as well, as the quality of the surviving playtexts suggests. Furthermore, most plays of the period made their appeal to an audience on a number of levels, and the combination of humour, moral instruction, biblical exegesis, and spectacle would have pleased a wide variety of tastes in an age which depended entirely on 'live' activities for its recreation. Besides, if performances were open to all free of charge, as was certainly the situation at some centres,[70] then their power to pull in spectators would have been considerably improved.

Certainly there can have been little doubt in the minds of the authorities and organizing personnel that the staging of drama was a serious obligation. One of the most eloquent illustrations of the point comes from the 'Early Banns' drawn up at Chester in 1539–40, which offer a unique insight into the thinking which lay behind the cycle presentations there, and doubtless elsewhere, and into the problem arising from coping with large numbers anxious to view them:

for asmyche as of old tyme not only for the Augmentacion & incresse
of the holy and catholyk faith of our savyour Cryst Iesu and to
exhort the myndes of the comen peple to gud devocion and holsom
doctryne ther of but Also for the comen welth and prosperitie of
this Citie A play and declaracion of many and dyvers stories of the
bible . . . to be declared & playde now in this Whison weke . . .
wherfore mr Mair in the kinges name straitly chargith and
comaundyth that every person and persons of what astate degree or
condicion so ever he or they be resorting to the said playes do use
theym selff peceably without making any Assault Afrey or other
disturbans wherby the same playes shalbe disturbed . . . Apon peyne
of imprisonyment of theire bodies and making fyne to the king at
Maisters Maires pleasure . . .[71]

These banns are a fitting reminder that in participating in the experience which was medieval theatre its original spectators both as individuals and as citizens were also considered to be its principal beneficiaries, and as a result were expected to behave themselves accordingly. Affrays and assaults might break out among them (and indeed among the players) from time to time,[72] but there can be little doubt that in general, their response to what was presented for their enlightenment and pleasure was a favourable one.

The reasons are not far to seek: medieval theatre was designed for the community as a whole rather than for a privileged or educated section of it. It frequently constituted a venture in which large sections of the population were active participants, and one in which the presence of an audience was freely acknowledged and gratefully relied upon to such an extent that its members could be addressed from the stage. Not only choric figures did so, but personages ostensibly immersed in the drama proper. Christ could launch his reproachful words from the cross not simply at the characters with him on stage, but to the spectators standing round the pageant-waggon. The actor playing Joseph could confide his fears about Mary's pregnancy directly to his real-life cronies in the crowd. Physically, too, medieval onlookers formed an integral part of the stage action, for on many occasions they impinged on the playing-area and on the actors' awareness to such an extent that they had to be told to stand still or to 'make room' or had to dodge aside when Herod raged 'in the pagond and in the strete also'. Quite clearly this led to an audience-response which was not only uninhibited and immediate, but also credulous. Proximity to the stage, far from destroying credibility, actually strengthened it.

Despite an evident unconcern for verisimilitude, much of the power of the medieval theatre lay in its ability to inspire such innocent affirmations of theatrical faith from its spectators. Allusions to the sense of belief engendered among audiences abound. Many witnesses of medieval presentations in Britain would surely have echoed the praise bestowed by a typical eye-witness of the celebrated performances of *Le Mystère des Actes des Apôtres* at Bourges in France of 1536, which included the comment that the plays were

> soundly and excellently set forth by serious-minded men who understood how to portray the characters they represented by signs and gestures so well, that the greater part of the audience viewed the whole matter as actually taking place, and not as a piece of make-believe.[73]

Such a testimony is an eloquent tribute to the undimmed attraction of the medieval stage.

Notes

Preface

1 All quotations are taken from *Everyman*, ed. A. C. Cawley, Manchester, 1961, to which I am also indebted for its stimulating introduction.
2 In the author's modern-dress production in North Wales in December 1981 Goodes was conveniently immobilized in a wheelchair decorated with banknotes, but the device is unlikely to have occurred to a medieval producer!
3 For instance, figures virtually identical to that shown in the woodcut of Everyman himself appear in Wynkyn de Worde's *Hyckescorner* (c. 1513) and in John Copland's *The Enterlude of Youth* (c. 1562), depicting their eponymous heroes.

Part I The Repertoire

1 Gāmini Salgādo, *English Drama: A Critical Introduction*, London, 1981.
2 For fuller discussions, see *MDC*; *EES* I; O. B. Hardison Jr, *Christian Rite and Christian Drama in the Middle Ages*, Baltimore, 1965; V. A. Kolve, *The Play Called Corpus Christi*, London, 1966; and Glynne Wickham, *Shakespeare's Dramatic Heritage*, London, 1969, pp. 7–23.
3 See Kolve, *op. cit.*, pp. 44–50, and *EES* I. 313–14.
4 See Rosemary Woolf, *The English Mystery Plays*, London, 1972, *MD*, and *MES* pp. 1–14, for some discussion of the origins of the cycles.
5 For a summary of the relative positions see *TMA* pp. 127–31.
6 See *DMC* II. 542.
7 For Geoffrey, see *TMA* p. 63; Hilarius's play appears in Latin in *DMC* II. 338–41. For locations of saints' plays see *Annals of English Drama*, ed. cit., pp. 2–16. For discussions of the genre, see Glynne Wickham, 'The Staging of Saint Plays in England' in Sandro Sticca (ed.), *The Medieval Drama*, Albany, 1972, pp. 99–119; David L. Jeffrey, 'English Saints' Plays' in Neville Denny (ed.), *Medieval Drama*, Stratford-on-Avon Studies 16, 1973, pp. 75–86.

8 *Duk Morawd* is printed in *NCP* pp. 106–113.

9 For texts of the two Digby plays see *Digby*, pp. 1–23, 24–95; they are also printed in *MD*. For *Beunans Meriasek*, see Whitley Stokes (ed.), *Beunans Meriasek: The Life of St Meriasek: A Cornish Drama*, London, 1872.

10 See below, pp. 69–70. For the Croxton *Play of the Sacrament* see *NCP* pp. 58–89. It is also printed in *MD*.

11 The text of *The Pride of Life* appears in *NCP* pp. 90–105.

12 The texts of *The Castel of Perseveraunce*, *Mankynde*, and *Wisdom* all appear in *Macro*, with a useful introduction to each play.

13 See Markham Harris (trans.), *The Cornish Ordinalia*, Washington, 1969. On its date, see David C. Fowler, 'The Date of the Cornish *Ordinalia*', *Mediaeval Studies* 23 (1961), 91–125.

14 See *TMA* pp. 97–104 for a summary of the position. For performances by London clerics, see *ibid.*, p. 198.

15 See Siegfried Wenzel, 'An Early Reference to a Corpus Christi Play', *MP* 74 (1977), 390–4.

16 For texts of the major cycles, see *Chester*, *Coventry*, *LC*, *Towneley*, and *York*; individual plays and fragments are printed in *NCP*.

17 For selected references to secular dramatic activities, see *TMA* pp. 14–21.

18 For text see J. A. W. Bennett and G. V. Smithers (eds), *Early Middle English Verse and Prose*, Oxford, 1966, pp. 196–200.

19 See Henry Jenner, 'Descriptions of Cornish Manuscripts: II', *Journal of the Royal Institute of Cornwall* 20 (1915–21), 41–8; R. Morton Nance, 'The Charter Endorsement in Cornish Brit. Mus. Add. Chart 19491', *Old Cornwall* II. 4 (1932), 34–6.

20 See Norman Davis (ed.), *The Paston Letters*, 2 vols, Oxford, 1971, I. 461. For the play see W. W. Greg (ed.), Malone Society *Collections* II, Oxford, 1908, 117–24, and David Wiles, *The Early Plays of 'Robin Hood'*, Cambridge, 1981.

21 *Nature* was reprinted in 1905 as Volume 12 of W. Bang (ed.), *Materialen zur Kunde des alteren Englisches Dramas*, 44 vols, Louvain, 1902–14; *Fulgens and Lucres* was edited by F. S. Boas and A. W. Reed, Oxford, 1926, and by Glynne Wickham in *EMI*. The allusion to Thomas More occurs in Roper's *Life*, Everyman Library edition, 1963, p. 3.

22 For the text see R. H. Robbins (ed.), *Secular Lyrics of the Fourteenth and Fifteenth Centuries*, Oxford, 2nd edn, 1956, pp. 110–13. For the Norwich Christmas ceremonial, see *MES* p. 123.

23 Lydgate's mummings are printed in H. N. MacCracken (ed.), *The Minor Poems of John Lydgate*, EETS (OS 192), 1923, II. Secular Poems, 668–701. See also *EMI*, pp. 204–13.

24 For civic ceremonial, see *EES* I. 51–111. Lydgate's pageants appear in MacCracken, *ed. cit.* II. 630–48; for others see Carleton Brown, 'Lydgate's Verses on Queen Margaret's Entry into London', *MLR* 7 (1912), 225–34; F. J. Furnivall (ed.), *Political, Religious, and Love Poems*, EETS (OS 15), 2nd edn. 1903, p. 5; Robbins, *ed. cit.*, pp. 115–17.

Part II Plays in performance

Chapter 1 The Booth Stage: **Mankynde**

1 I have derived considerable assistance in writing this chapter from the editions of the play printed in *Macro*, *MD*, and *EMI*. Although I disagree with Southern as to the siting of *Mankynde* and on other points of interpretation, I owe a great deal to *SPS* pp. 21–45, 143–5; I have been greatly helped by Paula Neuss, 'Active and Idle Language: Dramatic Images in *Mankind*', in Neville Denny (ed.), *Medieval Drama*, Stratford-upon-Avon Studies 16, 1973, pp. 41–67, and by Neville Denny, 'Aspects of the Staging of *Mankind*', *Medium Aevum* 43 (1974), 252–63.

2 See *Macro*, pp. xxxvii–xlv for essential remarks on the play's characteristics.

3 See *SPS*, and J. Q. Adams (ed.), *Chief Pre-Shakespearean Dramas*, Boston, 1924, p. 304, for the chief arguments for and against inn-yard performance. Wickham in *EMI* supports Southern's arguments for Great Hall presentation, though Eccles, *Macro*, prefers the traditional notion of an inn-yard. On medieval inn architecture, see Margaret Wood, *The English Mediaeval House*, London, 1965, pp. 192–3.

4 See Stanley J. Kahrl (ed.), *Records of Plays and Players in Lincolnshire, 1300–1585*, Malone Society *Collections* VIII, Oxford, 1969 (1974), p. 92, and *TMA* p. 21. On 'professional' performers, see *TMA* p. 221.

5 All quotations from the text of *Mankynde* are taken from *Macro*.

6 See *EMI* p. 5.

7 See *SPS* pp. 27–8, 143–4; my solution is a more satisfactory response to Southern's justified belief that the voices 'sound almost as if they came out of the audience' (p. 143).

8 See *ibid.*, p. 509 for examples of stage-figures wearing such 'labels'.

9 See *ibid.*, pp. 31–2.

10 See *ibid.*, p. 34.

11 *Ibid.*, p. 36.

12 Southern (*SPS* p. 40) takes the view that in order to collect the jackets both New Gyse and Nought exit through the indoor audience, but even in such an environment the security of costumes lying unattended remains a problem.

13 *EMI* p. 29.

14 *Ibid.*, p. 31.

15 Wickham's usually excellent edition in *EMI* omits this vital entrance (p. 31).

Chapter 2 Scenic Structures: the Croxton **Play of the Sacrament**

1 For this and other essential information I am indebted to *NCP*, pp. lxx–lxxxv; all quotations are from this text. I have also been grateful for many remarks in *MD*, pp. 754–6.

2 *MD*, p. 754.

3 *NCP*, p. lxxxiv.

4 See Giles E. Dawson (ed.), *Plays and Players in Kent, 1450–1642*, Malone Society *Collections* VII, Oxford, 1965, pp. 208, 209.

5 Although some commentators reject Cailleau's extended platform (which depicts nine principal structures) on the grounds of its length, its 'pictorialism', or what it omits from the locations apparently required by the play's content, the principle demonstrated is acceptable provided the structures are not unduly proliferated. For a cogent argument that the frequently-employed French term *mansion* for such components should be abandoned, see Graham A. Runnalls, ' "Mansion" and "Lieu": Two Technical Terms in Medieval French Staging?' *French Studies* XXXV (1981), 386–93. I am grateful to Mr Runnalls for bringing his article to my attention.

6 What follows is based on observations made during a visit to Croxton in September 1981.

7 See, for example, *TMA*, pp. 15–16, 126, 127, 133.

8 See Arthur Freeman, 'A Source for *The Jew of Malta*', *N & Q* 207 (1962), 139–41.

9 See Stanley Kahrl, *Traditions of Medieval English Drama*, London, 1974, pp. 119–20.

10 It is succinctly set forth in *MD*, p. 755.

Chapter 3 *Theatre in the Round:* **The Castel of Perseveraunce**

1 For a salutary caveat see Sumiko Miyajima, *The Theatre of Man*, Avon, 1977, pp. 157–68; the danger is illustrated by Merle Fifield's stimulating but single-minded *Castle in the Circle*, Muncie, Indiana, 1967. Nor is Henri Rey-Flaud, *Le Cercle Magique*, Paris, 1973, always immune from the temptation to make large claims for staging in the round, despite some impressive evidence.

2 Among the objectors to Southern's thesis have been P. M. Ryan in *Quarterly Journal of Speech* 44 (1958), 444–6, and Natalie Crohn Schmitt, 'Was there a Medieval Theatre in the Round? A Re-examination of the Evidence', *TN* 23 (1968–9), 130–42; 24 (1969–70), 18–25. For a rejoinder to Schmitt, see Catherine Belsey, 'The Stage Plan of *The Castle of Perseverance*', *ibid.*, 28 (1974), 124–32, which tends to re-assert Southern's views, although interpreting the plan symbolically rather than literally.

3 For the staging of the *Thrie Estaitis* at Cupar, see John MacQueen, '*Ane Satyre of the Thrie Estaitis*', *Studies in Scottish Literature* 3 (1966), 129–43; Glynne Wickham, 'The Staging of Saint Plays in England', in Sandro Sticca (ed.), *The Medieval Drama*, Albany, 1972, 99–119; Robert Potter, *The English Morality Plays*, 1975, pp. 81–8; Peter Happé (ed.), *Four Morality Plays*, Harmondsworth, 1979, pp. 58–9.

4 See *TMA*, pp. 229–31 for some details of admission charges and the absence of them.

5 See *ibid.*, pp. 135, 158; also Rey-Flaud, *op. cit.*, pp. 118–22.

6 See especially Schmitt, *op. cit.*, *passim*.

7 All textual references are taken from *Macro*.

8 See Schmitt, *op. cit.* Not all her ingenious arguments for rejecting Southern's theories need be accepted *en bloc*. Her claim, for example, that many of Fouquet's designs depict a scene within a barrier, ignores the fact that only the St Apollonia miniature actually shows spectators on scaffolds engaged in watching a scene from a stage-play. She also omits any reference to the plans which accompany the texts of the Cornish *Ordinalia*, and clearly show a circular 'theatre'. See too the objections voiced by Belsey under Note 2 above.

9 See *TMA* pp. 158–9.

10 See E. K. Chambers, *English Literature at the Close of the Middle Ages*, Oxford, 1945, p. 55.

11 See *NCP*, p. 60.

12 See *Macro*, pp. 186–7 (note to line 138); also *MD*, p. 803. On timing the play, see *MTR*, p. 112.

13 In what follows I have been greatly helped by *MTR*, Schmitt, *op. cit.*, and by the editorial matter in *Macro*, *MD*, Happé, *op. cit.*, and in Edgar T. Schell and J. D. Shuchter (eds.), *English Morality Plays and Moral Interludes*, New York, 1969.

14 One of the best discussions of the topic will be found in T. W. Craik, *The Tudor Interlude*, Leicester, 1958, pp. 49–92. For the daughters of God, see *Macro*, p. 185 (notes).

15 Nevertheless this view is taken by Arthur Forstater and Joseph L. Baird, ' "Walking and wending", Mankind's opening speech', *TN* 26 (1971–2), 60–4.

16 Eccles in *Macro*, p. 192 (note to line 1369) is inclined to read this line proverbially, but it can be taken literally as evidence of a modest celebratory feast served on the scaffold.

17 Fifield, *op. cit.*, p. 17; for continental passages and their use, see *TMA* pp. 163–4, 178. Happé, *op. cit.*, p. 78, thinks that a boy may have played the Soul, and been concealed in the cupboard!

18 *Macro*, Glossary, p. 249.

Chapter 4 *Processional Staging: the York Passion Sequence*

1 See Lucy Toulmin Smith (ed.), *York Plays*, Oxford, 1885, pp. xi, xxxi. All quotations from the York Cycle are taken from Richard Beadle (ed.), *The York Plays*, 1982, though I have not employed its Roman numeration for the plays. The earliest version of Rogers's *Breviary* is transcribed from an unnumbered manuscript in the Chester City Archives in *REEDC*, pp. 238–9.

2 See Toulmin Smith, pp. xxxii–xxxiii.

3 See M. L. Spencer, *The Corpus Christi Pageants in England*, New York, 1911; Hardin Craig, 'The Corpus Christi Procession and the Corpus Christi Play', *JEGP* 13 (1913), 589–602.

4 See H. F. Westlake, *The Parish Guilds of Medieval England*, London, 1919, p. 57.

5 Neil C. Brooks, 'Processional Drama and Dramatic Processions in Germany in the Late Middle Ages', *JEGP* 32 (1938), 141–71.

6 *Ibid.*, pp. 169–70.

7 See A. C. Cawley (ed.), *Everyman and Medieval Miracle Plays*, London, 1956; second edition, 1957, p. xii.

8 Martial Rose (transl.), *The Wakefield Mystery Plays*, London, 1961, pp. 9–48.

9 *Ibid.*, pp. 24–6.

10 Nelson's views were first advanced in 'Principles of Processional Staging: York Cycle', *MP* 67 (1970), 303–20, and reprinted with slight changes in *MES*. See also Martin Stevens, 'The York Cycle: from procession to play', *LSE* (NS) 6 (1972), 37–61.

11 See particularly Margaret Dorrell, 'Two studies of the York Corpus Christi Play', *LSE* (NS) 6 (1972), 63–111.

12 See Stanley Kahrl, *Traditions of Medieval English Drama*, London, 1974, especially pp. 43–7.

13 In describing the processional route and the location and leasing of stations, I am greatly indebted to Anna J. Mill, 'The Stations of the York Corpus Christi Play', *Yorkshire Archaeological Journal* 37 (1951), 492–502, Appendix III, and Meg Twycross, ' "Places to hear the play": pageant stations at York, 1398–1572', *REEDN* 2 (1978), 10–33.

14 For some of what follows I am grateful to the authors of papers published in *METh* 1 (1979), and 2 (1980), notably Peter Meredith, John Marshall, Philip Butterworth, and Reg Ingram.

15 See Alexandra F. Johnston and Margaret Dorrell, 'The Doomsday Pageant of the York Mercers, 1433', *LSE* (NS) 5 (1971), 29–34.

16 For the full indenture, see *REEDY* I pp. 55–6. I side with Peter Meredith (*PFRC*, p. 49) in thinking 'costers of lewent brede' is unlikely to mean 'an eleventh's breadth' as the editors of *REEDY* assume.

17 See *ERD* 123–4, *EES* I. 173, and *MDC* pp. 68–9; for a response see John Marshall, 'The Chester Pageant Carriage – how right was Rogers?', *METh* 1 (1979), 52–3, and *TMA*, pp. 105–6.

18 See Philip Butterworth, 'The York Mercers' Pageant Vehicle, 1433–1467: Wheels, Steering, and Control', *METh* 1 (1979), 72–81.

19 *REEDY* II. 713–15; for 1468 records see *ibid.*, I. 100–2, II. 772–4.

20 *Ibid.*, p. 25.

21 *Coventry*, p. 27.

22 See *ibid.*, p. 97, and Reginald Ingram, ' "Playng geire accustumed belongyng & necessarie": guild records and pageant production at Coventry', in *PFRC*, p. 89.

23 See *OED* under 'nail', meaning II. 4 (quotation c. 1440), and 'stub', meaning 6, but more importantly, meaning 7 b. For the widespread use of 'woode pins' in medieval life, see Dorothy Hartley, *The Land of England*, London, 1979, pp. 207–8.

24 I am much indebted here to some of the observations contained in David
Parry, 'The York Mystery Cycle at Toronto, 1977', *METh* I (1979), 19–31.

25 This was in fact the method adopted when the present writer staged a
selection of the cycles in Bangor Cathedral in March 1972. For their
practical experiments on the mechanics of the Deposition I have to thank
my colleagues Geoffrey Elliott and Michael Heath who played Nicodemus
and Joseph of Arimathea respectively.

Chapter 5   Great Hall Theatre: **Fulgens and Lucres**

1 For indoor entertainments in the medieval and Renaissance periods see
TMA, pp. 63–4, 70–9.

2 *Handlynge Synne* edited by F. J. Furnivall appears in *EETS* (OS) 119, 123
(1901, 1903); for a modern transcript of a major portion of the *Tretise* see
Anne Hudson (ed), *Selections from English Wycliffite Writings*, Cambridge,
1978, pp. 97–104; for the allusion from Bury St Edmunds, see Karl Young,
'An *Interludium* for a Gild of Corpus Christi', *MLN* 48 (1933), 84–6.

3 There is useful information in F. S. Boas and A. W. Reed (eds), *Fulgens
and Lucres: A Fifteenth-Century Secular Play* by Henry Medwall, Oxford,
1926, pp. ix–xxvii, and in *EMI*, pp. 37–40.

4 For a most helpful account of Great Hall theatre, see *SPS*, pp. 48–55.

5 *Ibid.*, pp. 53–5.

6 All textual references are to Boas's and Reed's edition of 1926, although
occasional capitalizations have been introduced for the sake of clarity.

7 *SPS*, p. 101.

8 For a more fully developed treatment of this aspect, see Robert C. Jones,
'The Stage World and the "Real" World in Medwall's *Fulgens and Lucres*',
MLQ 36 (1971), 131–42.

9 *EMI*, p. 46.

10 See *TMA*, pp. 18–19.

11 For the ensuing remarks I am indebted to Peter Meredith ' "Farte Pryke in
Cule" and Cock Fighting', *METh* 6.1. (1984), 30–9, and to Meg Twycross's
spritely production of *Fulgens* at Christ's College, Cambridge in March 1984.
Much as I admire Meredith's ingenious reconstruction, I still feel 'in cule'
suggests spearing *in the buttocks*, a feat seemingly impossible in the version
of the game adopted on this occasion.

12 *SPS*, p. 114.

13 *Ibid.*, p. 122.

14 *EMI*, p. 98.

Part III   The English Medieval Theatre

1 This part of the book owes an immense debt to Ian Lancashire's superlative
collection, *Dramatic Texts and Records of Britain*, Cambridge, 1984, *passim*.

2 See *TMA* p. 134 for continental examples.

3 On the 'game-place', see *EES* II. 1 (1963), 166–7, 361; David Galloway, 'The "Game Place" and "House" at Great Yarmouth, 1493–1595', *TN* 31 (1977), 6–9; Richard Beadle, 'The East Anglian "game-place": a possibility for further research', *REEDN* 1 (1978), 2–4; David Galloway, 'The East Anglian "game-place": some facts and fictions', *ibid.*, 2 (1979), 24–6. For Norwich, see *MES*, p. 135.

4 See W. O. Hassall, 'Plays at Clerkenwell', *MLR* 33 (1938), 564–7.

5 J. D. A. Ogilvy, *'Mimi, scurrae, histriones*: entertainers of the Middle Ages', *Speculum* 38 (1963), 603–19 contains invaluable references to early performers.

6 See Martin Stevens, 'The York Cycle: from Procession to Play', *LSE* (NS) 6 (1972), 37–61, and A. M. Nagler, *The Medieval Religious Stage*, New Haven and London, 1976, pp. 59–60.

7 See *TMA*, p. 47.

8 For the 'play-field', see Anna J. Mill, *Mediaeval Plays in Scotland*, Edinburgh, 1927, p. 351; for *Thrie Estaitis*, see Mill, 'Representations of Lyndsay's "Satyre of the Thrie Estaitis" ', *Proceedings of the Modern Language Association of America* 47 (1932), 636–51, and Peter Happé (ed.), *Four Morality Plays*, Harmondsworth, 1979, pp. 56–61.

9 See Kenneth M. Dodd, 'Another Elizabethan Theater in the Round', *Shakespeare Quarterly* 21 (1970), 125–56, which transcribes the quoted document on pp. 126–7.

10 On the Cornish sites, see *TMA*, pp. 134–5; also Trevor Holm, 'Cornish Plays and Playing Places', *TN* 4 (1950), 52–4; on the *plen-an-gwary* see R. Morton Nance, 'The "Plen an Gwary" or Cornish Playing place', *Journal of the Royal Institution of Cornwall* 24 (1933–6), 190–211, and Natalie Crohn Schmitt, 'Was there a Medieval Theatre in the Round? A Re-examination of the Evidence', *TN* 23 (1968–9), 130–42; *ibid.*, 24 (1969–70), 18–25; repr. in Taylor and Nelson (eds), *Medieval English Drama: Essays Critical and Contextual*, Chicago and London, 1972, pp. 292–315.

11 For a general survey, see G. H. Cook, *The English Mediaeval Parish Church*, London, 1954, pp. 31–4.

12 The Latin source of the Beverley incident is in *DMC* II. 539–40; see also *TMA* p. 126. John Bromyard in his *Summa Predicantium* (c. 1325–50) says that players 'in the play which is commonly called a *Miracle* use masks' (G. R. Owst, *Literature and Pulpit in Medieval England*, Cambridge, 1933, p. 395.)

13 Many of the relevant documents are printed in F. M. Powicke and C. R. Cheney (eds), *Councils and Synods with other Documents relating to the English Church, II. 1205–1313*, Oxford, 1964.

14 See F. J. Furnivall (ed.), *Robert of Brunne's 'Handlyng Synne'*, EETS (OS) 119 and 123, 1901, 1903. G. C. Britton, reviewing *TMA* in *N&Q* 225 (1980), 541–2, contends that Mannyng's condemnation applies only to such diversions as took place during Mass, but the diocesan statutes to which I have referred tend not to support such a view.

15 See David Klausner's contribution under 'Research in Progress', *REEDN* I (1979), 20–4, and Cook, *op. cit.*, p. 33. De Grandisson's injunction will be found in F. C. Hingeston-Randolph (ed.), *The Register of John de Grandisson, Bishop of Exeter, (A.D. 1327–1369)*, 1899, III. 1213–15.

16 See John C. Coldewey, 'The Last Rise and Final Demise of Essex Town Drama', *MLQ* 36 (1975), 239–60.

17 Printed in *EES* I. 332–9.

18 See *MS* II. 244, and R. B. Dobson, *Durham Priory 1400–1450*, London, 1973, pp. 97–8. For Maxstoke, see *MS* II. 384.

19 See C. B. Thomas, 'The Miracle Play at Dunstable', *MLN* 32 (1917), 337–44.

20 On *Wisdom*, see Milton M. Gatch, 'Mysticism and Satire in the Morality of Wisdom', *Philological Quarterly* 53 (1974), 342–62.

21 See *TMA* pp. 216, 19, 220.

22 On staging church-dramas, see Fletcher Collins Jr, *The Production of Medieval Church Music-Drama*, Charlottesville, 1972, much of which must be speculative; see also *TMA* pp. 49–63.

23 For a recent view of the staging of *La Seinte Resureccion*, see Henri Rey-Flaud, *Pour Une Dramaturgie du Moyen-Âge*, Paris, 1980.

24 Sundry examples of such effects are given in *TMA*, pp. 176–7.

25 Texts of both plays are found in *Digby*, pp. 1–23, 24–95, and *MD*, pp. 665–86, 689–753. Quotations are from *MD*.

26 For differing views on the staging of *The Conversion of St Paul*, see Mary del Vilar, 'The staging of The Conversion of St Paul', *TN* 25 (1970–1), 64–8; Glynne Wickham, 'The Staging of Saint Plays in England', in Sandro Sticca (ed.), *The Medieval Drama*, Albany, 1972, pp. 99–119; Raymond J. Pentzell, 'The Medieval Theatre in the Streets', *Theatre Survey* 14 (1973), 1–21; John Coldewey, 'The Digby Plays and the Chelmsford Records', *RORD* 18 (1975), 103–21; A. M. Nagler, *op. cit.*, pp. 64–7.

27 Examples of the use of animals and birds in medieval plays will be found in *TMA*, pp. 175–6.

28 *MD*, p. 688.

29 See Orville K. Larson, 'Bishop Abraham of Souzdal's Description of *Sacre Rappresentazione*', *Education Theatre Journal* 9 (1957), 208–13.

30 See, for example, Peter Meredith, 'The Development of the York Mercers' Pageant Waggon', *METh* I (1979), 5–18, on just one such technical problem and the response to it.

31 One instance is quoted by Martin Stevens, 'Illusion and Reality in the Medieval Drama', *College English* 32 (1970–1), 448–64.

32 See *TMA*, p. 40.

33 The Fleury *Visitatio* is found in *DMC* I. 393–7; the Herod plays in *ibid.*, II. 84–9, 110–13; the *Planctus* in *ibid.*, I. 507–12.

34 Text in *MD*, pp. 80–121.

35 The staging of *Adam* is still subject to much speculation; see Grace Frank, 'The Genesis and Staging of the *Jeu d'Adam*', *Proceedings of the Modern Language Association of America* 54 (1944), 7–17 (summarized in *TMA*,

pp. 121–4) for the '*al fresco* view'. Willem Noomen, '*Le Jeu d'Adam*. Etude descriptive et analytique', *Romania* 89 (1968), 145–93, Tony Hunt, 'The Unity of the Play of Adam (*Ordo Representacionis Ade*)', *ibid.*, 96 (1975), 368–88, 497–527, and M. Accarie in *Mélanges Jonin*, Senefiance, 7, Aix-en-Provence, 1979, 1–16, all favour indoor performance.

36 See Urban T. Holmes Jr, '*Ludos Scenicos* in Giraldus', *MLR* 57 (1942), 188–9.

37 *Councils and Synods*, p. 195.

38 Quoted in translation in *TMA*, pp. 187–8.

39 J. W. Robinson, 'Medieval English Acting', *TN* 13 (1959), 83–8, in my view over-stresses the formalized elements in liturgical performance, though I am greatly indebted to his discussion in many other respects.

40 *REEDY* I. 109.

41 All references to Beverley records are from *MES*, pp. 94–9.

42 *REEDY* I. 24–5.

43 See Robinson, *op. cit.*, and Meg Twycross's contribution recorded in Sheila Lindenbaum, 'Informal Report of the 1976 MLA Medieval Drama Seminar', *RORD* 20 (1977), 87–90.

44 F. N. Robinson (ed.), *The Poetical Works of Chaucer*, Second Edn., 1957; *The Canterbury Tales*, VI. 395–9.

45 David Bevington, 'Discontinuity in Mediaeval Acting Traditions', in G. R. Hibbard (ed.), *The Elizabethan Theatre* V, London, 1975, pp. 1–16.

46 R. W. Ingram, ' "To find the players and all that longith therto": Notes on the production of Medieval Drama in Coventry', in *ibid.*, pp. 17–44.

47 See Kenneth Cameron and Stanley J. Kahrl, 'Staging the N-Town Cycle', *TN* 21 (1967), 122–38; for the paid actors, see p. 133.

48 See Peter Meredith, ' "Item for a grone – iijᵈ – records and performance" ', in *PFRC*, p. 33. For references see *REEDC*, pp. 96, 108.

49 See Alexandra F. Johnston, 'The Guild of Corpus Christi and the Procession of Corpus Christi in York', *Mediaeval Studies* 38 (1976), 372–84; for Lincoln, see Stanley J. Kahrl, 'Medieval Drama in Louth', *RORD* 10 (1967), 129–33. For the York ordinance of 1475, see *REEDY* I. 104; for Thomas Colclow, see *Coventry*, p. 83.

50 Translated from the Latin in *MES*, p. 92.

51 *REEDC*, p. 33. For the York document of February 1568, see *REEDY* I. 352–3.

52 Cited by Stanley Kahrl, 'Learning about local control' in *PFRC*, p. 110. For Crow, see note 46 above; also *EES* I. 299. For Gover Martyn, see Giles E. Dawson (ed.), *Records of Plays and Players in Kent, 1450–1642*, Malone Society *Collections* VII, Oxford, 1965, pp. 202–11; for William Jordan, see Paula Neuss, 'Memorial Reconstruction in a Cornish Miracle Play', *Comparative Drama* 5 (1971), 129–37, and 'The Staging of The "Creation of the World" ', *TN* 33 (1979), 116–24; for Burles, see John C. Coldewey, *op. cit.*, and 'That Enterprising Property Player', *TN* 31 (1977), 5–12.

53 *REEDY* I. 102–3. For the Creed play, see *ibid.*, pp. 352–3.

54 See *MS* I. 109, 344; *MDC*, p. 119; Stanley J. Kahrl, *Traditions of Medieval English Drama*, London, 1974, pp. 138–9. For Tamworth, see Ian Lancashire, 'The Corpus Christi Play of Tamworth', *N&Q* 224 (1979), 508–12.

55 See *TMA*, pp. 227–8 and references.

56 See E. W. Ives, 'In Aid of the Restoration Fund: A Medieval Example', *N&Q* 207 (1962), 162–3; John C. Coldewey, *Early Essex Drama: a History of its Rise and Fall . . .*, Boulder, 1972, p. 9.

57 See *TMA*, p. 228 and references. The 'Reynes Extracts' are printed on pp. 121–3 of *NCP*.

58 See Reginald Ingram, '"Pleyng geire accustumed belongyng & necessarie": guild records and pageant production at Coventry' in *PFRC*, p. 73. For Pisford, see *Coventry*, p. 105. For Lincoln, see Stanley J. Kahrl (ed.), *Records of Plays and Players in Lincolnshire, 1300–1585*, Malone Society *Collections* VIII, Oxford, 1969 (1974), p. 49.

59 See Coldewey, 'Last Rise', *MLQ* 36 (1975), pp. 239–60, 253–7.

60 See F. S. Boas, 'Tewkesbury Abbey's Theatrical Gear', *Times Literary Supplement*, 16 March 1933, p. 184, and Leslie Brooke, *The Book of Yeovil*, Yeovil, 1978, p. 133.

61 All the information (though not its collation) is derived from *REEDC*, pp. 49–50.

62 See *ibid.*, p. lv. The Smiths' data for 1571–2 appears on pp. 90–1, the Coopers' record for 1575 on pp. 108–9.

63 *REEDC*, pp. 77–8. For the Painters and Glaziers, see pp. 81–3.

64 Anne Hudson (ed.), *Selections from English Wycliffite Writings*, Cambridge, 1978, pp. 97–104, prints a substantial extract from the *Tretise*.

65 Printed in *DMC* II. 416–17.

66 See Priscilla Heath Barnum (ed.), *Dives and Pauper*, EETS (OS) 275 (1976), pp. 293–4.

67 See *TMA*, pp. 197–8, and references.

68 See Bevington, *op. cit.*

69 Texts of *Duk Morawd*, and the 'Durham Prologue' are found in *NCP*, pp. 106–13, 118–19.

70 See *TMA*, pp. 229–32, for admission arrangements in Britain and Europe.

71 *REEDC*, p. 33.

72 See *TMA*, pp. 233–4.

73 See Raymond Lebègue, *Le Mystère des Actes des Apôtres*, Paris, 1929, p. 100.

Select bibliography

The following lists contain only a small fraction of the available material which deals with medieval English drama. However, I have narrowed the field by concentrating attention chiefly on those works which contribute significantly to our understanding and knowledge of methods of staging. A list of abbreviations used appears on pp. xiii–xiv above. Place of publication is London, unless otherwise stated.

Editions: Texts

Donald C. Baker et al. (eds), *The Late Medieval Religious Plays of Bodleian Mss Digby 133 and E Museo 160*, EETS (OS) 283 (1982).

Richard Beadle (ed.), *The York Plays*, Arnold, 1982.

David Bevington (ed.), *Medieval Drama*, Houghton Mifflin, Boston, 1975.

K. S. Block (ed.), *Ludus Coventriae, or The Plaie called Corpus Christi*, EETS (ES) 120 (1922 for 1917).

F. S. Boas and A. W. Reed (eds.), *Fulgens and Lucres: A Fifteenth-Century Secular Play*, Clarendon Press, Oxford, 1926.

A. C. Cawley (ed.), *Everyman*, Manchester University Press, 1961.

Hardin Craig (ed.), *Two Coventry Corpus Christi Plays*, EETS (ES) 87 (1902), re-edited, 1952.

Norman Davis (ed.), *Non-Cycle Plays and Fragments*, EETS (SS) 1 (1970).

Mark Eccles (ed.), *The Macro Plays*, EETS (OS) 262 (1969).

George England (ed.), *The Towneley Plays*, EETS (ES) 71 (1897).

Peter Happé (ed.), *English Mystery Plays*, Penguin Books, Harmondsworth, 1975; *Four Morality Plays*, Penguin Books, Harmondsworth, 1979.

Markham Harris (transl.), *The Cornish Ordinalia*, Catholic University of America Press, Washington, D.C., 1969.

R. M. Lumiansky and David Mills (eds.), *The Chester Mystery Cycle*, I., EETS (SS) 3 (1974).

Martial Rose (transl.), *The Wakefield Mystery Plays*, Evans Bros, 1961.

Whitley Stokes (ed.), *Beunans Meriasek: The Life of St Meriasek: A Cornish Drama*, Trubner & Co., 1872.

Glynne Wickham (ed.), *English Moral Interludes*, Dent, 1976.

Editions: Records

Lawrence M. Clopper (ed.), *Records of Early English Drama: Chester*, University of Toronto Press, 1979.

Giles E. Dawson (ed.), *Records of Plays and Players in Kent, 1450–1642*, Malone Society *Collections* VII, Oxford University Press, 1965.

R. W. Ingram (ed.), *Records of Early English Drama: Coventry*, University of Toronto Press, 1981.

Alexandra Johnston and Margaret Rogerson (eds), *Records of Early English Drama: York*, 2 vols., University of Toronto Press, 1979.

Stanley J. Kahrl (ed.), *Records of Plays and Players in Lincolnshire, 1300–1585*, Malone Society *Collections* VIII, Oxford University Press, 1969 (1974).

Ian Lancashire (ed.), *Dramatic Texts and Records of Britain: A Chronological Topography to 1558*, Cambridge University Press, 1984.

Peter Meredith and John Tailby (eds), *The Staging of Religious Drama in Europe in the Late Middle Ages: Texts and Documents in English Translation*, Western Michigan University, Kalamazoo, 1983.

Books

Jane A. Bakere, *The Cornish Ordinalia: A Critical Study*, University of Wales Press, Cardiff 1980.

David M. Bevington, *From "Mankind" to Marlowe: Growth and Structure in the Popular Drama of Tudor England*, Harvard University Press, Cambridge, Mass., 1962.

A. C. Cawley *et al.*, *Medieval Drama*, Revels History of Drama in English I, Methuen, 1983.

E. K. Chambers, *The Mediaeval Stage*, 2 vols., Oxford University Press, 1903.

Fletcher Collins Jr., *The Production of Medieval Church Music-drama*, University Press of Virginia, Charlottesville, 1972.

Hardin Craig, *English Religious Drama of the Middle Ages*, Clarendon Press, Oxford, 1955.

T. W. Craik, *The Tudor Interlude: Stage, Costume and Acting*, Leicester University Press, 1958.

W. A. Davenport, *Fifteenth-Century English Drama*, D. S. Brewer, Cambridge, 1982.

Clifford Davidson *et al.* (eds), *The Drama of the Middle Ages*, A.M.S. Press, New York, 1982.

Neville Denny (ed.), *Medieval Drama*, Stratford-on-Avon Studies 16, Arnold, 1973.

Joanna Dutka (ed.), *Records of Early English Drama: Proceedings of the First Colloquium*, Toronto, 1979.

Merle Fifield, *The Castle in the Circle*, Ball State University, Muncie, Indiana, 1967.

Harold C. Gardiner, *Mysteries End: An Investigation of the Last Days of the Medieval Religious Stage*, Yale University Press, New Haven, 1946.

Peter Happé (ed.), *Medieval English Drama: A Casebook*, Macmillan, 1984.

O. B. Hardison Jr., *Christian Rite and Christian Drama in the Middle Ages*, Johns Hopkins University Press, Baltimore, Maryland, 1965.

Stanley J. Kahrl, *Traditions of Medieval English Drama*, Hutchinson, 1974.

George R. Kernodle, *From Art to Theatre: Form and Convention in the Renaissance*, University of Chicago Press, 1944.

V. A. Kolve, *The Play Called Corpus Christi*, Arnold, 1966.

Anna J. Mill, *Mediaeval Plays in Scotland*, St Andrews University Publications 24, Blackwood, Edinburgh, 1927.

Sumiko Miyajima, *The Theatre of Man: Dramatic Technique and Stagecraft in the English Medieval Moral Plays*, Clevedon Printing Co., Avon, 1977.

A. M. Nagler, *The Medieval Religious Stage: Shapes and Phantoms*, Yale University Press, New Haven and London, 1976.

Alan H. Nelson, *The Medieval English Stage*, University of Chicago Press, 1974.

Paula Neuss (ed.), *Aspects of Early English Drama*, D. S. Brewer, Cambridge, 1983.

Robert Potter, *The English Morality Play: Origins, History and Influence of a Dramatic Tradition*, Routledge & Kegan Paul, 1975.

F. M. Salter, *Mediaeval Drama in Chester*, University of Toronto Press, 1955.

Richard Southern, *The Medieval Theatre in the Round*, Faber, 1957; second edition, 1975.

The Staging of Plays before Shakespeare, Faber, 1973.

Sandro Sticca (ed.), *The Medieval Drama*, State University of New York, Albany, 1972.

Jerome Taylor and Alan H. Nelson (eds), *Medieval English Drama: Essays Critical and Contextual*, University of Chicago Press, 1972.

William Tydeman, *The Theatre in the Middle Ages*, Cambridge University Press, 1978.

Glynne Wickham, *Early English Stages, 1300–1660*, 4 vols, Routledge & Kegan Paul, 1959–81.

Arnold Williams, *The Drama of Medieval England*, Michigan State University Press, East Lansing, 1961.

Rosemary Woolf, *The English Mystery Plays*, Routledge & Kegan Paul, 1972.

Karl Young, *The Drama of the Medieval Church*, 2 vols, Clarendon Press, Oxford, 1933.

Articles

Catherine Belsey, 'The Stage Plan of *The Castle of Perseverance*', TN 28 (1974), 124–32.

David Bevington, 'Discontinuity in Mediaeval Acting Traditions', in G. R. Hibbard (ed.), *The Elizabethan Theatre* V, Macmillan, 1975, pp. 1–16.

Bing D. Bills, 'The "Suppression Theory" and the English Corpus Christi Play: A Re-Evaluation', *Theatre Journal* 32 (1980), 157–68.

Philip Butterworth, 'The York Mercers' Pageant Vehicle, 1433–1467: Wheels, Steering and Control', *METh* 1 (1979), 72–81.

Kenneth Cameron and Stanley J. Kahrl, 'Staging the N-Town Cycle', *TN* 21 (1967), 122–38.

John C. Coldewey, 'The Digby Plays and the Chelmsford Records', *RORD* 18 (1975), 103–21.

'The Last Rise and Final Demise of Essex Town Drama', *MLQ* 36 (1975), 239–60.

'That Enterprising Property Player', *TN* 31 (1977), 5–12.

Mary Del Vilar, 'The Staging of *The Conversion of St Paul*', *TN* 25 (1970–1), 64–8.

Neville Denny, 'Aspects of the Staging of *Mankind*', *Medium Aevum* 43 (1974), 252–63.

Kenneth M. Dodd, 'Another Elizabethan Theater in the Round', *Shakespeare Quarterly* 21 (1970), 125–56.

Margaret Dorrell, 'Two Studies of the York Corpus Christi Play', *LSE* (NS) 6 (1972), 63–111.

Anne Cooper Gay, 'The "Stage" and the Staging of the N-Town plays', *RORD* 10 (1967), 135–40.

Reginald W. Ingram, ' "To find the players and all that longith therto": Notes on the production of Medieval Drama in Coventry', in Hibbard (ed.), *op. cit.*, pp. 17–44. (See under Bevington above)

' "Pleyng geire accustumed belongyng & necessarie": guild records and pageant production in Coventry', in *PFRC*, 1979, pp. 60–100.

'The Coventry Pageant Waggon', *METh* 2 (1980), 3–14.

David L. Jeffrey, 'English Saints' Plays', in Neville Denny (ed.), *Medieval Drama*, Stratford-on-Avon Studies 16, Arnold, 1973, pp. 75–86.

Alexandra F. Johnston, 'The Guild of Corpus Christi and the Procession of Corpus Christi in York', *Mediaeval Studies* 38 (1976), 372–84.

Alexandra F. Johnston and Margaret Dorrell, 'The Doomsday Pageant of the York Mercers, 1433', *LSE* (NS) 5 (1971), 29–34.

'The York Mercers and their Pageant of Doomsday, 1433–1526', *ibid.*, 6 (1972), 10–35.

Robert C. Jones, 'The Stage World and the "Real" World in Medwall's *Fulgens and Lucres*', *MLQ* 36 (1971), 131–42.

Stanley J. Kahrl, 'Medieval Drama in Louth', *RORD* 10 (1967), 129–33.

'Learning about local control', in *PFRC*, 1979, pp. 101–27.

John Marshall, 'The Chester Pageant Carriage – how right was Rogers?', *METh* 1 (1979), 52–3.

Peter Meredith, 'The Development of the York Mercers' Pageant Waggon', *METh* 1 (1979), 5–18.

' "Item for a grone – iijᵈ – records and performance', in *PFRC*, 1979, pp. 26–60.

' "Farte Pryke in Cule" and Cock-fighting', *METh* 6.1 (1984), 30–9.

Anna J. Mill, 'The Stations of the York Corpus Christi Play', *Yorkshire Archaeological Journal* 37 (1951), 492–502.

David Mills, 'Characterisation in the English Mystery Plays: A Critical Prologue', *METh* 5.1 (1983), 5–17.

Alan H. Nelson, 'Principles of Processional Staging: York Cycle', *MP* 67 (1970), 303–20.

Paula Neuss, 'Memorial Reconstruction in a Cornish Miracle Play', *Comparative Drama* 5 (1971), 129–37.
　'Active and Idle Language: Dramatic Images in *Mankind*', in Denny (ed.), *op. cit.*, pp. 41–67. (See under David L. Jeffrey above.)
　'The Staging of The "Creation of the World" ', *TN* 33 (1979), 116–24.

J. D. A. Ogilvy, '*Mimi, scurrae, histriones*: entertainers of the Middle Ages', *Speculum* 38 (1963), 603–19.

David Parry, 'The York Mystery Cycle at Toronto, 1977', *METh* 1 (1979), 19–31.

Raymond J. Pentzell, 'The Medieval Theatre in the Streets', *Theatre Survey* 14 (1973), 1–21.

J. W. Robinson, 'Medieval English Acting', *TN* 13 (1959), 83–8.

Natalie Crohn Schmitt, 'Was There a Medieval Theatre in the Round? A Re-Examination of the Evidence', *TN* 23 (1968–9), 130–42; *ibid.*, 24 (1969–70), 18–25; reprinted in Taylor and Nelson above.

Martin Stevens, 'The Staging of the Wakefield Plays', *RORD* 11 (1968), 115–28.
　'Illusion and Reality in the Medieval Drama', *College English* 32 (1971), 448–64.
　'The York Cycle: from procession to play', *LSE* (NS) 6 (1972), 37–61.

Meg Twycross, ' "Places to hear the play": pageant stations at York, 1398–1572', *REEDN* 2 (1978), 10–33.

Siegfried Wenzel, 'An Early Reference to a Corpus Christi Play', *MP* 74 (1977), 390–4.

Glynne Wickham, 'The Staging of Saint Plays in England', in Sandro Sticca (ed.), *The Medieval Drama*, State University of New York, Albany, 1972, pp. 99–119.

M. James Young, 'The York Pageant Waggon', *Speech Monographs* 34 (1967), 1–20.

Index